Hidden Treasures

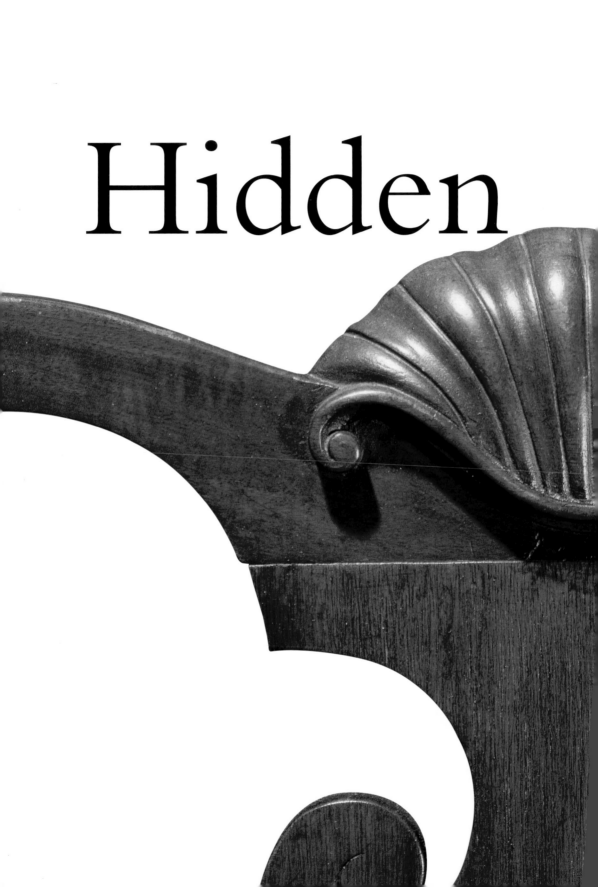

Hidden

Leigh Keno & Leslie Keno

with Joan Barzilay Freund

Treasures

Searching for Masterpieces of American Furniture

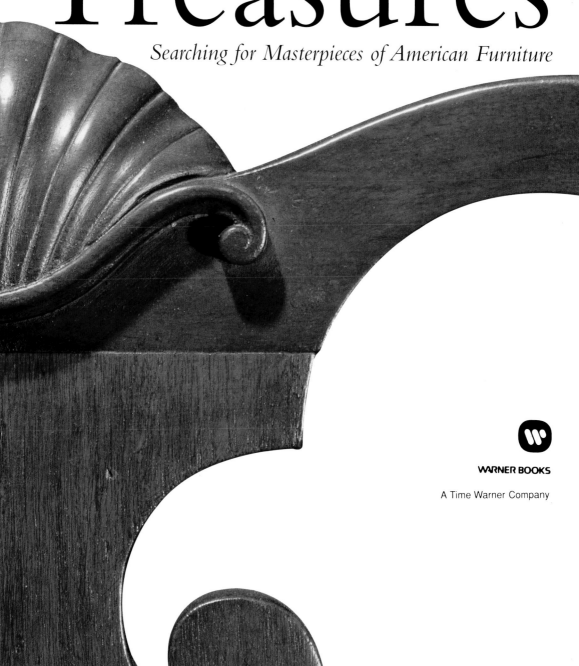

WARNER BOOKS

A Time Warner Company

ANTIQUES ROADSHOW
is a trademark of the BBC. All rights reserved.
Produced under license from BBC Worldwide.

Leigh and Leslie Keno offer special thanks
to the Chubb Corporation for their support
of this terrific program.

Warner Books, Inc., 1271 Avenue of the Americas, New York, NY 10020
Visit our Web site at www.twbookmark.com

 A Time Warner Company

A Time Warner Company
Printed in Great Britain
First Printing: November 2000
10 9 8 7 6 5 4 3 2 1
Library of Congress Cataloging-in-Publication Data

Keno, Leigh.
     Hidden treasures : searching for masterpieces of American furniture / Leigh Keno and
Leslie Keno with Joan Barzilay Freund.
        p. cm.
     Includes bibliographical references and index.
     ISBN 0-446-52692-4
     1. Keno, Leigh. 2. Keno, Leslie. 3. Antique dealers--United States--Biography. 4.
Furniture--United States. I. Keno, Leslie. II. Freund, Joan Barzilay. III. Title.

NK1133.26.K46 A2 2000
749.213--dc21
                                                                                    00-039891

Book design by David Larkin

This book
is dedicated
to our parents,
Norma
and
Ronald Keno

Acknowledgments

Hidden Treasures: Searching for Masterpieces of American Furniture has been realized only through the generous efforts of many individuals. We owe our first debt of gratitude to Joan Barzilay Freund. She understands us and our crazy passion for *things* and the stories that surround them in a way that no one else can. Without Joan, this book would not have been possible.

We thank Aida Moreno for her ongoing encouragement and enthusiasm. We are grateful for the support of Betsy Groban, Peter Cook, Lou Wiley, and Peter McGhee of WGBH. Warm thanks also go to those who graciously shared their personal and poignant recollections: Robert Backlund, Claire Beckmann, Richard Dietrich, Robert Fileti, Tom Lloyd, Thierry Millerand, Alexandre Pradère, Chris Machmer, Morgan MacWhinnie, John Nye, Ron DeSilva, Kevin Tierney, Nate Wallace, and Ed Weissman.

So many people are deserving of our thanks for their valuable advice. We are most grateful to Luke Beckerdite for his insights into Newport and Philadelphia cabinet-making techniques. We also acknowledge Dede Brooks, Wendy Cooper, Dan Farrell, Dean Failey, John Hays, Peter Kenney, Barbara Livy, John Marion, Michael Moses, Robert Mussey, Bill Samaha, Bill Stahl, and Jim Tottis. Personal thanks also go to the collectors Ted and Barbara Alfond, Peter Brant, Stuart Feld, Jesse Price, George and Linda Kaufman, Ned and Lillie Johnson, Tim and Lisa Robertson, Peter Terian, Tony and Lulu Wang, Irving and Joy Wolf, and Martin and Ethel Wunsch.

Countless individuals provided generous assistance with photographs: Lisa Abitol of WGBH; Put Brown; Mark Anderson of Winterthur Museum; John M. Driggers of Robert Mussey Associates, Inc.; Linda Eppich, curator, and Jennifer Bond, assistant curator, of Graphics, The Rhode Island Historical Society; Alan Gorsuch of Sanford & Son Auctions; Valerie Hardy of the College of William and Mary; Stephen Harris of the Dallas Museum of Art; Kelly K. Leu, curator of collections, Jefferson County Historical Society; Clayton Pennington, Lita Solis-Cohen, and David Hewett of *Maine Antique Digest*; Debbie M. Rebuck, curator, and Jacqueline M. DeGroff, associate curator, The Dietrich American Foundation; Dr. John Reese; Joel and Betty Schatzberg; Scudder Smith of *Antiques and the Arts Weekly*; and Laura Beach of *Antiques America,* and Jonathan Thomas. We also thank the photographic services departments of Christie's, Colonial Williamsburg Foundation, Harvard University Art Museum, The Metropolitan Museum of Art, and Sotheby's.

Many photographers are deserving of our appreciation for contributing their efforts. Jeff Dunn unselfishly donated his time and photographs. Gavin Ashworth, Leslie Jean-Bart, Ben Cohen of Sotheby's, Lynn Diane De Marco, Tom Jenkins, Duncan Livingston, Kelly J. Mihalcoe, and Sally Neeld have all been very helpful. We are especially grateful to Lady Ostepeck for sending the long lost photograph of us with our mother at a flea market.

We offer special thanks to our agent, the dynamic Susan Ginsburg of Writer's House. We are also grateful to John Hodgman and Elizabeth Gilbert for their early assistance, as well as our attorney, Mark Lawless, for his excellent guidance and brilliant sense of humor. Thanks are also due to the staff at Katy Gallagher's, where we spent long hours working on the book.

We are grateful to Angela George for her skillful fact checking and research on various objects, Janis Mandrus for coordinating the photography, and Amy Coes for organizing the bibliography and glossary. We also wish to thank our colleagues Clifford Harvard, Carisa Koontz Sykes, and Marnie Reasor of Leigh Keno American Antiques, as well as Tanya Hayes and Beth Koules of Sotheby's.

We were fortunate to have worked with a fantastic team at Warner Books. We thank especially Maureen Egen, President of Time Warner Trade Publishing. Our wonderful editor, Les Pockell, who convinced us to trust our story to Warner Books and who, together with Harvey-Jane Kowal, expertly guided us once we arrived. We also acknowledge Christine Dao, Jean Griffin, Karen Melnyk, Jackie Meyer, Jennifer Romanello, and Flamur Tonuzi. We are especially grateful to our book designer, the visionary David Larkin.

Deep thanks are due to Alex Acevedo, who believed in Leigh and offered his support when Leigh first started his business.

We express our most appreciative thanks to Joan's husband, Tony Freund, and son, Thomas, for allowing us to take so much of her time, and to her parents, Robert and Alice Barzilay, for pinch-hitting on babysitting. Finally, we extend our deepest gratitude to members of our own families for their unfailing support and encouragement: Leslie's wife, Emily, and daughter, Ashley; Leigh's son, Brandon, and his mother, Jasmin Español; our brother, Mitchell, who is now working with Leigh; Grandma Wava; and of course our parents, Ronald and Norma Keno.

When you are born a twin, the first lesson
you learn is about sharing—be it a toy, a blanket,
or time with your parents—
and that has certainly colored our strategy
for writing this book. Since we wanted to
make *Hidden Treasures* a chronicle of *both* our
adventures in antiquing, we knew from the start
that even here we would have to abandon any
competitive urges and politely take turns.
So as you embark on reading this
book, please realize that our voices alternate
from chapter to chapter (although there are
a few exceptions). We've tried to leave enough
signals and clues in the text so that it is easy
to pick up on which of us is the narrator.
As to which of us is the better storyteller?
You be the judge.
Enjoy!
—LEIGH AND LESLIE KENO

CONTENTS

1

Going Once . . .

"LOT NUMBER 701, THE CARVED MAPLE BEDSTEAD . . . And we have a $1,500 bid to start it, bidding at $1,500. I have $2,000 . . . now $2,500 . . . on the phone now $3,000. . . ."

When I heard auctioneer Bill Stahl open the bidding on that bed frame, at Sotheby's Important Americana sale of January 17, 1999, my heart began to race. Run-of-the-mill New England bedsteads don't usually have that effect on me. After all, I have been with Sotheby's for over twenty years—seventeen of which have been spent as the director of the American Furniture and Decorative Arts Department—so I've seen my share of maple beds.

My pulse quickened, however, because I knew that within moments that Federal bedstead would be sold and the bidding would open on the next lot—a large mahogany secretary-bookcase made in Newport, Rhode Island, in the 1740s. This particular bookcase was unlike any other piece of American furniture that I had ever seen before. From the moment I first laid eyes on it, in a set of hazy, unprofessional photographs sent in through our Paris office some years before, I had been consumed by its mystery and beauty. And indeed, during the week prior to the sale, when potential buyers and the merely curious are invited to preview the furniture, I noticed the secretary working its magic on others, as well. As viewers tried to take in its nearly nine-foot facade, I heard words like *sexy, beguiling,* and *enigmatic* being used to describe it—words that might just as easily be used to describe a wife or lover. Quite simply, the piece seduced all who crossed its path.

Bill Stahl, my friend and colleague, was conducting the sale from behind a raised corner podium that serves as the visual apex of the main auction room at Sotheby's. I, as was usual at such sales, stood just a few feet to his right, behind a smaller podium, which was more centered on the dais. Bill, a large man with gray hair and a handsome, still-boyish face, lends a great presence to the auction room, for he exudes confidence without bravado. One of his more theatrical gestures involves cocking his head to one side as he softly recites incoming bids. Then, as the numbers begin to climax, he'll start to move his head from side to side, as if he's straining to catch the melody of a favorite old song playing somewhere beyond the room. However disarming, there is nothing casual about this movement. Bill is, in fact, deeply aware of the whereabouts of every player in the room and is actually focusing intently on each one. Invariably, he seems able to draw out an additional bid from those who are about to fold.

I hoped I had what might be perceived as an easy, expectant smile on my face as I listened to Bill's voice while scanning the packed auction room with nervous anticipation. In the past few days, I had fielded an unusually high number of calls from members of the press. All had been curious about my expectations for the secretary, and they were in attendance that day. I had ordered two hundred extra folding white chairs for the sale, to supplement the approximately one thousand seats that are usually set up in the high-ceilinged auction room, and now almost every one was filled. As was customary, the walls of the salesroom were lined with many of the larger pieces of furniture being sold that day, including a fair number of high chests of drawers and six secretary-bookcases. This is done because the pieces are simply too heavy to be hoisted onto the revolving platform set behind me on the dais, where each item up for sale dramatically rotates into view during the bidding (just as quickly they rotate away when the bidding is over). At present, however, I could hardly see the furniture lining the room, because within the last few minutes, the aisles in front of them had visibly swollen with people. Clearly I was not the only one who was excited about the upcoming lot. The crowd was particularly thick in the back of the salesroom, where many dealers like to stand so they can get a good view of who's bidding. There, the clients and spectators must have been packed nearly ten-deep.

In fact, the only spot in the room that wasn't jammed with people was the podium behind me. And it was there, to the right of the revolving display area, that the object of my (and everyone else's) attention stood—the exquisite Newport secretary. That morning, I had asked the staging crew to redirect a number of the spotlights that hang from the rafters, so that they would shine directly onto the dark wooden facade of the piece, which dramatically accentuated its form. Light splashed across the closed slant lid of the desk section, or secretary (from which the piece gets its abbreviated name), and lengthened the almost-imperceptible shadows of the four drawers stacked below. The probing beams also brought into high relief the fluted scallop shells rigorously carved at the top of the upper section's two doors. Like a pop star caught in the spotlight, the secretary's form demanded attention, from the high spring of the arched dome top with its unusual trio of flame-twist finials to the magnificent mottled grain of the rare plum-pudding mahogany that activated the surface and gave it great character.

Elaborate case pieces such as this secretary are among the priciest furniture ever crafted in the colonies, and they certainly evoke the wealth and sophistication of their original owners. Only the most learned of men had need for the many pigeonhole compartments and drawers that lay hidden behind the cabinet doors and desk lid, making it the Colonial era's answer to a computer. During the week leading up to the sale, a number of visitors to Sotheby's viewing galleries had speculated that this particular secretary might have been the most expensive piece ever made in eighteenth-century America. One reason for this theory was that its exquisitely crafted exterior was accented throughout with solid-silver hinges, drawer pulls, and elaborate bird-shaped lopers (the pull-out supports for a slant-front desktop) initialed by their maker, the Rhode Island silversmith Samuel Casey. Until this secretary came to light, solid-silver hardware on a piece of Early American furniture was simply unheard of. It was an extravagance of such magnitude that few patrons could have so much as considered, let alone commissioned, such ornamentation.

But it was not just its obvious good looks that made this secretary so compelling. There was perhaps a greater beauty (of the more mysterious sort) contained within its closed doors, drawers, and slant-top desk lid— a beauty to be savored by a fortunate few. Furthermore, what I had learned about this secretary's long journey from the Newport cabinet shop where it was made to the small Right Bank apartment where it was found by a Parisian antiques dealer only added to its allure. And so, as this piece—without question, the most significant piece of American furniture ever offered for sale in Sotheby's 255-year history—commanded the stage behind me, I couldn't help but feel a tremendous awe in its towering, silent presence. It seemed to face the buzzing, fidgeting crowd with centuries-old wisdom and perspective.

"I have $5,500—my bid is on the phone—and down it goes, all done for $5,500." Bill Stahl's voice boomed in my left ear, shaking me from my reverie. The New England bedstead spun out of sight, soon on its way to a new home, and the Newport secretary was next on the block.

In the world of Americana, there is only a handful of top collectors capable of buying a piece of furniture of this secretary's caliber. As objects go, such pieces are simply not for beginners. So as my eyes roamed the room at an ever-increasing pace, I took mental note of the few members of that elite cadre who were present: In the front row was Albert Sack, who, along with his brothers Harold and Robert, heads the venerable firm of Israel Sack, Inc., founded by their father in 1905. Albert is affectionately known in the business as the "Godfather of American antiques," and he and his brothers are all great heroes of mine. Albert was the only one in attendance that day, however. A man of uncommonly good taste, he has advised, among other collectors, a certain billionaire client who paid $12.1 million for the legendary Nicholas Brown desk and bookcase when it sold at Christie's in 1989.

I spotted the New England collectors Ted and Barbara Alfond about ten rows behind Albert. They have a marvelous collection of American furniture, particularly strong in Boston and Newport examples. I briefly focused on Bill Samaha, who was sitting about fifteen rows behind the Alfonds and all the way to the left. A Massachusetts- and Ohio-based dealer, Samaha often advises Ned Johnson, the chairman and owner of Fidelity Investments, who owns one of the largest collections of New England furniture in private hands, in addition to an extraordinary collection of Chinese furniture and porcelain. All week long, I had watched Samaha's appreciation for the Newport secretary gain momentum. As a whole, this well-seasoned group looked eager, expectant, yet remarkably poker-faced.

Having completed my scan, I noticed just one more heavyweight in the crowd, a man who could certainly figure prominently in what I expected to be a fight for the secretary. A furniture dealer—one of the field's best—he sat in the front row of the auction room, arms crossed above his green-and-tan tweed sports jacket. Over the past ten years at auction alone, he had spent over $35 million on American furniture. The man's head was tilted downward, obscuring his sharp, angular features, which were very familiar to me. Suddenly, the light bounced off his blond hair as he raised his head and his blue eyes locked with mine. I saw his eyebrows quiver for a moment and the edges of his lips come together, and then his eyes moved on. It was only a second that he held my gaze, but that glance spoke volumes to me, for this was my twin brother, Leigh.

As I looked at my brother Leslie standing behind the podium at Sotheby's—a place I had seen him stand many times before—I could sense the turmoil he was going through. The great secretary looming behind him on the stage was the most exciting piece of furniture he had ever discovered—and, quite possibly, that he would ever come across again. I knew how bittersweet that felt. At forty-three, Leslie and I both like to think we are still young, so to keep the game fun (the pursuit of antiques should always be a game, at least to some extent), we find it necessary, if not crucial, to believe that there are always greater, rarer treasures to be found just around the bend. It's a motivational theory that's applied every day at the dog races: If the greyhounds ever catch the mechanical rabbit, it is said, they will forever lose their hunger for the chase.

Well, I knew neither of us was anywhere near ready to retire from the track, and the reason I say "us" is because the Newport secretary that meant so much to my brother was also of intense interest to me. When wonderful objects such as that secretary enter the marketplace, clients turn to me for advice. They want to know that the furniture that interests them is authentic as well as beautiful. In the weeks preceding the sale of the Newport secretary, I had committed to a relatively new client—a person of intense intellect and privacy—who had grown nearly as passionate about this object as Leslie and I. I use the word *committed* because, like most dealers, I make it a standard practice to look at an object for one customer at a time. To put it simply, I would lose my clientele if they found themselves bidding against one another.

The passion that this person and I now shared for the Newport secretary made me a player that day. So if I managed to win the secretary for my client, in what promised to be some high-stakes bidding, I would conceivably have bought the finest piece of American furniture that I would ever handle. Like Leslie, I found that prospect both thrilling and daunting.

Throughout our lives, Leslie and I have spent so much time in auction rooms that being in them tends to open up the floodgates of memory. No matter how pressured the moment, I inevitably feel the tug of things familiar: a face in the crowd that reminds me of a past sale; a piece of furniture that takes on a new elegance as it spins to attention on the revolving stage; a lull in the bidding that allows time for retrospection.

On the day of the sale of the secretary, I sat in the front row of the packed auction room, trying my utmost to appear outwardly calm. As a dealer, it is important for me to show minimal advance interest in items for sale. Any extra attention I pay to an object may indicate to my competitors that I vouch for its quality. Not only is that free advice but it might encourage them to dig a little deeper into their pockets when they bid. That, in turn, runs up the final price of the furniture for my clients, which is not a good thing. In addition, for reasons of security, many buyers do not want to be seen publicly spending large sums of money. That is why even after a sale has gone through, a new owner may choose to remain anonymous.

So as I sat in my chair, trying to avoid the curious stares of those around me (particularly from members of the press, who tend to keep tabs on the progress of a sale from the front of the room), I took a glance up at Leslie. I was not surprised to see him looking straight back at me. During the past week of previews, things had grown unusually tense between us, and the Newport secretary was the reason why. The blanket of secrecy that I had drawn about myself to protect my client in the days preceding the auction had also shrouded my intentions from Leslie. He was and is my best friend and brother, and yet I couldn't breathe a word, not even to him, about the level of my client's interest. My silence on the subject was in no way indicative of a lack of trust or confidence in him; after all, I would trust him with my life. It was simply another way of maintaining the anonymity that this and most clients preferred.

We're almost there, I wanted to reassure him. A few more minutes and it's done.

Of course I couldn't say any of that. Instead, I simply looked at him a fraction of a second more and then looked away. But I was left with a feeling of surprising tenderness, given the packed auction room. Leslie looked vulnerable up there. Despite his position of prominence upon the raised sales dais, his easy stance behind the slim burnished mahogany podium, and the confident lines of his navy London-cut suit, he looked to me like the brother of my youth. I was just a few yards away, but at that moment, I might as well have been miles, if not years, away. This was no time for memories, but all I could do was sit back and think of how far we had come, my brother and I, from the small upstate New York town where we were born. Back then, we would never have imagined that our shared passion for antiques—one that we had nurtured side by side for virtually our entire lives—would have brought us to this precipitous moment, standing, as it were, on opposite sides of a single perfect object.

At three and a half.

When you are born with an identical twin brother, you never lack for companionship, and Leslie and I were pretty much inseparable throughout our early years. Some people like to shed their pasts as they grow older, but we found our bearings as children, so we never had reason to rebel. So much of who we are today germinated in our shared adventures as children. I look back now and marvel at how many perfect moments there were, even before we began to pursue our common, almost-instinctive love for antiques seriously.

In 1960, when Leslie and I were three and our older brother, Mitchell, was nearly seven, our parents purchased the ninety-five-acre farm where we grew up, just outside of Mohawk, a small village set deep into the crescent of the lower Mohawk Valley. It was a beautiful spot, which Dad, who had grown up in the area, could remember driving by as a child and loving the way the farm buildings fanned out across the hillside.

The main farmhouse, a white clapboard structure with dark green shutters, might best be described as a nineteenth-century Greek Revival—with a twist. There wasn't much logic to the arrangement of rooms inside the L-shaped house, in which two of the bedrooms stood adjacent to the dining room and the second story was pretty much consumed by the attic, save for an additional bedroom. It wasn't anything fancy, but it was home to us and we loved it.

At the time our parents bought the property, little of the place had been altered, although it had not functioned as a working farm for half a century. Behind the house stood a small horse barn that had a particularly intricate rafter system, which was great for climbing. Occasionally, Dad rented out a few of the stalls to a farmer up the road who raised Appaloosas. At day's end, Mitchell, Leslie, and I would straggle outside to bring the horses in, and the sight of them at the crest of the hill, silhouetted against the darkening sky, is still etched in my memory.

Some of the other outbuildings included a large red barn—originally used as a dairy—with a gray slate roof topped with two cupolas, and a small stone structure that we always called "the smokehouse" (running along the interior walls, there were long wide hooks on which meat might have hung), but that we now think was probably an old icehouse, given the building's dirt floor. There was also a low two-story structure

Home.   The red barn.

built directly into the slope of the hillside; it housed a root cellar on the bottom level and a bee house on the top. The root cellar was lined with shelves, some still stocked with large turn-of-the-century stoneware jugs left by previous owners, and the whole dank space bore traces of a once-pungent vinegary aroma. We never raised bees, however, so Dad, who is an artist by training, stored his canvases in the rising dome of the upper level, until the roof caved in just a few years ago. It was there, sneaking a peak at Dad's art school nudes, that Leslie and I got our first glimpse of the female form.

When we were really young, that property, and the vast fields and woodlands around it, was our playground. There was nothing Leslie and I enjoyed more than heading up onto the hillside and digging around to see what we might find. Our brother Mitchell wasn't really a party to this stage in our lives, because of the age difference between us. While we wanted to search for treasures, Mitchell wanted to listen to rock and roll (when he was fifteen, he and some friends formed a band called the Diplomats, which met with great local success). Leslie and I were extremely absorbed in our daily hunts for hidden treasures—really to the exclusion of anyone else. As our mother liked to say as she watched us dart out the back door as soon as we'd swallowed our breakfasts, "There go the twins, off into their own little world."

Our rooting around the property was well justified, though, given the rich history of the lower Mohawk Valley. Our farm alone, which was built around 1845, had seen more than a century of use by at least three previous families, and there had been enough civilization in the extensive woods behind us for remnants and refuse to have been left tantalizingly behind. For example, one winter day when Leslie and I were probably about six, we spotted three nineteenth-century U.S. military-issue bullets trapped in a patch of ice behind the smokehouse. How they had come to be deposited there, and why we hadn't noticed them just sitting there on the ground in the warm-weather months, was and still remains a mystery to us. Then there was the rare nineteenth-century child's marble that we found lodged nearly a foot down in the wet, sloppy mud beneath the long trough next to the horse barn. The swirled threads of blue, red, and lavender glass seemed suspended in the one-and-a-half-inch orb, and otherworldly in their vibrancy. We were so amazed by its magnetic beauty that Leslie and I more or less convinced ourselves that it had been left there by men from Mars.

As we grew older, we cast our nets farther away from the watchful gaze of our parents, and the focus of our searches expanded. At first, the snaking path of Fulmer

Scenes from our lives.

19

Creek, which surged through the middle of our property but ran for miles in the hills behind the house, served as our conduit. Our paternal grandfather, Leslie Lamont Joseph Keno, for whom my brother was named, was a great fisherman, and he instilled in us, at a very early age, his passion for the sport. Today, when we think about our love of discovery—the actual process of spotting and zeroing in on the jewels of our trade—we find constant analogies in terms of fishing. A stream might appear to most eyes as merely water rippling over rocks, but an experienced fisherman can see where a big trout rises as it feeds on tiny nymphs, its head not even breaking the water. It's a trophy trout, and he sees it right away. This is a talent—exactly like scanning for that rare treasure at a flea market—which takes the angler many years and countless miles of water to develop.

When we were about eleven, a large work crew from the Tennessee Gas Transmission Company came through the woods behind our house and cleared a huge swath of land. They were laying a trench for a natural-gas pipeline that

eventually ran through Mohawk to the village of Ilion, and then farther west toward Frankfurt, Fort Plain, and Utica. In time, the brush closed in again around the pipeline, but for a few years, it pretty much provided us with a superhighway for adventuring east and west across the county, without ever needing to use roads or state highways. It was also about that time that our parents gave us a 120-cc Suzuki trail bike to share, and then we really began to cover great distances. Riding tandem, we would zoom down any dirt trail that we could make out, searching for ruined barns and old house foundations, in which we saw enormous potential for discovery. In particular, we were on the lookout for late-eighteenth- and early-nineteenth-century wrought-iron hinges and door handles. We were fueled by the idea that among the fallen beams and rotting doors of these once-proud buildings were artifacts that had been handcrafted upward of 150 years ago, now sinking slowly into the earth. By the mid-nineteenth century, iron hinges (the jointed devices that allow a door to swing) were widely mass-manufactured, but what we were in search of were ones that had been individually hammered on a forge by local blacksmiths. It amazed us that someone had crafted something so simple and beautiful out of the most basic, rugged material. We could almost hear the rapid-fire report of the hammer hitting the hot metal when we handled their elongated shapes and roughened surfaces.

Some wrought-iron hinges from our childhood collection.

We graded the hinges and door handles that we unearthed, based on their quality, intricacy, and the presumed level of craftsmanship that was involved in their manufacture. For example, the simplest hinge was a strap hinge, which actually looks like a leather belt or strip, binding the door to the frame. They were quite mainstream, and not particularly valuable. Next came bean hinges, so called because they feature an oblong lima bean shape, usually half an inch to two inches wide, on the end piece, or terminal, that attach to a door. Rarer still were those that featured a heart-shaped terminal, ideally with a curled or winding tip (often called a "rat tail"). We loved the juxtaposition of the straight, tapered rodlike body of the hinge with the winding, free-form end. The contrast spoke volumes about the balance that must always be struck between practicality and creativity in the decorative arts. These were very functional pieces, so whatever creativity shone through in the design came from something deep inside the maker.

Once, when we were approaching an old foundation at a site about five miles east of our house, we spotted a door with rat-tail hinges and a matching handle lying faceup in the bramble. We were still on our bike, so we just kept shouting our thoughts to each other over the roar of the engine as we weaved among the trees. I still get excited about barn hinges and their counterpart door handles, which have gone up in value since our early days in the woods, when a really great set might have fetched one hundred dollars. A few years ago at Sotheby's, I bought an incredible pair of large heart-handle latches for forty times that amount. They now sit on a low chest next to my bed, and I will never sell them.

*A rare pair of large
wrought-iron door handles.*

Prying these iron treasures off dilapidated barn doors was sort of like pulling out teeth that don't have cavities. It was hard work, which is why Leslie and I always carried a couple of thirty-inch crowbars with curved ends on one side (with V-shaped cuts in the center of the curve that were good for pulling out nails) and an angled back end that was ideal for prying up large rocks. They were our main tools, although we also carried sizable hammers with mallets on both ends and heavy-duty work gloves, although they never seemed to be any help. A few years later, when we were in college, Leslie and I took classes in archaeology, where we learned proper excavation techniques, which, of course, left us pretty much appalled at the memory of our earlier field work. We really were not as respectful of the sites as we should have been, and we left few clues for future researchers who might stumble across the same area a hundred years from now.

However clumsy our technique, our intentions were only the best. In particular, we were fueled by the knowledge that both our parents came from families with deep roots in the territory we explored. It was a concept that fed our imaginations and personalized our scavenging. We liked to wonder about the people who first handled those cold iron latches and pushed open those weathered exterior doors. Mom's family, the Sweets, had been in northern New York State for two generations, and Dad's paternal grandfather, Albert Peter Cuenot, was born on a farm just a mile from our house. His family was originally from the Alsace-Lorraine region of France, just near the Belgian border. When Albert was a boy, he was sent to a country school four miles outside of Mohawk, where his teacher encouraged him to anglicize his name. Cuenot became Keno, and our family name was born.

In 1888, Albert, by then a dealer in cattle, horses, and hay, with a sideline business in milk and cheese, married Delphine Devenpeck, our great-grandmother. She, too, had roots in the area, having been born and raised in East Herkimer, on the banks of the West Canada Creek. It had always come down in the family that Delphine was a direct descendant of the Revolutionary War hero Gen. Philip Schuyler (1733–1804), a scion of one of New York's great landholding families. Before our grandmother (Delphine's daughter-in-law) died, she used to take us to visit the old Schuyler Mansion in Albany, by that time (as it is now) a museum. When Leslie and I toured its elegant interiors with Grandma, she explained with great solemnity and pride that this was all a part of our cultural heritage. With this romantic notion, she fed our imaginations, although we always wondered, half in jest, why our family hadn't gotten any of the furniture.

Recently, we learned that our presumed rights to the Schuyler fortunes and furniture were, well, tangential at best. Although we can trace our roots directly to a German-born Philip Schuyler (1718–1784), who moved to New Jersey in his early youth and later to upstate New York, the general was likely a distant cousin, which makes his great house a wonderful place to visit, but not exactly the family homestead. Regardless, the beauty of the place, and Grandma's enthusiasm, left a strong impression on our developing aesthetic sense.

After a long day in the woods, working toward the future and dreaming about the past, we might have uncovered two or three sets of hinges and handles. We would carry these home and take them to a corner of our parents' horse barn that we had staked out for our treasures. There, we would wipe the pieces down with a cloth or towel and lay them out, pair by pair, on a blanket spread across the floor. Later that night, after dinner, we would take out our copy of Wallace Nutting's *Furniture Treasury,* and return to the barn to compare our most recent discoveries to the black-and-white pictures in the book. Nutting was an early and extraordinary collector, and he compiled nearly five thousand images of American furniture, hardware, and household utensils in a three-volume set, first published in 1928. Although his work contains minimal text (and a fair number of the artifacts pictured have since been proven inauthentic or misattributed), it remains a wonderful visual source. Back then, however, it was our bible.

Barn hardware was not the only thing we ferreted out of those wooded sites, however. The decaying foundations of old houses, for example, stood as signposts to old refuse pits—literally, nineteenth-century garbage pits—which were another source of potential treasures. After hunting the surface of a site for all that we could find, we turned our attentions farther away, to the area that immediately surrounded it, and asked ourselves, If we had lived in this place, where would we have thrown our trash? The answer usually lay over the nearest hillock, just out of view of the surviving structure, because the low rise acted as a natural buffer to what originally must have been an unsightly pile. We discovered that lilac bushes often sprouted over these waste sites, perhaps attracted to the moist, dark soil, so if we spotted that fragrant bush, we made sure to dig near the roots.

Leslie and I would often work silently together for hours, clad only in our work boots and jeans, sifting through the ground as the shifting shade of the trees above sheltered us from an otherwise-relentless summer sun. There was suspense in each shovelful of moist, gritty soil, which was further sweetened by the aroma of the earth itself. For us, these were times filled with the kind of unadulterated intensity—a purity of focus—that I think is reserved for children, try as we might to recapture it throughout our lives.

Sometimes our excavations yielded nothing more than broken bits of oatmeal-colored stoneware—that practical, daily-use ceramic that might be best described as the Tupperware of the nineteenth century—but occasionally we uncovered an old inkwell or pieces of fancier tableware, such as English soft-paste pearl ware (a form of cream-colored earthenware) or blue-and-white Chinese export porcelain (made in China specifically for export to Europe and the United States). More often, though, we found fractured bottles of colored glass—ones that had probably been used for alcoholic beverages or for medicinal purposes—and occasionally came up with a perfect, unbroken specimen.

Just as with the wrought-iron hardware, there were levels of rarity to the shapes and colors of the glass bottles. We sometimes carried a price guide to antique glass bottles with us when we worked, so we could immediately determine the value of our discovery. The most desirable colors were amber and sapphire blue, followed by assorted shades of yellow-green. Next were the aquamarine examples, followed by colorless or clear bottles, which were the most common.

For weeks in the summer, we could spend every day combing the same site, over and over, deeper and deeper. It was addictive, because the lower we dug, the earlier the vintage and more rare the samples we might uncover. One memorable bottle that we discovered was an aqua-toned pocket flask that resembled a pumpkin seed in shape. It had a flat oval body leading to a short, narrow neck, and we called it the "Christmas flask" because it carried a raised imprint of what looked to be a fir wreath on one side. By the early nineteenth century, glassmakers began hand-blowing the glass directly into a mold that could yield any pattern they fashioned. Politically inspired portraits of men like George Washington, Benjamin Franklin, and Andrew Jackson proved incredibly popular, as were images of the American eagle and ships flying the American flag. Our small flask not only displayed a less mainstream (and therefore rarer) image and a sumptuous color; it was also in absolutely mint condition: not a chip or scratch, despite the small colony of black beetles and other residue that we shook from its clogged interior. When we first spotted that piece peeking out from the soil like a gem, our whoops of joy bounced off the rocky ravine where we worked and rose high into the valley around us.

Introduction:
In this book are listed things that we bought and sold from July 16 to Sept. 30. _1969_ We hope that you will enjoy our _writings_!

Leigh & Leslie   (at this time)

12 years old

We are antique dealers.

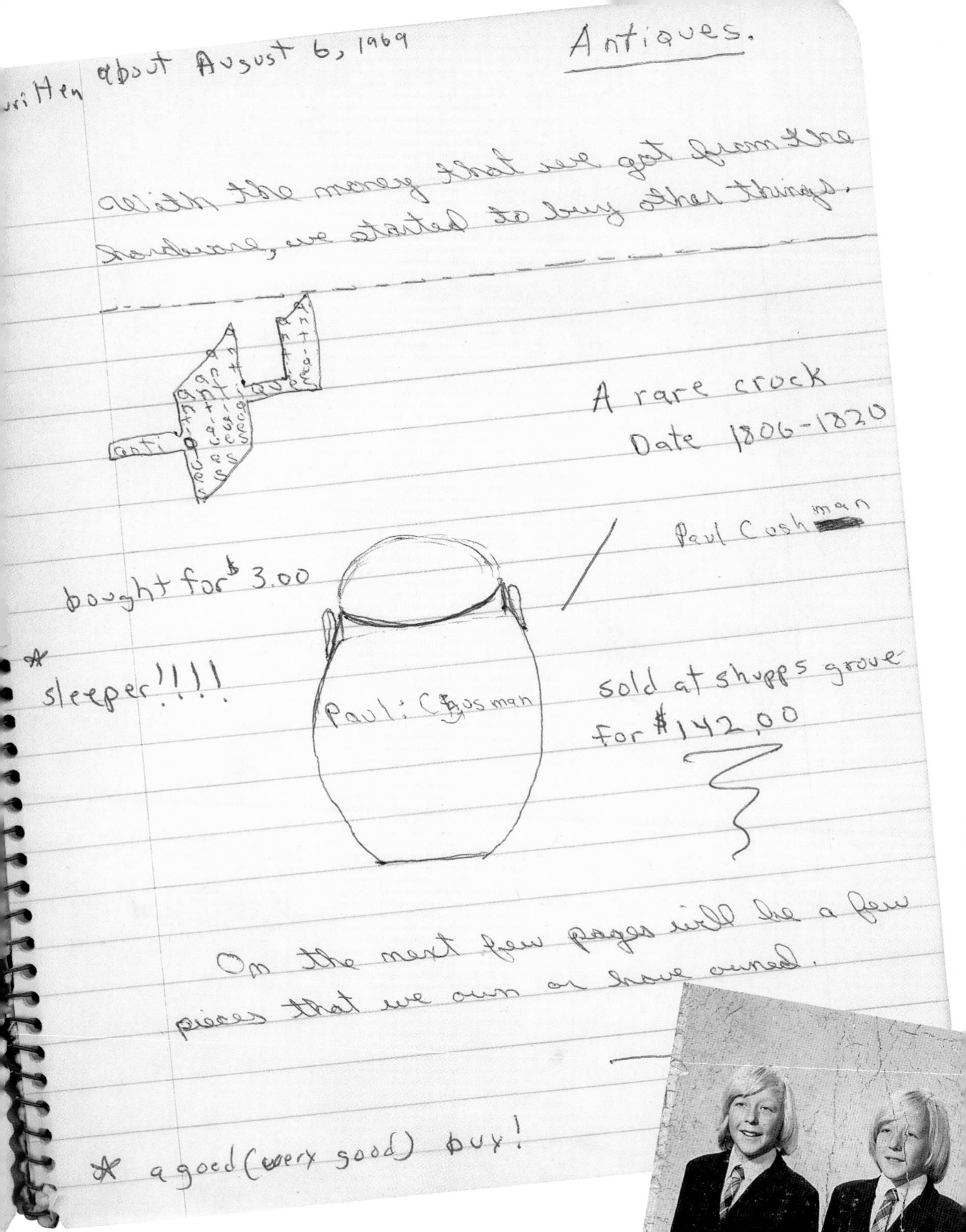

With the money that we got from the hardware, we started to buy other things.

A rare crock
Date 1806-1820

Paul Cush man

bought for $3.00

sleeper!!!!

Paul: C. gus man

sold at shupp5 grove for $142.00

On the next few pages will be a few pieces that we own or have owned.

* a good (very good) buy!

Circa 1969, about the time we started our diaries.

27

<u>HAPPY NEWS</u>!! JUST now our

mother (mom) told us that she
had a birthday present picked.
And better than that, the present
is stoneware. mom says that the
piece has incising, but, thats the
only hint she'll give. Now all that
we can do is wait untill our birthday —
6 days away. we hope that they
won't tell us "before our due" date.
As we might have said earlier the
lecture was enjoyed by the dealers
who attended. The room was a bit
cramped, but we survived. Mary Vail,
the person who owned the house where
the meeting was held, has a small
unmarked crock with an incised bird.
but, the problem is the crock has
the woman's name on it. Ms Vail
(in blue) after we noticed this.
we didn't question any more about
whether she would sell it or

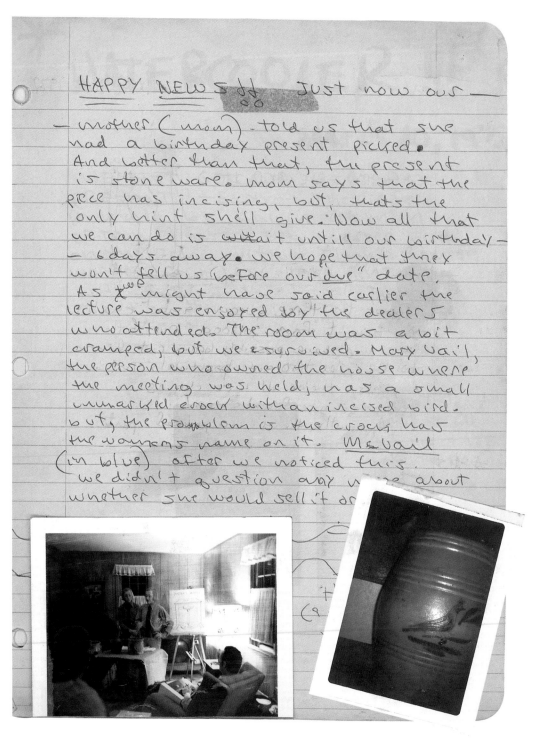

Teenaged lecturers.

A prized early-nineteenth-century water cooler.

2

"We Are Antique Dealers"

WHEN LEIGH AND I WERE TWELVE, we decided to start a joint diary. Like many children that age, we had begun to develop a sense of our own personal history. Finally, we had lived enough actually to *have* a past significant enough to recall—and, of course, we were beginning to dream about our future. Unlike most other children, however, our dreams revolved around antiques, and not just the kind that we were finding in the woods. Flea markets, tag sales, and antique shops also loomed large in our early childhood, and with a diary, Leigh and I decided, we could chart the progress of our expanding interests. We resolved to record and research in the greatest detail the many objects we admired and sought.

When my brother and I first decided to write this book, we revisited those diaries, which had somehow come to be stored in a large brown cardboard box in the back room of Leigh's Madison Avenue gallery. On a cold winter's night not too long ago, we hauled the box out into the wide arena of the gallery's main show space and set it down on top of a rare Philadelphia piecrust tea table. We then pulled up a pair of walnut side chairs made in Boston around 1740, lifted the long rectangular top off the box (inhaling the musty scent of aging paper), and began to weed through its jumbled contents.

We were immediately sent back in time by the well-worn pages of each battered notebook filled with our alternating immature hand—replete with misspellings, food stains, and doodles. I am still amazed by our first and rather prophetic entry, dated July 15, 1969, in which we unabashedly declared, "We are antique dealers. Leigh & Leslie 12 years old (at this time)."

I think we saw those words as our mission statement. We felt we were making official our entry into the world of antiques. Our mutual love and appreciation for old things, stems, of course, from our parents, who were, and still are, avid collectors and dealers. As we wrote in our diary that first year, "We actually owe part of the intellegence that we have in antiques to . . . our Mother and Father. They got us interested in this fabulous hobby. We think that they diserve a good hand. We want at least 1/2 the credit to go to our fantasticly wonderful parents."

Misspellings notwithstanding, Leigh and I got a good laugh from the line that directly followed that statement, which reveals just how focused we were: "By the way, we are writing on an early Hepplewhite table (tiger maple) that we estimate is worth $150.00. It is a very fine piece of furniture." What we were referring to was a trim little drop-leaf table (often termed a Pembroke table) that sat in our parents' living room. It had a rectangular top with two hinged leaves on either side that could be pulled up and supported by a pair of wings, or braces, that extended like fingers on the underside (open, it probably measured close to thirty-five inches in width). The table's triptych top featured a wonderfully charged tiger-maple wood, so called because its distinctive rippled pattern (caused by an aberration in the grain) resembles a tiger's stripe. It was an elegant, well-proportioned piece that probably dated to the 1820s. That is why in our diary we made reference to the English cabinetmaker George Hepplewhite, whose influential book *The Cabinet-maker and Upholsterer's Guide* (first published in 1788) forever linked his name with Neoclassical style, in both England and America. Until our parents sold the table a few years back, it was the oldest piece of furniture in the house.

It may seem unusual that Leigh and I were so consumed with the search for and study of antique artifacts, but I don't think we ever had a choice in the matter. It was simply in our blood. What Dad has always called the "antiquing thing" began with our paternal grandmother, Anna Keno, who, around the time our parents married, developed an interest in trivets, the small short-footed stands, usually made of cast iron, that were used to protect tabletops from oven-hot pots and dishes. After rooting around in her attic one day, Grandma found one that had belonged to her mother. The trivet's base formed a scripted letter *W*, which likely stood for Westermann, her mother's family name. Grandma decided to hang the piece in her stairway hall, and within a short time, that single trivet was joined by another and another, just as Grandma herself would be joined by one collecting Keno after another.

Our parents married quite young. Mom was eighteen and had just graduated from the Herkimer County High School, while Dad, aged twenty-one, was a junior at Syracuse University. After their marriage, our folks moved into a small two-bedroom apartment that Dad built over the garage of his parents' place. That's when they began accompanying our grandparents on visits to small antique shops in the area. Our grandparents were still on the lookout for trivets, but it wasn't long before Mom and Dad began pursuing objects that caught their own fancy.

Their first purchase was a late-nineteenth-century dry sink made in New York. It still carried its original buttermilk red paint (so called, according to Dad, because the deep brickred color could be formulated at home by mixing a powder pigment with any convenient liquid medium, such as buttermilk). Nowadays, many people use these freestanding wooden washbasins as planters, but originally they were used for cleaning dishes in kitchens that lacked running water.

Soon after our parents took the dry sink home, Dad did what many others did at that time: He scraped the old red paint right off. This was, of course, the worst thing he could have done, but back in the early 1950s, people didn't respect old finishes the way we do today. Regardless, a few weeks later, our parents spotted a chest of drawers that they thought would prove more useful in their newlyweds' home, so they sold the sink (actually managing to double their investment) to buy the chest of drawers. Antiquing was not only fun, they quickly discovered, but it could be profitable, as well.

By the time Mitchell was born in December 1952, Dad had also begun to pursue another passion of his, collecting classic cars. Some people find it surprising that Mom indulged Dad as much as she did. At one point in the early 1970s, Dad was storing eight cars on our property, including a silver 1938 3.5 liter SS100 Jaguar and a white 1954 XK120 Jaguar coupe, two of the world's sexiest sports cars. At times, our property may have resembled a parking lot, but, then as now, if Dad was happy, Mom was happy, too. So, while other young couples bought sensible Dodges, Fords, Chevys, or Plymouths, the growing Keno clan piled into an old Jaguar, Cord, or Auburn, none of which qualified as a typical "family car."

With Dad on the fender of a rare 1931 L-29 Cord.

The family.

Despite our parents' growing interest in antiques and automobiles, they were by no means wealthy people. As Leigh mentioned before, Dad was a trained painter; for a living, he taught art at Mom's alma mater, the Herkimer High School. But he also supplemented the family's income as a structural ironworker, working on bridges and buildings around Utica during school vacations. Leigh and I remember taking him lunch with our mother while he was working on the South Washington Street Bridge, which now spans the Mohawk River and the Erie Canal (in parts of Herkimer County, the two run side by side) from north to south. There, we gazed up in complete awe at Dad, our hero, skirting the exposed network of metal support beams rising eight stories into the sky.

Right after our parents moved to the farm, Mom took a more serious stab at the antiques business and set up a small shop in our home. As it turned out, Mom was a born seller. Her success as a saleswoman came from her direct and low-key approach to her customers. She would tell visitors just what she knew about a piece and leave the rest up to them. And when clients came to the house, Mom placed Leigh and me—then about five or six—in charge of minding the shop, which of course pleased us no end. We loved cautioning browsers to handle the merchandise with care, although, in hindsight, I suspect it was Mom's tender way of ensuring that we were the ones who were careful.

"The Homestead"—where we first learned about original condition.

A few years later, Mom moved the shop across Creek Road to an early-nineteenth-century homestead that was part of our property. (Sadly, that house—which had probably been built by the people who originally settled our land—has since been torn down to make way for a state highway.) Despite its run-down condition, the house was a magical place, with the original bean-shaped wrought-iron handle on the front door, wide pine floor boards, plaster walls, low-beamed ceilings, and a neatly built green-painted pine corner cupboard in the large parlor room that Mom converted into her shop. Walking in there, you were immediately enveloped by the spicy smell of old wood and warm fires extinguished long ago. It is an unforgettable scent, one that I regularly catch inside the many high chests and corner cupboards that I examine at Sotheby's. As teenagers, Leigh and I used to spend time down in the homestead, hanging out with our buddies, sneaking cigarettes, and listening to the Grateful Dead and Tranquillity. But that was only after Mom had moved her shop off the premises, to a storefront in Fly Creek, a town about thirty miles south, toward Cooperstown.

The shop may have been Mom's domain, but our parents were a team when it came to acquiring antiques. Dad has a wonderful eye for objects, probably because of his training as an artist. One of the questions he always asks when evaluating a new object reverberates with Leigh and me to this day when we look at American furniture: "Does it speak to you?"

A piece may be authentic and unaltered and possess the right color and finish, but if it lacks an inner light, Dad believes, there is nothing even the best salesman can do to convince you of its greatness. Great objects should trigger reactions that are visceral. And this criterion applies as much to high art or masterpieces as it does to work done by blacksmiths, carpenters, or nonacademic painters—folk art, or innocent art, can also be breathtakingly beautiful in its natural expression.

The first purchase that Leigh and I recorded in our joint diary was a small Canton ginger jar, about six inches high, which we bought from a woman named Myrtle Dicker for fifteen dollars. In retrospect, acquiring that porcelain jar (probably made around 1840 and shipped from China's port of Canton to the United States) was not a particularly significant event in our early collecting history, but meeting Myrtle Dicker certainly was. Myrtle was a retired schoolteacher who had taught in the Poland Central School just outside of Cold Brook, the small village where she lived, a few miles north of Utica. During the early 1940s and 1950s, Myrtle had run an antiques business as a sideline from her home. But by the time we met her in 1969, she was all but retired from antiques as well, and whatever signage she had posted outside the large yellow Victorian house had long since fallen down and never been replaced.

As with so many folks in this business, Myrtle was a character. Quite simply, she was the most stubborn, ornery, unpredictable woman we had ever come across in our young lives, but she had her reasons. By the time we met her, she was well into her seventies and so crippled by arthritis that she needed a walker to get around. A large woman with shoulder-length gray hair, she spoke with a German accent that seemed forever colored with pain and frustration. I think we first met Myrtle through a friend of our parents named Roger Johnson, who was also an antiques dealer (and also quite a character). In the thirty-five years or so that we have known Roger, he has always driven a battered van stocked with the tools of his trade: old receipt books scattered across his windshield, quilted packing blankets stacked high in the trunk, and a few boxed items that are always for sale.

By contrast, Myrtle's house, and all its glorious contents, sat virtually undisturbed and forgotten in that sleepy little village nestled deep in the foothills of the Adirondacks. In all the years that we visited Myrtle, the phone never rang and no one ever came to call. After our first visit, though, Leigh and I were captivated by the beautiful things that we saw there and insisted that our parents take us back as often as they could (usually about twice a month). Every cabinet, dresser drawer, and visible surface above or beneath her chairs, tables, and even the beds held a gem.

Myrtle's taste in objects was exceptional. She had a great eye. She owned a number of large country pieces. In particular, I recall a tall eighteenth-century pine corner cupboard in the living room. It had three open shelves on the upper half and inset paneled doors below. There was also a wonderful tiger-maple kettle stand with a circular top and three cabriole legs, which was kept in an upstairs bedroom. But the strength of her collection was in early "smalls," items that could be easily handheld or carried. The reason for this was that back when she was actively acquiring antiques, in the 1940s and 1950s, she bought most of her stock out of the homes of her neighbors. Usually, that meant eighteenth- and early-nineteenth-century ceramics, pewter, glassware, woodenware, and iron— all items that could have been easily transported to the area by the earliest settlers. This was also the reason why Leigh and I chose to focus on those same categories when we first entered the field. We liked the early things—and still do today—and the oldest pieces that had survived in our rural pocket of New York State tended to be smalls.

In some ways, Myrtle was a mentor to us—albeit, an unorthodox one—for she insisted that we understand the merits of the objects that we enjoyed and studied in her home. "Has anything been done to this cupboard?" "Is this the original surface?" "Do you think this painting has been altered?" "Why is this burl bowl better than the others?" she'd query us firmly.

But even if we made it through the rigors of her questioning, it was still never clear that we would be allowed to buy anything. In fact, nothing in Myrtle's house ever displayed a price tag or sticker, so we might jump through her hoops for hours on end, only to discover that the object we coveted was not for sale. Or she might agree to sell something and then abruptly change her mind and ask us to leave. On Mom's advice, we always came bearing a quart of vanilla ice milk to soothe our way into Myrtle's good graces, but she still pushed the limits of our twelve-year-old patience.

On the day that we bought the Canton ginger jar (so named because the form was traditionally used in China for storing shaved bits of ginger root), we were having an impromptu lesson on Chinese export porcelain. Myrtle asked us to collect two similar jars from the top shelf of the tall pine corner cupboard and debate the merits of each vessel. Leigh and I each grabbed one of the fragile blue-decorated white jars from the upper shelf and carried it back to the dining room, where she waited for us on a small couch. We sat down on either side of her and began to study the pair.

Both were ovoid (or egg-shaped), but one was clearly more refined than the other. Its silhouette featured a delicate narrow collar, or neck, that sloped gracefully outward toward the rounded belly of the jar and then cut inward again at the bottom to form a perfect circle. An eggshell-thin flat lid capped this exquisite vasiform, or vaselike shape. The jar seemed particularly successful in its design because the bulbous shape was strikingly enhanced by the brilliant cobalt blue flower pattern that encircled it. The flowers seemed to bloom most expressively at the broad middle of the piece. By comparison, the floral pattern that ran along the body of the second ginger jar was ever so slightly blurred, but that imprecision was enough to damage the impact of the overall design. Furthermore, the proportions of that jar were just a little off—the neck seemed a bit too short, the body a bit too broad. Myrtle was pleased with our analysis and invited us to buy the first jar.

I have sometimes wondered why Myrtle allowed us to visit as often as we did. Usually, we went there in the evening, when our parents were the most free to drive us, and stayed a number of hours. In fact, it wasn't unusual for Mom and Dad to head for the car and nap until we were finished with our dealings. Perhaps Myrtle liked our company, or perhaps she had seen in us a genuine interest that touched her teacher's soul and made her think she could make a difference. Regardless of the reason, she did leave her mark on us. Whatever skills Leigh and I now have as negotiators, we first honed in Myrtle's living room, for she had as much difficulty parting with items like that fifteen-dollar ginger jar as some of the people we meet today who ask us to handle long-treasured family heirlooms.

About this time, Leigh and I began to foster a budding interest in stoneware, the heavy-duty nonporous pottery jugs, jars, and crocks that were commonly made for food storage from the early 1700s through the late nineteenth century. The piece that jump-started our own pursuit of stoneware, however, was a large crock that we found at a yard sale about forty-five minutes from our farm. Interestingly, the sale was held at the home of a late-nineteenth-century balloonist, so some artifacts that would have amazed anyone interested in early aviation were offered in the barn with the rest of the merchandise. There was an enormous deflated cloth balloon, and a giant wicker basket large enough to fit four men and a cluster of oblong ballast bags comfortably. As intriguing as that assemblage was, what caught our

The Allman brothers? No, just us inspecting some of our favorite pieces.

attention was a large ovoid crock lying on its side in a pile of hay to the right of the large basket. It measured about thirteen inches high and had a small hairline crack that ran from the edge of the top down about two inches, toward the swelled center of the piece. The crack didn't bother us, however, because the overall sweep of the form was so expressive, it immediately recalled to our minds the broad-knuckled hands of the potter molding the wet clay as it spun on his wheel. Similarly, the mottled brown tone of the glaze spoke to the scorching heat (roughly 2,300°F) of the wood-burning kiln in which it had been fired so long ago. Boldly stamped across the center of the piece, as an advertisement of his craft, was the name of the man who had made it, Paul Cushman, an Albany-based potter who was active between 1806 and 1820.

Since Cushman was an upstate New York potter, Leigh and I were already somewhat familiar with his work. But this was the first piece of his that we purchased (we tried our best to remain straight-faced when we paid the woman who had owned it the three dollars she was asking for the crock). After we took the piece home, we researched Cushman, who had worked as a building contractor on Albany's waterfront before he switched to the pottery business. Perhaps it was his late start at the craft, but a surprisingly high number of Cushman's pots dropped while they were being baked in the kiln (a complicated process that involved stacking dozens, if not hundreds, of pots on top of one another, separated only by small, narrow tiles). This usually resulted in an off-kilter, or lopsided, vessel. Leigh and I were anything but discouraged by such imperfections. Rather, we found them incredibly compelling because they reminded us of the laborious and unpredictable process of making the pots.

My brother and I held on to that Cushman crock for a long time, although sometime before college we sold it to a private collector for upward of two thousand dollars. Eventually, it was joined by nearly fifty more pieces of stoneware, all housed on a set of shelves that we had erected with gray weathered barn boards at the end of the first-floor hallway, near the living room. Most nights after dinner, the two of us would each grab a cup of coffee from the kitchen—always poured into a pair of memorable blue-decorated stoneware mugs that our mother had purchased in Bennington, Vermont—and make our way to those shelves. There, in between gulps of coffee, we would go through the collection piece by piece, carefully handling and examining the spun surfaces and swelled bodies of each one. In time, the peculiarities of each crock—the steady rise of the wheel-spun form and the subtle shifts from brown to gray in the mottled glaze—were fixed in our minds like the words of a favorite song.

Flea markets were another great source for stoneware, and the checkerboard grid of booths on their grounds was as familiar to us as our own backyard. Our parents had taken us to shows from the time we were infants, and we loved the whole process. First there was the drive, which was plotted so that we would hit as many small antique shops as possible. Back then, the shops, much like our mom's, were usually set up in a home, garage, or barn. The intimacy of walking onto someone's private

Our collection on display at the end of the hall.

property lent an aura of freshness to the objects, as if they had just been carried down from the attic or acquired from a neighbor. The group-shop phenomenon, where various vendors pool their goods and resources together, was still a long way off, and I have to say that a sense of intimacy was lost when all those independents began to disappear.

At each stop, our parents, Leigh, and I would pile out of the car and head inside for a quick go-around. My brother and I would separate from them and scan the territory for "sleepers," a trade term for undervalued merchandise. If we spotted one, he and I might hold a hasty huddle in a corner to strategize, then approach the proprietor and try to strike a deal. I think store owners were sometimes taken aback at the sight of us: a matched set of young boys with an almost-exaggerated sense of purpose, our shoulder-length blond hair combed to one side, our T-shirts tucked into low-slung blue jeans held up with two-inch-wide brown leather belts.

I remember one shop in Massachusetts where Leigh and I spotted an incredible early-nineteenth-century Leeds bowl, so called then because it may have been manufactured in Leeds, England, probably as an export item for the American market. This particular piece had a cream-colored body and unusually large polychrome, or multicolored, floral decoration. After many hours in the car, Leigh and I were in the mood for some horseplay and, thinking we were out of view of the shop owner, took turns putting the valuable bowl on our heads like a helmet and marching around the front of the store. We were not out of view, however, and the owner was, not surprisingly, appalled. She thought she had a pair of hoodlums in her shop and didn't know what to do. We quickly settled down, however, and ended up having a great conversation with her about the merits of eighteenth-century ceramics: how the fragile, thin surfaces can feel creamy to the touch and how the deeply saturated blue, red, yellow, and green tones may have influenced the palette of so many American folk painters. Ultimately, we bought the piece at a reduced, dealer's price. As an adult, I have since run into the proprietor, only to have her shake a finger at me in playful reference to our first encounter.

After the long ride to a show, made longer by all our stops and starts, we would arrive at the grounds, usually around nightfall. There, our parents would take their place at the end of what could easily grow to be a mile of cars, vans, and trucks snaking away from the gated and locked entrance. As soon as our parents parked,

Leigh and I would be out of the van and on our way, walking the length of vehicles with a pair of high-powered flashlights, hoping to spot some hidden treasures in the packed trunks and perhaps strike an early deal. Our hunger for the search really knew no bounds. As the night wore on, we would repeat this procedure again and again as the line continued to grow. Sometimes, folks would be trying to catch some sleep in the back of their cars. I remember plenty of times when I would shine my light into a darkened van, looking for sleepers, but seeing instead a sleeping dealer throwing up an angry arm to block the beam from our lights.

Eventually, when Leigh and I grew tired ourselves, we would find space on the floor of our parents' own van and curl up to sleep beneath the heavy quilted packing blankets used to protect the folk art and country furniture in which they specialized. Sometimes, the van was so stocked with merchandise—in the mid-1970s, they branched out into old arcade equipment such as slot machines and jukeboxes—that we had to spend the night outdoors in sleeping bags placed on folding cots covered by large plastic sheets in case of rain. I remember waking up one morning at the big three-day flea market in Brimfield, Massachusetts, barely able to move my arms. During a long night's rainstorm, what felt like five gallons of water had pooled along the contours of my body, so when I finally managed to roll off the cot, the rainwater came rolling off right with me, hitting the ground with a heavy splat.

As young flea market attendees, we'd already found our direction.

Our parents often brought a trailer along to rest in themselves, but actually, they never seemed to sleep. Our wake-up call was usually the sound of Mom revving the van engine sometime around 5:30 A.M. That meant she had spotted the show manager preparing to throw open the gates to the grounds. Despite the early hour, this was the time that Leigh and I lived for. Within moments, our van would join the line of cars lumbering through the gates and then dispersing through the dew-wet grass to their appointed spots. Then as our parents began to unpack their wares, we two hunters would set off through the rising mists of the brightening fields.

The start of the shows was always an adrenaline-rushing, heart-accelerating time. I remember seeing buyers lined up at the gates, ready to run at full speed to the just-opening booths as the trucks were still rolling in. It was the golden age of antiquing—only no one knew it at the time. It seemed as if it would never end. The reason it felt like a new frontier was because there was so little information available, other than a handful of guides and books on collectibles. Particularly with the early pieces that Leigh and I loved, issues of quality, age, and condition called for seat-of-the-pants judgments. There were simply no established guidelines or standards. As a result, we cut our analytical teeth on the pottery, painted boxes, weather vanes, and furniture that we found. For us, the open vistas of the flea markets—like the fields and woods behind our house—summoned unending possibilities for discovery. I remember one annual show in Amherst, New Hampshire, that was particularly thrilling, simply because it was held on rolling grounds (unusual for a flea market). The landscape really rose and dipped, and certain parts of the field were shielded by small groves of trees, all factors that only intensified our hunger for the search.

The best thing about sleepers, of course, is that they appear without warning. We might scan table after table of disheartening junk, only to be startled back to life by something stupendous. Such was the case at a show we attended when we were fourteen, held on the grounds of the Shaker Museum in Chatham, New York. The gates had been open for about twenty minutes when we came upon a man unpacking the contents of a small four-drawer chest (probably made in New York around 1840) onto an oatmeal-colored wool blanket thrown across the open bed of a pickup truck. Perhaps it was the bib overalls he was wearing, paired with the truck, but he looked as if he had decided that very day to switch from farming to the antiques business. The man had yet to open the bottom drawer, so when Leigh and I reached the booth proper, we asked if we might take a look inside. With a nod and a smile, he gave his consent, so we bent over in unison and pulled open the drawer.

We found ourselves peering down at the broad domed lid of a large rectangular painted tin box. Measuring about twelve inches in length, it featured a brownish black ground that shone like Japanese lacquer, and it had a narrow border of highly realistic cherries and strawberries running about half an inch from the edge. The fruit was so carefully delineated that we could see the evenly spaced grid pattern of white seeds on each strawberry. Mounted at the center of the top was a small bail, or curved hoop handle, which one of us seized and used to pull the box up and out of the drawer. As we held it aloft, the squared form rocked slowly in the cool morning air, revealing a

Above: Setting up shop with Mom at a flea market.

Left: Inspecting Dad's latest purchase—a 1939 6C 2500 Alfa Romeo sport coupé with coachwork by Touring.

Opposite: A journal page.

Sept 17, 1969.

7.  sandwich whale oil lamp
(pewter top) blown

8.  sandwich tieback
(green)

9. 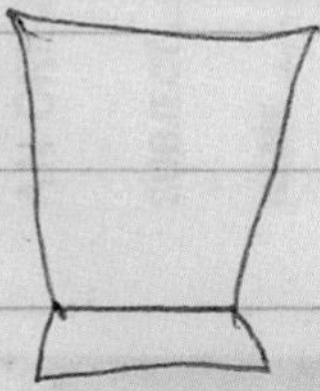 American pewter cup
1806-1820   J.D. Locke

10.  sandwich plate
(chipped) (small crack)

(12 in) diameter
early unlevel crooked
piece of graphite
in glass.

many
antiques but not
enough room

cluster of brilliantly painted floral sprays on its front and back. As with the fruit running along the top, the rendering of the highly stylized orange-red flowers was superbly colored, making it an incredible piece of folk art.

Painted and decorated tin, or toleware, was America's answer to imported French *tôle*, which was, in turn, made as an alternative to Oriental lacquerwork. Toleware was popularized in the United States during the early nineteenth century, and many households had at least one toleware canister, tray, teapot, or document box, generally decorated with a pattern involving brightly colored flowers or fruits. The document box that we were passing back and forth in our hands, however, was the largest, most exquisitely rendered example of toleware we had ever seen in our lives—even in books. But there was just one problem: It showed virtually no signs of age.

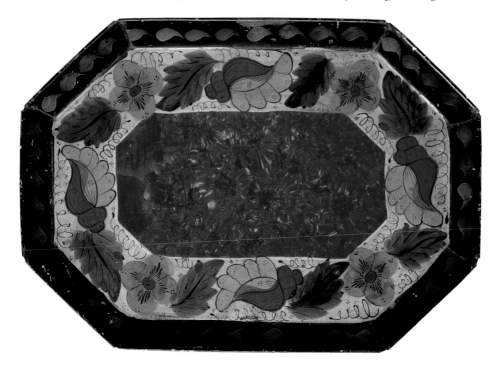

An early-nineteenth-century American toleware tray.

Realizing this, Leigh and I continued to open and shut the box (the fit was intentionally tight to protect important papers from mice and insects), run our fingers along its contours, and occasionally hold it up to the early-morning sun in an effort to detect some clues to its past. We asked ourselves how this piece could have survived nearly two centuries of use without any wear to its paint. There should have at least been dulled halos in the areas surrounding the lock and bail handle, where the box would have been most frequently touched. Even the finish on the bottom was intact, as if the box had never been dragged across a tabletop. Still, Leigh and I were inextricably drawn to this piece. We asked the man what he knew about the box, but his answer was fairly vague. "My guess is that it had been in our family for some time," he said, "but I'd never seen it before I looked inside that drawer a few weeks ago."

The man had an open, honest face, and we decided to give the piece a chance. Perhaps the box had been tucked away for safekeeping and then forgotten, which would account for its pristine condition. We bought it for his asking price of eight dollars, and I remember feeling like we had just robbed a bank as we turned and left the booth. But as we made our way out into the field of dealers, already in search of our next sleeper, a most peculiar thing happened. We began to sense a commotion behind us. Looking back over our shoulders, we noticed a small group of people pointing and gesturing to the box that we held between us. The auburn light of the rising sun was bouncing off those incredibly rendered fruits and flowers with an intensity that further deepened the richness of the colors. Suddenly, two people broke away and approached us. They were joined by two more, and then two more. All were interested in our newly acquired box. We could have held an auction right there on the spot. Someone offered us forty-five dollars for the box, another sixty-five dollars, but, with matching grins, we assured them that it wasn't for sale.

We did sell it, though, not very long after the Chatham show, to a prominent dealer in American folk art for about ninety-five dollars (a tidy profit, even though today it might be valued at closer to ten thousand dollars). After all, hoarding objects was not the full thrust of our purpose, for we were quite serious about nurturing our business as dealers. We took a great deal of satisfaction from selling off most of the objects we acquired, for a completed sale is the ultimate barometer of taste—it means that your aesthetic instincts are good. Leigh and I had been selling items on our own from about the age of ten. First, there were the iron hinges and handles that we found in the woods behind our house, which we sold from a blanket in our parents' booth at shows. Later, we branched out into other areas we enjoyed, such as pottery, porcelain, and pewter, and we often brought in a bigger weekend profit than our parents did.

Buying our first piece of American furniture, in the winter of 1972, was a memorable event. It was a black-painted banister-back armchair (the back was formed of a series of four evenly spaced vertical spindles) that had been made in New England, probably around 1760. We found the chair, which cost about two hundred dollars, at an antiques shop in Amherst, Massachusetts, that was run by a retired Amherst College professor of classics and literature named Reginald Foster French, who looked and sounded every inch of his name—tall, distinguished, and thoroughly profound.

We loved the piece right away because it was so old. At some point in the early nineteenth century, a previous owner had converted the chair into a rocker, and we thought that gave it a real Wallace Nutting–type charm. We particularly enjoyed the way the chair showcased the art of the turner, the craftsman who supplied the many lathe-turned parts, including the legs, arms, and signature banister back. A lathe is a large machine, still in use today, in which a piece of wood can be clamped on a horizontal axis and then spun rapidly while a cutting tool is simultaneously used to whittle away at the surface.

With Professor French looking on, we admired all the permutations of the turner's craft as they appeared on that chair. There were the well-articulated rear posts, which included the legs and the vertical side supports of the chair (called the stiles), ending in

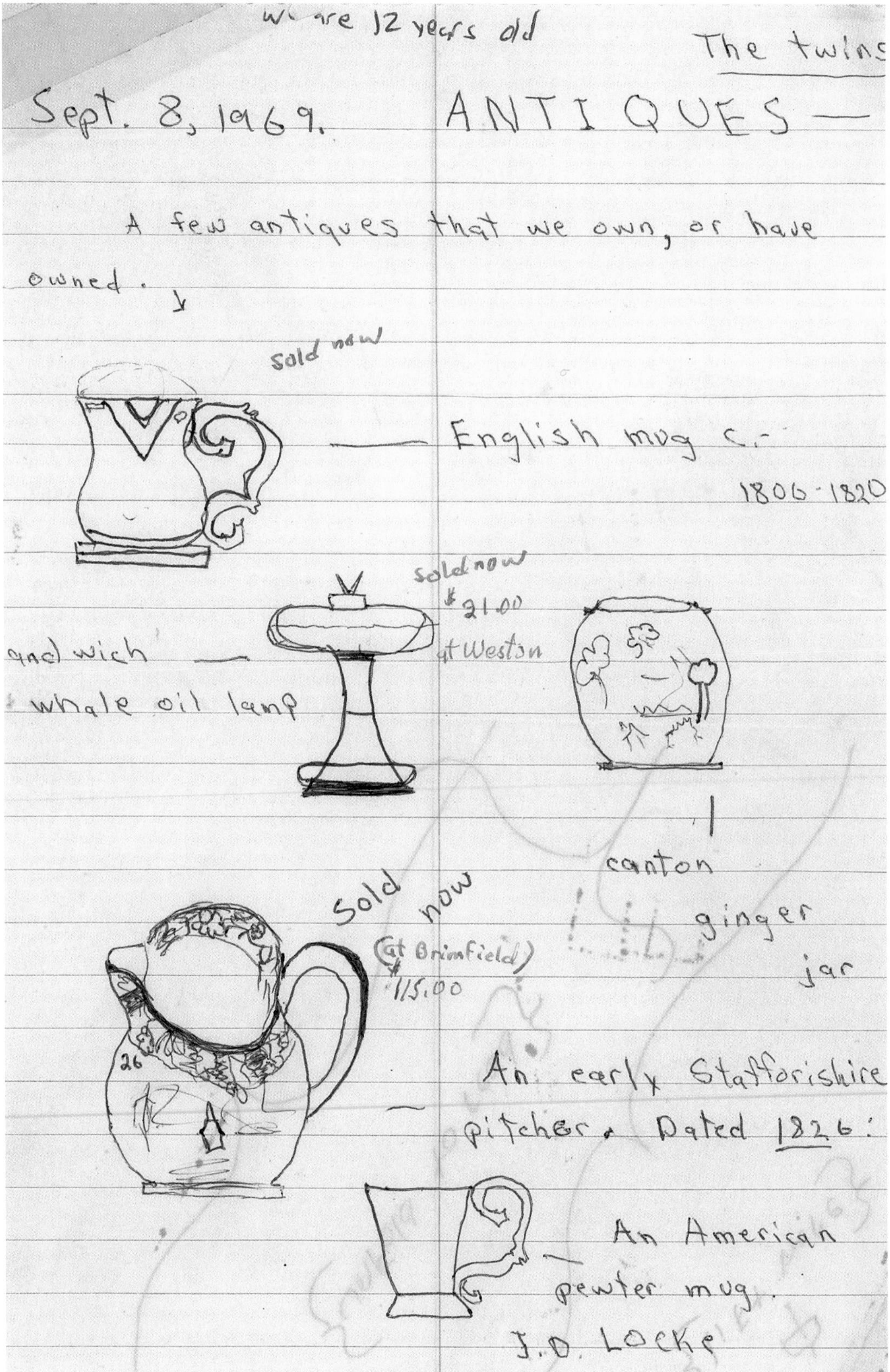

we are 12 years old

The twins

Sept. 8, 1969. ANTIQUES —

A few antiques that we own, or have owned. ↓

sold now

— English mug c. 1806-1820

sold now $21.00 at Weston

Sandwich — whale oil lamp

canton ginger jar

Sold now (at Brimfield) $115.00

— An early Staffordshire pitcher. Dated 1826.

— An American pewter mug. J.D. Locke

Left: A page from our diary documenting, among other prized possessions, Myrtle Dicker's ginger jar.
Above: Highly prized animal-decorated stoneware.

45

Various treasures, including (lower left) our first furniture purchase, an eighteenth-century New England banister-back armchair.

a pair of small decorative finials. The bulbous swells of the decorative turnings narrowed slightly as they rose along the legs into the stiles, thrusting the viewer's eye upward. The same occurred with the front posts, where the line of each leg grew more slender as it rose and gradually transformed into an arm support. At the back the chair featured four reeded slats of wood suspended between two cross rails. More ornate versions of these banisters or balusters required the chairmaker to take a piece of wood sized for the lathe, split it, and then lightly glue it back together. He then lathe-turned the entire glued piece and resplit the spindle when he was through. That left him with a flat surface to face the front of the chair (against which the user's body would presumably rest) and a decorative curved half baluster in the back. It was an ingenious process.

As with so many of the things my brother and I owned and enjoyed, we followed our dealer's instinct and eventually sold the chair a few years later for around four hundred dollars. I always think it fortunate that Leigh and I were never rivals in our search for antiques. We always worked and bought objects as a team. Honestly, I don't think it even occurred to us to go it alone. We just took so much pleasure in our partnership and dialogue, it would have been unnatural, if not boring, to have competed for things. At shows, however, we would very often split up in order to cover more ground. And until dealers got to know us, it was all but inevitable that some mix-ups would occur because we were twins. For example, I might notice something in a booth, ask the dealer some pointed questions, and then move on. A few moments later, my brother would pass through the same booth, spot the same item, follow up with the same line of questioning, and then get lambasted by the dealer for wasting his time once again.

But such run-ins were rare, and they certainly never slowed us down. We continued to collect objects and information wherever and however we could, always pushing the scope of our expanding interests. We also combed the countryside for antiques at shops, shows, and auctions, and to nurture our particular passion for rare stoneware. After high school, Leigh and I both enrolled at Herkimer County Community College. But we resolved to apply ourselves diligently in order to get the good grades we would need to transfer out after our sophomore year and switch to a school better equipped to propel our interest in antiques to a new level. To finance the switch to a private college, we knew we would have to sell off most of our beloved stoneware collection, which we gradually began to do, most often privately to other collectors.

My calling came from Williams College, which I first visited in the fall of 1976. To my mind, the school and its setting in Williamstown, Massachusetts, is one of the most beautiful spots in the country (it was used as a backdrop for the early college scenes in *The Way We Were*). The college itself, one of the oldest in New England, was chartered in 1793, so a good percentage of the campus architecture dates to that period, including the Admissions Office, which is located right on the town's main street.

When I walked into the front room of that proud nineteenth-century structure, I was stopped dead in my tracks by the sight of a tall maple high chest of drawers with an upswept, arched bonnet top. The mellow grain of the wood seemed to smolder in the dappled sunlight that streamed in through the small-paned windows that lined the room. I could barely move my eyes away from the chest in order to speak to the receptionist. But when I did, I realized that she was seated at an incredibly rare eighteenth-century butterfly table (so called because when open, its double leaves are supported from beneath by a bracket shaped like a butterfly's wing). I stammered my name as I lightly touched the worn rounded edge of the small table. After finding my appointment in her book, the receptionist gestured for me to take a seat. I turned and quickly saw that the chair to which she pointed—much like the others that lined the room—was an early-nineteenth-century high-backed Windsor chair (so named because a prototype for the form is said to have been used by George I of England as lawn furniture at Windsor Castle). The chair's signature design featured a curved multiple-spindle back that fit like an arched comb into the solid wood seat that rose and dipped at the center like a saddle and was supported below by slender lathe-turned legs that splayed outward.

I was floored by my surroundings, literally. Before I could stop myself, I was down on the floor, studying the legs of the high chest of drawers that had first caught my eye. All around me the nervous chatter of parents and their teenagers quieted down, and it wasn't long before I felt a quick tap on my shoulder. I edged out from beneath the chest, to see an admissions officer ready to usher me in for my interview. I noted the concern and sympathy on the faces of the parents as we walked by, but they needn't have worried. That day, I had found my future on the floor of the Williams College Admissions Office.

During my interview, I learned that the objects I had so admired all came from a large collection of American furniture that had been donated to the school in 1943 by a former graduate, Charles M. Davenport. There were 168 pieces of furniture in the collection, none of which had ever been properly researched or cataloged. After being admitted to Williams, I would spend the better part of the next two years devoting myself to that task. (Leigh had a parallel experience when he transferred to Hamilton College in Clinton, New York, and found that they, too, had an Americana collection for which he would also produce a catalog.)

Dissecting the Davenport Collection was my first long-term, hands-on experience with a wide range of high-style American furniture. There were, for example, rich mahogany chests of drawers, dazzling walnut tilt-top tea tables, and a number of seventeenth-century chests that were so simple and elegant in form. Being able to handle and compare the appearance and construction of these varied pieces was a gift, for previously I had gotten no closer than a roped line at a museum. The college's Davenport Collection also featured an astounding *fifty-three* Windsor chairs. This sizable inventory gave me an opportunity to examine for the first time the way a standard form was reinterpreted again and again. During my senior year, I prepared an exhibition and catalog based upon my research. Taking a cue from a show I had seen at Yale's art gallery, I hung the chairs from fishing line strung at eye level around the rotunda of the Williams College Museum of Art. Doing so forced visitors to confront the chairs as sensual, sculptural forms rather than as merely utilitarian pieces of furniture. Just as the texture and shapes of the early hardware and hinges that Leigh and I had found in the woods nearly made audible the rapid-fire report of the black-smith's hammer, the bulbous turnings of these spindled chairs made the turner's lathe whirl and whistle in my ear. Those sounds reverberate within me to this day.

Our first business card.

3

Putting It Together

LESLIE AND I HAD LONG SET OUR SIGHTS on moving to New York City, so it seemed only a matter of course that in late August 1979, with our newly minted degrees in hand, we finally made the move. We had gotten our first real taste of the city back when we were sixteen, a visit that had coincided with our earliest brush with the New York auction scene. Together, they had left an indelible impression. We had decided to part with an unusual salt-glazed stoneware jug that we owned, one that was decorated with a pair of acrobats—a man grasping a woman upside down by the ankles. Human or figurative decoration is very rare in stoneware, followed by animals (such as deer or lions), birds, and, finally, flowers. We had owned the jug since we were fourteen, when we bought it at a small country auction for $3,500, which at the time was a world record for American stoneware (there was more than a moment of sustained applause in the room after the hammer fell). Because we had so much money invested in the piece and we wanted an infusion of cash to buy more things, we thought we would try our hand at a New York auction house. We took the jug to Sotheby's for an evaluation by their folk art expert, Nancy Druckman (who within a few years would become a colleague of Leslie's), and agreed to consign the piece.

On the day of the sale, we drove down to the city from Mohawk with our parents. I remember how thrilling it was to walk into the salesroom proper and see the rows of furniture lining the walls (the jug had been consigned to an Americana sale that included both furniture and decorative arts) and all the activity up on the dais. Everything had a very white-glove feel. We were entranced as we watched the auctioneer move the proceedings along. His wit and style seemed a far cry from the country auctions we were used to, where the pace and timbre of the sales tended to resemble something closer to a cattle auction. Unfortunately, the auctioneer's charms that day did nothing to boost the sale of our jug above $2,800. It was disappointing to take a loss (in retrospect, I believe that our suggested estimate of from $3,000 to $3,500 was too high and probably dampened interest in the piece), but I think the experience left us with a great sense of determination to return to that environment and learn more about its wily ways. We have since gained some vicarious satisfaction in knowing that in 1986 the same jug sold again at Sotheby's for $28,600 and then in 1994, in a private sale, for over $60,000, meaning our teenage instincts weren't all that bad.

When we moved to the city in 1979, we entered a landscape for Americana that looked vastly different from what it is today. Sotheby's, the auction house with the firmest footing in the field, had yet to move to its York Avenue space and was still headquartered in the old Parke Bernet building at Madison Avenue and Seventy-sixth Street (ironically, the same building where my gallery is today). Christie's, the London-based auction house, had established their stateside flagship in New York only two years previously, and with it, a newly minted American Furniture Department. Harold and Albert Sack were the favorite sons of American antiques, having taken over (with their brother Robert) the firm started by their father, Israel, almost seventy-five years earlier. They had some rivalry in the persons of John Walton and Bernard and S. Dean Levy, among others. Meanwhile, the finishing touches were being made on the Metropolitan Museum of Art's newly expanded American Wing, which was to give it a sixfold increase in size. In other words, change was in the air, and we had just arrived: young, eager, and ready to prove ourselves.

In September, Leslie entered a rigorous one-year training program at Sotheby's—which worked as a feeder into the firm. I, on the other hand, decided to try my hand at a smaller outfit called William Doyle Galleries, which had been founded by its namesake, Bill Doyle, in 1963. Bill built his business the old-fashioned way, through hard work and perseverance. In the early years, he used to drive through the New England countryside, buy all kinds of antiques, throw them into his truck, and return to the city to sell them off the back. He was a bighearted, charismatic man and had one of the greatest minds for antiques I have ever known. It was not unusual for Bill to overpay for an estate (even after his auction business was off and running, he continued to buy furniture outright) simply because he liked the owners. After his unexpected death in 1993, the firm passed into the capable hands of his dynamic wife, Kathleen, who runs it to this day. I thought that by going with Doyle's I would get a crash course on the ins and outs of the auction world, and I was not mistaken. I also liked the way Bill hired me, fresh-faced and totally green, within moments of our meeting, saying by way of explanation, "I understand from my friend Bob Skinner [the owner of a Massachusetts auction house] that you've been in the business since you were a kid. Well, that's good enough for me."

I worked for Bill for nearly four years, beginning as general appraiser, then quickly moving up to the position of an estate buyer, and eventually inaugurating and heading Doyle's American Furniture and Decorative Arts Department. When I left Doyle's in 1984 for Christie's to become a vice president in the appraisals department, I found it particularly hard to say good-bye to Bill, whom I had come to look upon as a great friend and mentor. The move was a necessary one for me, however, because I felt I needed to understand thoroughly the workings of an international auction house like Christie's if I ever hoped to fulfill my long-term dream of becoming a private dealer in top-notch American furniture.

Within a year, however, I left my job in appraisals (where I assessed general estate property from all over the country) when a position opened up in Christie's burgeoning American Furniture Department, then running smoothly under the smart, easygoing guidance of Dean Failey. The move catapulted me to a place that I had long hoped to reach—the exclusive domain of American furniture at the highest level. More important, I was doing it at a time when the marketplace for Americana was really changing. Five years earlier, when I was still at Doyle's, more than 85 percent of the furniture purchased at auction was bought by dealers (who then turned the merchandise around and sold it at a markup in their galleries). It was very rare to see a private collector bypass this well-entrenched system and bid independently.

But by the mid-1980s, a new generation of buyers had arrived on the scene—many of them born negotiators, flush from their successes on Wall Street, who were willing to spend heretofore-unheard-of prices for Americana. They were a tenacious group, who often liked to bid on their own, but they needed some help analyzing the merchandise and the conditions of the market. Their need for guidance was great for me because I loved American furniture and could honestly think of nothing more enjoyable than getting others excited about it, as well. Because dealers had long dominated the field, I don't think the auction houses were accustomed to reaching out to retail customers. In that way, the shifting marketplace was a boon to me at Christie's (and for Leslie at Sotheby's), because we were there in the thick of things, developing and educating clients, just as a new generation of collectors was finding its way.

One such client was a man named Eddy Nicholson, a compact, intensely driven character (with a predilection for custom-made alligator cowboy boots), who was then president and CEO of Congoleum Corporation. Eddy well represented the new guard in Americana collecting. He had the means and intellect to seek out great objects, he enjoyed bidding for himself, and yet, as bullish as he was, his taste in furniture never strayed beyond absolute elegance. Eddy collected in earnest for a little over a decade, beginning in 1982, and during that time he probably felt a certain kinship to the wealthy colonists who had originally commissioned the many sumptuous pieces that he bought. (In 1995, Eddy abruptly decided to divest himself of his entire hard-won collection in a now legendary $13.6 million sale at Christie's.)

Eddy's strategy, like that of many elite collectors of American furniture, was to home in on the purest examples of a particular furniture style, be it the lilting S curves of the sensuous baroque, the excessive and brilliant carved ornament of the rococo, or the intricate inlaid designs of America's early Federal period. Searching for the finest examples meant that he did not limit himself to objects produced in any one city or region—a key factor to smart collecting.

Targeting a place of manufacture is important to collectors because design and construction techniques, such as the interpretation of the claw-and-ball foot or the design of a chair's back splat, generally developed in a manner unique to each Colonial port town, particularly those at the manufacturing hubs of the major Northeast ports. The reason for this was that the close quarters of early American cities allowed for a lot of cross-pollination and mutual inspiration among the furniture masters. Craftsmen in the port towns tended to set up shop near the waterfront, where the shipbuilding industry kept them busy and mercantile traffic was heaviest. In places like Boston and Newport, the wharves were literally lined with woodworking shops, which meant a short stroll near the dock was all an artisan needed to do to survey the competition. Today, furniture scholars have been able to trace many eighteenth- and early-nineteenth-century design features to individual towns, and even to specific shops, which makes collecting American furniture all the more exciting. It allows a rich historic context to be built up around each object, which in turn informs and enhances our appreciation for the piece as a whole.

Further compounding this interest in regional provenance is the fact that each of the major Colonial ports experienced what might be termed a golden age—a time when the town's fashions were at the forefront of Colonial style. This makes the furniture of certain areas more desirable than examples from other regions. Boston was in the forefront of American style from roughly 1690 through the 1740s. Newport achieved its peak between the 1760s and 1780s. Philadelphia overlapped a bit with Newport, thanks to its fantastic rococo designs in the early 1750s through the 1770s, while New York furniture makers attained their distinctive mastery at the turn of the nineteenth century.

A few collectors make a game of this area of study by buying only the furniture of one region. Some prefer Boston or Newport furniture; others collect Connecticut River Valley pieces made of maple or cherry wood; still others restrict themselves to Philadelphia. Eddy Nicholson preferred to buy the best of every region, which offered him the widest range of possibility. I was still a recent arrival to Christie's American Furniture Department when Eddy made auction history by purchasing the first piece of American furniture to top the $1 million mark at auction—an exquisite Philadelphia tea table. Nearly ten years later, in 1995, long after I had become a private dealer, I would buy that table for a client at Nicholson's housecleaning sale for $2,422,500, a price that again set a record for the form.

The first time I saw the table close-up, it was sitting in the office of my boss, Dean Failey, having just been delivered from the home of the consignor. Dean's office was a cluttered space that always seemed to be overflowing with the numerous bits of auction life that invariably build up before each sale—furniture files, receipts books, research materials, and hundreds of photographs and transparencies. With nothing more flattering than the fluorescent light radiating down from the drop ceiling to showcase its form, the table still managed to stand with the utmost of chic and poise.

The light bounced off the table's largest horizontal face—the highly figured mahogany board of the circular top—warming the rich chocolate grain of the wood. Large, perfectly flat tops of this type require great talent to make and, in addition, this one featured a raised rim that moved in and out in a crisply delineated scalloped pattern (often termed a piecrust top because of its obvious resemblance to that baked form). The scalloped-edge design, inspired by contemporary London tea tray designs, was perfected by Philadelphia's cabinetmakers during the height of that city's rococo period, when this table was made.

Centered beneath the lush reflective surface of the top was a small open-air boxlike structure—often termed a birdcage—that featured four miniature balusters, one marking each corner. The birdcage was attached to the center shaft of the table, which in turn led down to the tripod base, and it housed a mechanism that allowed the table to pivot from a horizontal to a vertical position (thus inspiring a second popular name for the form, tilt-top tea table) and also rotate to facilitate the ceremony of tea. The action of the table played right into the mid-eighteenth-century fascination with theatricality and function-specific furniture. (How elegant, a table just for tea!) The tilt top allowed for the table to be stored easily at the perimeter of a room when it was not in use.

I pinched my right thumb and forefinger around the shaped edge of the rim and ran them along its undulant scalloped course—so perfectly planned and rhythmically proportioned. As expected, the dense mahogany wood felt smooth and cool to the touch. My hand remained on the edge of the pivot top as I crouched down to get a closer look at the shaft. I counted an astounding twenty-two flutes running down the face of its length, giving it the appearance of a Grecian pillar (twelve or fourteen of these concave channels is a more usual amount to see). By choosing so elaborate a design, the carver was effectively flaunting his virtuoso technique, yet the result was refined and seemingly effortless. Near the bottom of the shaft, the fluting was halted by a compressed sphere, or ball, that seemed to bulge outward in response to the weight of the large top above. I marveled at the craftsman's technique—that he was able to convey such plasticity of form with so unforgiving a medium as dense mahogany wood.

Beneath the ball was a reel-like passage in the shaft that was shaped rather like an empty spool of thread. It fed into the tripod base, which was formed by a trio of cabriole legs that each curved outward and then down into a tapering reverse curve. Each leg was finished with a foot designed to emulate the taloned grasp of a bird of prey, clutching a ball instead of its next meal. As with the compressed ball I had admired on the shaft, the cabinetmaker had manipulated the animalistic spring of the legs to convey the ample weight of the top. Like the legs of a weight lifter grasping barbells on the rise, each leg seemed braced in order to bear the heft of the tabletop above. Meanwhile, the balls trapped between each claw flattened in added response to the gesture.

I lingered over this table for such a long time because I knew another example of similar eloquence and beauty probably would not cross my path again soon. During the twenty-five years or so of Philadelphia's reigning rococo style, only a handful of top-level craftsmen were able to produce tables as graceful and powerful as this one, and very few have turned up. Adding to its rarity was the fact that a table such as this would have been produced for only the wealthiest of customers—one who was willing to pay extra for the highly figured mahogany wood, the vivid scalloping, and the elaborate carving of the shaft and legs. Each detail added to the final price of the piece at the time it was made, and adds to its value today.

Admiring the table in Dean's office brought to mind only one other nearly identical

example, at New York's Metropolitan Museum of Art. When Morrison Heckscher, the curator of American Decorative Arts there, heard of the piece at Christie's, he invited my colleague John Hays (now the director of the American Furniture and Decorative Arts Department at Christie's) and me to bring the table to the museum so that we could do a side-by-side comparison of the two. So on a Monday morning, when the museum was closed, we took the table over there. Seeing this magnificent pair, certainly born of the same cabinet shop, united in the hushed gallery was really a thrill. The two tables were clearly twins in terms of their design, with only the subtlest variations in the surface decoration to distinguish them. Most of the differences were found in the handling of the wavy leaf carving that edged down the front of each leg and spread around the curve of the compressed ball, like a series of vines growing around a garden folly. In each case, the carving—so fluid, it seemed to have been hewn from soft butter—added up to the essence of rococo style. Even the bottoms of the feet were fitted with identical brass casters imported from England, which were quite expensive in the eighteenth century. (Later research done by Luke Beckerdite, an exceptional scholar in the realm of Philadelphia's rococo furniture, revealed that both tables were the work of an immigrant craftsman named Hercules Courtenay [1744?–1784]. Before he moved to Philadelphia, Courtenay had been a student of the great London craftsman Thomas Johnson [1714–1778], one of the most active proponents of English rococo style.)

On the day of its sale, the table turned on the dais, facing what was, not surprisingly, a near-capacity crowd. Auctioneer Brian Cole opened the bidding at $550,000, after which the room grew unusually still. Nothing happened—no paddles, no hands—for what seemed an eternity. Suddenly, one of the staff signaled a telephone bid of $575,000 and the numbers began to climb, not stopping until they reached $950,000. With the buyer's 10 percent premium added, that made the final price for the table $1,045,000. A handful of reporters covering the sale rushed to catch a word with Eddy Nicholson, the new owner, who had been bidding openly in the room.

An interesting footnote to the sale of that table is that when I purchased it in January 1995, I learned that during his period of ownership, Eddy had sent the table to the conservators at the Henry Francis du Pont Winterthur Museum in Delaware for a cleaning. *Cleaning* is a dirty word in American furniture because most experts have come to view the grunge and dirt that settle into the finish of an object over a period of two centuries as a valuable commodity. Original finish sells because it helps guarantee authenticity. Why remove a patina that has taken so long to develop? It's like hitting the erase button on a tape recording of the object's life.

But the type of cleaning Eddy had in mind for the table was similar to the painstaking work done on an old master painting. The piece was worked over in a lab, quarter inch by quarter inch, with nothing larger than a cotton swab, and the original shellac finish was never penetrated. I wouldn't have recommended it, but at least he approached it the right way. When I bought the table in 1995, I received a packet from Mark Anderson, the vigilant Winterthur conservator in charge of the project. It was a plastic bag filled with the table's original dirt—cotton swabs and all. I later sent it on to the table's present owner, thinking to myself, Well, now he has the *whole* table.

When I left Christie's to start my own firm in March 1986, Eddy Nicholson was one of the first people to offer his congratulations and support. His encouragement meant a great deal to me. It was my ambition, of course, to work with savvy clients such as Eddy, so the fact that he expressed confidence in my abilities and was not put off by my youth (I was twenty-eight) felt like a hearty slap on the back.

I had long looked forward to opening my own shop and no longer having to answer to a corporate boss, but it was still unsettling when the day finally arrived. I felt as if I had taken a leap forward, but I couldn't quite make out the place where I would land. In the beginning, my tiny studio apartment in an old baroque-style town house just off Fifth Avenue on East Seventy-fifth Street doubled as my office. I still remember the first inquiry I received, literally the day after I had incorporated myself. It was from a man who wanted to know if I handled old cigar boxes. After explaining to him that collectibles really weren't my focus, I hung up the phone, praying that things would get better.

Not five minutes later, the phone rang again. This time, the call was from Gary Sergeant, a Connecticut-based antiques dealer specializing in English and European furnishings, who was familiar to me from the salesrooms at Christie's. Gary was calling on behalf of a New Jersey clock dealer named Steve Petrucelli, who had recently puchased from a neighbor a pair of chairs that he believed were American. Steve wanted the chairs to be examined by someone with expertise in American furniture, and Gary had suggested me (with the understanding that if I bought the chairs, he would get a commission on the deal).

Well, the chairs sounded far more promising than the cigar boxes, so the next morning I found myself entering Steve Petrucelli's modest home in Cranbury, New Jersey, in the company of Gary Sergeant. The pair of chairs—or what was left of them— stood just to the left of the entrance foyer. *Chair* is actually a generous term for what I first saw that day. These things looked like a matched pair of stools, each with a seemingly incongruous post rising off its back, and nothing else.

I approached the two with a combination of wonderment and awe, for despite all that was obviously missing from their design, there was something unmistakably beautiful about the forms that remained. I bent over and picked up one of the pair and was immediately struck by the heft of the wood. No doubt it was constructed of dense mahogany, an exotic plum-toned hardwood imported from places such as Honduras, Suriname, and the West Indies. Mahogany was used on the priciest furniture throughout the colonies, but it found particular favor in Newport during that city's stylistic heyday, the 1760s through the 1780s. As I bent closer to study the flecked grain of the wood, I began to suspect that I might be in the presence of two highly unusual pieces.

Lifting and tipping the chair also brought the legs into full view. The rear legs were simple, unadorned backswept squared shafts, but the front legs were far more elaborate. They each took the form of two sturdy S-curved cabriole legs that narrowed at the ankle to end in full-blown claw-and-ball feet. There was something very distinctive about the execution of these feet, and I had seen it a few times before, always on furniture attributed to the Newport cabinetmaker John Goddard (1723/4–1785).

Goddard, a cabinetmaker of considerable skill, was part of a family of craftsmen who, along with their neighbors the Townsends, were largely responsible for Newport's brief rise to artistic prominence just after the mid-1700s. These two Quaker families were closely bound by ties of apprenticeship and marriage, and together they managed to produce an astounding number of exceptionally talented craftsmen, most of whom achieved a profoundly elegant yet conservative aesthetic. Drop either family name in reference to a piece of furniture near a serious collector of Americana and you are bound to elicit a smile (and perhaps an increase in pulse).

John Goddard was a fairly prolific member of the clan. Perhaps the most distinctive feature of his work is the robust manner in which he carved his claw-and-ball feet. His claws look far more animalistic than, say, the birdlike talons that I had admired on the Philadelphia tea table when I was still at Christie's. The knuckles always appear slender and tall, although swollen at the joints, with each digit well delineated. Furthermore, Goddard tended to carve the balls held within the claws, taller than they were wide, thus forcing a powerful tension into the tendons stretching taut above the spheres below. Such were the feet of the chair I held in my hands.

I set the chair back down on the ground and placed both my palms down on the center of the seat. I took a breath and then spread my hands in opposite directions across the equator of its balloonlike shape, ignoring the busy Victorian needlework pattern that passed beneath my moving fingertips. When I reached the opposite ends of the seat, my hands dipped down across the smooth exposed mahogany sides to the underbelly of the chair and then continued inward until they met again at the center of the seat. I arched my hands and pushed gently up at the center, easily slipping the seat (thus the popular term *slip seat*) out of the chair frame. I briskly flipped this over and was thrilled to see that beneath that loud nineteenth-century Victorian cover, the original eighteenth-century maple seat frame still existed, complete with the chair's original linen webbing, muslin, and horsehair stuffing. It is extremely rare to see original upholstery ingredients survive two hundred years of use, and I was excited. But as I returned the slip seat to the embrace of the chair's frame, I was also reminded of the problems looming just above seat level.

I was about to ask Steve what had happened to the rest of the chairs, when I noticed a small pile of dark wood gathered on the floor to the left of the pair. I must have visibly winced at the realization that in that pile lay the answer to my unasked question, for Steve quickly stepped in and began to explain the story of the chairs. They had been found, he said, on the second floor of a chicken coop at a local farm. For a short time, the space had been used as a clubhouse by some neighborhood kids, which probably accounted for their sorry state. The seat frames and legs had remained intact, but the rest of the parts had been scattered about in the hay (which accounted for the bits of straw that I found myself brushing aside as I crouched down to try to make sense of the jumble).

I shook my head in disbelief at the concept of this strange scenario. The places people choose to stash antique furniture never cease to amaze me. That these objects had somehow managed to survive the indignities of a chicken coop stood as a testament to the integrity of their design. I sifted through the pile and managed first to extract one perfect, unblemished crest rail, marked at the center by a wonderfully expressive scallop shell with a clearly delineated pattern of concave and convex channels carved in simulation of a shell's lobed back. The crest rail is the yoke-shaped top rail that is most often grasped when a chair is pulled back from a table. It is a key design component and acts like a lid to the rest of the chair's back. The stiles fit directly into the recesses of its ends, while the decorative back splat (the upright central

A voluptuous shell marks the center of a chair's crest rail.

support) locks into its center. Because the crest rail is one of the most heavily handled parts of a chair, it can, on occasion, loosen and fall off. Once the crest rail is missing, then the other parts of the back may soon follow.

Finding that freestanding crest rail and then moments later an identical one, also intact, gave me hope. Perhaps these chairs could be saved. Piece by piece, like a jigsaw puzzle, I reassembled the backs of the chairs on the floor. I sometimes think of back splats as the Rorschach test of American furniture. What will the viewer see in the design? Here, for example, the pattern could be interpreted a number of ways. Did the pair of matching back splats look like two large Grecian urns composed of curving ribbonlike lines, or did they appear more like two highly stylized pretzels? Then, too, there was the airy shape of a hawk-nosed bird formed by the negative space between the outer edges of the splat sides and the arched curve of the stiles. Whatever the interpretation, I thought the pattern of the chair backs closely resembled the back splats displayed on a well-photographed and much-celebrated roundabout chair (also called a corner chair because it features two back splats that face each other at a right angle) that had a history of ownership in the prominent Brown family of Providence. An image of that chair popped into my mind as I played with the pieces on the floor, particularly since that chair bore an attribution to the hand of John Goddard. The similarity in design among the chairs helped guide my still-forming opinion of the objects.

A pair of slip seats and the fragments of a single chair back.

63

Using a handful of red rubber bands that Steve found in a kitchen drawer, we slowly began to bind the disassembled parts to the two surviving chair frames. Miraculously, the pieces held, and in less than ten minutes we had one complete chair (save a few chips here and there) and the second one nearly finished. All that was missing was one twelve-inch section of a vertical stile from the backrest. It was frustrating to be just a foot away from a complete pair of chairs, particularly since I was certain the two could be linked to the Newport master craftsman John Goddard.

I looked at Steve and asked him if we definitely had seen all the broken pieces. He nodded his head in assent. I explained to him that I thought Goddard had made these profoundly beautiful chairs but that the missing passage definitely detracted from their value. Given their condition, I told him, I would be willing to pay a price in the low five figures. Steve agreed to my price and I wrote him my first check as a dealer. With the paperwork done, we loaded the chairs into the van that Gary and I had driven to New Jersey that day. Gary was already in the driver's seat and had the engine running when I slammed the back doors closed and turned to face Steve one more time. Something in my gut told me to try again.

"I know you said those were all the pieces," I told him, "but I would give you four thousand dollars if you could find that missing piece of wood."

Without missing a beat, Steve turned to his wife, Karen, who had come out of the house to watch the proceedings, and said, "Honey, get that box out of the garage."

Karen disappeared behind the corner of the house, then came back a few moments later with a large cardboard box of debris that Steve had swept from the chicken coop's floor on the day he found the chairs. I sank to my knees on the asphalt and began to sift through the contents of the box. I pulled out, among other things, a heavily carved crest rail belonging to a Victorian sofa, a couple of old Coke cans, a mouse skeleton, and a few fistfuls of straw. I fished deeper into the box, and soon my hand came across something distinctively cold, hard, and heavy. It felt different from the other bric-a-brac in the box. I quickly extracted the item from the tangle of stuff and held it up in the sunlight. It was a dense reddish piece of mahogany—a segment of the missing section of stile.

My heartbeat quickened as I gripped that lush piece of wood in one hand and plunged the other back into the box. A moment later, I came up with a second piece of wood. I brought my hands together and joined the two pieces. They fit together perfectly. I smiled broadly and looked up at Gary, who had by this time turned off the van's engine and gotten out. I then looked at Steve and his wife, each of whom wore a look of cautious expectancy.

"Yes, this is probably the most expensive piece of broken wood ever purchased," I said in answer to their looks as I passed the wood to Gary and took out my checkbook to write Steve my second dealer's check.

I had come up with the four-thousand-dollar figure on the spur of the moment, but in retrospect, it was a gamble worth taking. Without that extra part, I had merely purchased a chair and a half, but with that missing link, I suddenly had a potential pair of gems on my hands. When I got the chairs back to my apartment that evening, I began to think long and hard about the type of collector who should own them. I thought it best that the chairs be sold in their present condition so that the buyer could restore them to his or her liking. That meant whoever bought the pair needed to have a strong sense of vision and determination. I decided to contact Eddy Nicholson. But before I did, I called my dad, because I also knew that Eddy liked a good bawdy joke and that my dad always had a stockpile of them. Dad did not disappoint. He reached down and deep and dirty and gave me something Eddy was sure to love.

Eddy and I were still chuckling on the phone (he was out at his second home in Palm Springs) when I began to describe the chairs to him and the conditions under which they had been found. We talked about what measures would need to be taken to restore the two to their former dignity and how the best person for the job was no doubt a man named Alan Miller. Miller is a Pennsylvania-based restorer-cum-consultant and his hands are among the best in the business. I had, in fact, queried Alan earlier in the day about the chairs, in preparation for my pitch to Eddy. He had told me that he had some dark, dense Cuban mahogany in his shop that might be useful for filling in any small missing sections once the pieces were reassembled.

The restored chairs.

The John Goddard chairs find a more suitable home in Eddy Nicholson's front hall.

Within twenty-four hours, sight unseen, Eddy bought the chairs at the six-figure price I quoted him. That night, for the first time in years, I felt the profound urge to write in a diary. I found an empty notebook among my things and began to recount the events of the past few days. Near the end of that first entry, I wrote, "I am going to go to bed—but first want to say that I feel as if I stand at the threshold . . . of being directly involved in . . . handling the most important pieces in the world—mainstream. We'll see."

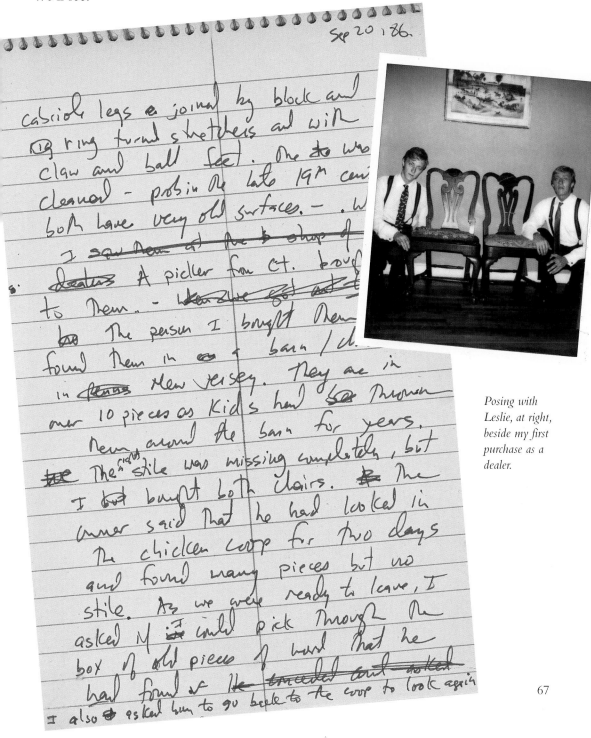

Sep 20, 86.

cabriole legs e joined by block and ring turned stretchers and with claw and ball feet. One do who cleaned - prob in the late 19th cent. both have very old surfaces. — . W I saw them at the shop of dealers A picker from Ct. brought to them. — The person I bought them found them in a barn / ch. in New Jersey. They are in over 10 pieces as kids had thrown them around the barn for years. The right stile was missing completely, but I bought both chairs. The owner said that he had looked in the chicken coop for two days and found many pieces but no stile. As we were ready to leave, I asked if I could pick through the box of old pieces of wood that he had found of the coop to look again. I also asked him to go back to the coop to look again

Posing with Leslie, at right, beside my first purchase as a dealer.

67

4

The Shell Game

WHEN I ARRIVED AT SOTHEBY'S in September 1979—a place where scholarship, commerce, and cultivation glamorously intersected under one roof—I was completely focused on my future. It was only the second time in the history of the auction house that a recruitment program had been offered to groom future specialists, and the competition for enrollment had been stiff. I now laugh at the memory, but my first day there, I somehow managed to corner Bill Stahl, then director of the American Furniture and Decorative Arts Department, and declare, "My name is Leslie Keno and I would like to work in American furniture." Ever the gentleman, Bill threw a few words of polite encouragement my way before promptly moving on.

Reaching that department, however, proved a harder task than I would have imagined. The end of my year's training coincided with Sotheby's move from its headquarters on Madison Avenue to its current, larger space (formerly a Kodak processing plant) on York Avenue and Seventy-second Street. The expansion left the auction house short-staffed in the new building, and I, as a recent graduate, was placed on the loading dock, where I was expected to receive and tag property for upcoming sales.

It was the summer of 1980, and the loading dock where I had been sent was located in the basement of the new headquarters. Not surprisingly, my "office" lacked air conditioning, which meant I spent most days drenched in sweat as I worked my way through an endless onslaught of furniture. Indeed, my beleaguered colleagues and I were forced to wear shorts simply to survive the oppressive heat on the platform.

To say I was miserable would be putting it mildly. Obviously, this was not what I had studied so hard to achieve. The black plumes of exhaust emitted from each incoming truck only deepened my dark mood, and I began to think seriously about contacting rival auction houses for work. Nonetheless, whenever a cargo of American furniture arrived, I'd linger over the new objects as long as I could, admiring their contours, examining their interior construction, and trying to pinpoint their origins as I filled out form after Sotheby's form.

One sultry afternoon, a pair of country maple chairs arrived, along with documents that described them as having been made in New England around 1760. The pair had been loosely wrapped in some off-white padded blankets, which I easily peeled back to uncover them. As the blankets slid to the concrete floor, they revealed a matched set of chairs with plain yoke-shaped crest rails, vase-shaped back splats, woven rush seats, and lathe-turned back posts and front legs that ended in simple splayed-brush, or Spanish, feet (both terms used to describe a carved scroll foot with vertical fluting that curves backward at the base). The chair form had met with great popularity throughout New England from about 1730 through the 1780s, and had in fact changed very little during that time. They were the kind of chairs that might be found in a grandparent's country house dining room—old, charming, but not particularly comfortable.

But it was something in the *appearance* of this particular set that made me uncomfortable. The turned stiles and legs seemed a little too fresh and blemish-free, the perfect edge of the back splats didn't look hand-hewn, and although the neat geometric patterning of the seats appeared to be original (woven or rush seats wear out with time and are often replaced), their bright yellow tone belied their age. Even the chairs' most vulnerable spots, such as the oft-handled crest rails or the tops of the legs (which usually bear the brunt of a careless shove), were clean. Furthermore, chairs of this type were almost always originally painted, but as I examined the various crevices and turnings on the pair before me, I found not a speck of paint remained, which was highly unusual, even if possibly they had been refinished.

The clamor of the loading dock swelled in my ears for a moment, but I quickly tuned it out as I grasped one of the chairs firmly by the back post and flipped it on end to examine the underside of its irregularly shaped brush feet. I was dismayed to see an absence of checking, the distinctive dark patterning that occurs over time as wood naturally loses moisture. Checking is usually most apparent at the feet because they are formed from end cuts of wood (sawn at right angles to the medullar rings). Such cuts leave the wood pores exposed, and over time, as the wood dries, a speckled or checked pattern begins to emerge. But the bottoms of the feet on these chairs were as smooth and unmarked as sea-washed stone. I studied them a minute longer, then set the chair back on the ground, completed the arrival notice, and sent the paperwork along.

A few hours later, I received a call from the American Furniture Department asking why I had labeled the chairs reproductions. I started to explain my reasoning but was quickly informed that Bill Stahl was coming down to hear and see for himself. When Bill appeared, he brought with him the department's senior cataloger, Tom Lloyd, a tall, rangy man with a long, solemn face that, I later learned, masked an incredible sardonic wit. I'm sure I would have broken into a nervous sweat at the sight of them if I hadn't already been drenched from the heat of the loading dock. If I was wrong in my analysis, I knew any chance of my joining their department would all but evaporate. Bill and Tom moved with efficiency over to the chairs and began to examine them, flipping them over and back and from side to side as I stood close by, shifting my weight from one leg to the other. When they were through, they straightened up and turned around to face me. Their matched looks of approval told me all I needed to know: They, too, thought the chairs were fakes that had somehow slipped through the cracks of a hasty appraisal. It was an unpleasant bit of news that they needed to break quickly to the consignor, but for me, the verdict stood as an endorsement. They turned to leave and were almost to the elevator when Bill turned back to look at me and said with a quick nod, "Don't worry, I'll get you out of here."

Those words carried me through the next few months, and by October, true to his word, Bill did get me off the loading dock and up into his department as a junior cataloger. I think the prolonged wait made my arrival in Americana all the more sweet. I savored every aspect of the job, from sorting the mail (I relished the possibility of untold treasures to be found in the daily stream of client inquiries) to the frenzied pace of the research that precipitated every catalog deadline. Suddenly, my opinion had the power of Sotheby's behind it and I began to feel that I had graduated from the small shops and flea markets of my past.

Nearly two years into my tenure in Americana, I came across an object that marked a turning point in my career. Sipping my morning coffee, I had just begun plowing through a sizable stack of mail that had built up over the Labor Day weekend when I came across a moderately sized ivory-colored envelope bearing a Ticonderoga, New York, return address. The envelope initially gave me pause because the carefully scripted blue-ink lettering on its front and back reminded me of my grandmother's own elegant hand. I opened the envelope and was just beginning to pull out a folded two-page letter when a small color photograph slid out from between the horizontal creases. I stopped it with my hand and righted it, only to be met by an astonishing sight: a Newport bureau table with a shell-decorated block-front facade—quite simply, an icon of American furniture.

As I gazed at this incredible image, I also felt an almost-intuitive awareness of the contents of the letter. Although I had yet to read a word, I could see the distinctive format of a family tree carefully drafted down one of the two pages, and that gave me cause for even greater excitement. *Provenance* is a word used in the business to describe the ownership history of a piece. The more complete that history, the greater our perspective on its life. Collectors at the most rarified levels delight in strong provenance because it helps personalize the furniture. They enjoy knowing who else has treasured and safeguarded an object through the centuries. Furthermore, a solid history in one family implies a certain "freshness" to a piece, which presumably has never left private hands.

Of course I wanted to share the news of my discovery with my colleagues, but I also wanted to savor the moment a few minutes longer. So rather than leap to my feet, I settled back into my chair, lit a cigarette (in those days we were still allowed to smoke at Sotheby's), and contemplated the beauty of the image, while the letter fell, unread, to my desk.

Initially, I was struck by the sculptural presence of the bureau. Its artistic impact clearly outweighed its practical use as a dresser and occasional writing table (usually found in a bedchamber). I was quite familiar with the form from books, and I knew that if the piece was authentic, it probably dated to sometime between 1760 and 1780. I can't think of an equivalent object found in the bedrooms of today. Shell-carved block-front bureaus were meant for a time when people still used the morning light to minister to their toilet, or occasionally received close friends or relatives in the bedroom, or drafted quick handwritten notes to be sent off in the morning post. In that sense, it was a decidedly old-fashioned piece, which, of course, was part of its great appeal.

The force of the bureau's tactile design came from two sources: the four expressively carved shells that punctuated the facade like a series of perfect half-moons (three evenly spaced on the top drawer, and one on the door of a central recessed kneehole compartment) and the wonderful, undulant, blocked surface. The shells all had voluptuously ribbed bodies that were identically made, save for the fact that the one appearing on the center of the drawer and the one fronting the kneehole door were hewn from

the surface of the piece, while the remaining two were convex and bulged outward.

The blocking (meaning the swelled projections seen on the two stacked columns of small drawers flanking the kneehole space) took its cue from the gesture and alignment of those two convex shells. Each raised passage began its descent directly beneath the end-points of the fan-shaped spread of the shell back, which gave a wonderful sense of undulant movement to the exterior. Not only did the projecting passages appear at once to thrust forward toward the viewer but they also channeled the energy of the design upward.

The photograph I held in my hand was amateurish and poorly composed, but I still felt the impact of the design. The outer ends of the case piece seemed to jump out from the glossy picture plane, luring me with their tightly crafted perfection. Every line and curve was crucial to the overall unity of the design—a delicate balance that gave the piece its power. To create such an effect required more time, materials, and skill than a traditional chest of drawers. The raised areas were carved from solid slabs of highly figured mahogany, which, given the tight grain of the wood, was no easy task. Furthermore, the swells in the façade were an extravagance that did nothing to increase the holding capacity of the piece, and thus spoke only to the mind-set and natural dexterity of the carver and the taste and wealth of the client who had originally commissioned the piece.

With those issues in mind, I finally turned to the owner's letter, which was lying open on my desk, and smoothed it flat across the crowded top. I quickly learned that the bureau had a history of descent in a prominent family that could trace its roots to eighteenth-century Newport. Its first owner, George Gibbs, Jr. (1735–1803), had been a senior partner in the Newport shipping house of Gibbs and Channing, which owned one of Rhode Island's largest merchant fleets. Gibbs's rank in the community made him a model candidate for such an elaborate and elegant piece of furniture. Moreover, the letter detailed the location of the Gibbs shipyard in Newport, right on the wharves of Easton's Point, a waterside enclave that was also the site of most of the Goddard and Townsend workshops. This was a thrilling bit of news, because the design of the shell-carved block-front bureau reached its apex with the genius of that close-knit clan of craftsmen, and from the moment I saw the photo of the Gibbs example, I was certain it could be traced to their collective hands.

At that point in my life, I had never actually seen a shell-carved bureau table, outside of New York's Metropolitan Museum, so beyond my responsibilities to the auction house, I was extremely eager to see and touch this incredible object. The last time a bureau like this had come up for auction was at Sotheby's much-celebrated on-site sale of the contents of Pokety Farms, the elegant home of Col. Edgar and Bernice Chrysler Garbisch, on Maryland's Eastern Shore. That example had born a later coat of white paint and had for years stood on an outside porch, but it still won pride of place on the cover of the May 1980 auction catalog (and was in fact purchased by the comedian Bill Cosby, who is a keen collector of American furniture). The only other block-front example that I could think of that came close to the Garbisch piece in importance was a three-shell chest of drawers from the collection of Mr. and Mrs. Walter B. Robb, which sold at Sotheby's in 1980 for $360,000. Now, some three years later, that price was still the standing world record for American furniture.

With the images and statistics of those two objects in mind, I scanned the rest of the letter, looking for a phone number. There was none. My heart rate quickened. I scanned the page again, this time flipping it over to check the back side, then the reverse of the photograph, and finally the envelope itself. Still no phone number. Now I was concerned. Due to the long weekend, the mail on my desk was a few days old, and I worried that the owner might have been anxiously awaiting a response. Also, I knew full well that clients often approach more than one auction house with a query, and I hated to think that Sotheby's had missed an opportunity to handle this incredible item because we hadn't responded promptly. Eventually, having tried Ticonderoga's directory assistance, police station, and post office, I finally found a phone number for the woman who had written the letter. Naturally, the line was busy. But when I eventually got through, she very graciously invited me up to her home to see the bureau, which I arranged to do within a couple of days, accompanied by my boss, Tom Lloyd.

Ticonderoga is a sleepy resort village in northeast New York, set on a spit of land in between Lakes George and Champlain (the name is an Iroquois word meaning "land between the waters"). Tom and I had arranged to meet the desk's owner on the grounds of nearby Fort Ticonderoga, the site of a number of battles of the French and

The foot of the Gibbs bureau reveals Edmund Townsend's characteristic carving—as well as a splash of red paint on the bracket, left behind by the former owner's sons.

Indian War and the American Revolution because its location was so strategic to the main inland water route to Canada. The reason for this unusual point of rendezvous was that the woman's family had a long-standing involvement with the place (one of her ancestors, William Ferris Pell, a wealthy New York merchant, had once owned the ruined fortress and its surrounding lands, and his great-grandson, Stephen, had spurred its early-twentieth-century renovation) and she had related work to do there that day.

The bureau's owner was a reed-thin, elegant older woman with an aristocratic bearing, and as she strode across the walled-in grounds to meet us, I was struck by her resemblance to Katharine Hepburn. Soon, Tom and I were trailing her in our rental car back to the modest home that she shared with her husband and two sons. The details of the house itself remain a bit sketchy to me, for almost immediately upon entering the house, I spotted the Newport bureau standing against a wall just inside the living room. Although it was partially shrouded by a white linen runner and covered with a wide array of silver-framed family photos, I still fell immediately for its wonderful form. Coming face-to-face with a masterpiece is like recognizing a famous actor or actress on the street and being hit by a wave of familiarity for someone (or something) you have never met before. But it is also at these moments that I am struck by the oddity of my job, which requires me to conduct serious business within the intimate confines of a family's home. It creates a strange dynamic that forces me to restrain my blatant curiosity about the furniture with extreme politesse. Sometimes I would like nothing better than to push past a client and fall to my knees before the object, like those far-off days in the woods with Leigh when I pawed through the earth unchecked in search of barn hinges and glass bottles.

On this day, however, there was no need to finesse the situation because the owner had immediately stepped forward to clear the bureau and Tom and I had only to pitch in and help. As we lifted away the white cloth runner, I noticed a few flecks of what looked to be red paint splashed across the glistening mahogany top and feet of the bureau. The owner, who saw me hesitate at the spots, explained that the bureau had done some hard time as a workstation for her now-grown sons, who had once shared a mutual interest in building model airplanes. The paint, she said, dated to that time.

There was a brief round of polite laughter in the room, but I thought I detected a flicker of concern in the owner's eyes, which I quickly tried to dispel. I explained to the woman that the paint had no effect on the value of the piece because it simply attested to the life it had lived (and, as it turned out, was easily removed with the flick of a thumbnail). Her eyes warmed with relief just as Tom, picking up on that thread of conversation, stepped back for a moment to elaborate on the subject. And as they launched into a discussion behind me about finish and condition, I reached for the handles of the uppermost drawer, marked by its magnificent trio of carved shells. As the drawer slid out, I looked over the top and saw that the finished drawer sides were made of poplar—a durable local wood often used on the interior of Newport case pieces. The sides joined the mahogany drawer front with wedge-shaped interlocking joints, or dovetails (the form resembles a dove's tail), cut with the precision of clock-gear sprockets. I soon found this attention to detail was typical of the entire piece.

I was pleased to see that where the posts from the handles screwed into the drawer front, no additional holes cut into the wood, which meant they were almost certainly not replaced. Nevertheless, to confirm their originality, I decided to loosen one of the handles by carefully unscrewing the irregularly cut washers, or nuts, that held it in place. I lifted the handle and back plate away and noticed with satisfaction that a distinct shadow remained, which mimicked the pattern of the hardware I had just taken off. For more than two hundred years, the brass plate had acted as a shield for the surface beneath it, protecting it from the daily pummeling of light and air that had faded the surrounding facade.

I reattached the pull when I was through and then moved on to examine the three carved shells marking that same upper drawer. Shells were popular decorative devices for much of the eighteenth century in many regions, but the Goddards and Townsends specialized in wide-bodied, robustly carved interpretations of the form (think of the smaller but no less tactile versions seen on the crest rails of Leigh's John Goddard chairs). I swept my hand across one of the two convex outer shells (both seamlessly applied with glue made from animal hide). My fingers rose and fell eleven times along the ripple of alternating lobes and fillets carved to imitate a shell's natural grooves. I followed the gesture of the channels to the point where the shell's lobes narrowed and gathered. Here, smooth wood gave way to texture: The area was filled with a series of stop-fluted intaglio petals that accented the heart of the shell. Stop fluting is a decorative device that involves concave carved channels, each one filled with small lines or reeding. It is another costly detail, and it signals the creativity of the man who had made it. There are plenty of important Newport pieces that don't have extra carving at the center of the shell, so to see it here was an unexpected bonus.

I stepped back from the piece for a moment to survey the entirety of the design. My eyes ran quickly from the top to the bottom of the bureau, then fixed for a moment on a subtle yet favorite detail of mine, typically found on Goddard and Townsend examples of this form—the distinctive treatment of the ogee bracket feet. Bracket feet are often found on low case pieces because they offer sturdy, load-bearing support.

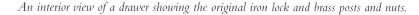

An interior view of a drawer showing the original iron lock and brass posts and nuts.

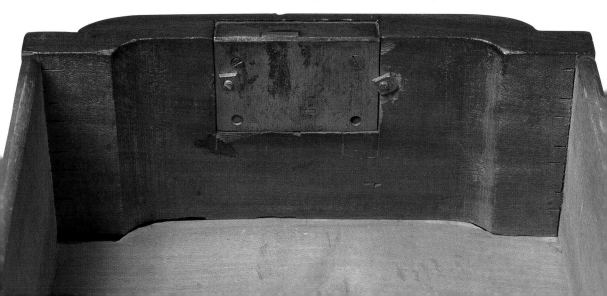

The desk that took my breath away.

They are formed by two pieces of wood that join at a corner, with the open side cut to follow a simple pattern, which in the case of the Gibbs desk was an ogee, or S-shaped line. Certainly other cabinetmaking centers, such as Boston or Salem, explored the contours of the ogee bracket foot, but in the hands of the Goddards and Townsends, the device was carried one step further. Here, each foot tapered slightly toward the bottom and was accented by a molded, rounded inner edge (often referred to as beading). At the ends, the beading trailed off into a delicate curlicue, or volute, which gave the design some added flare. Like the stop fluting seen in the carved shells, it was a minor detail, which at first glance might be overlooked but over time would be discovered and appreciated.

Collectors and scholars alike are often quick to call shell-carved block-front bureaus quintessentially American because the form was little influenced by London-made examples. Newport, unlike other coastal cities, such as Philadelphia, Boston, and New York, did not appear to draw high numbers of London-trained craftsmen who came fully conversant with the latest furniture fashions from abroad. Instead, the town's cabinet trade remained quite insular. Most of the Goddards and Townsends trained among themselves, which accounts for the localized construction and stylistic details found in their work. Furthermore, the two families had a near monopoly over the high-end cabinet trade of Newport, which meant they had little reason to change their ways.

The significance of that distinction is made clearer by comparing the Gibbs piece with the flagrantly London-influenced rococo scheme of the tea table once owned by Eddy Nicholson. The two objects were made almost concurrently in Colonial towns with strong Quaker identities, and yet they couldn't be more different. That contrast underscores the allure of regionalism to collectors and makes it clear that in order to appreciate American furniture, you need to place it within a social and historical context.

Tom and I probably spent about an hour and a half in the owner's home. Before we left, we explained to her how thrilled we were to have seen the piece and just how special we considered it to be. In preparation for our visit, we had scoured the existing literature for similar examples and we actually had a few photocopies in hand. We both agreed that the bureau was likely the handiwork of Edmund Townsend (1736–1811), a third-generation craftsman born to the highly skilled Job Townsend, with whom he likely apprenticed. Of the twenty-five or so shell-carved block-front examples known, only four are signed or labeled by their makers, two of them by Edmund. One labeled example is in the M. and M. Karolik Collection at the Museum of Fine Arts in Boston, and the other, held in a private collection, features the scrawled signature of the cabinetmaker in graphite on a drawer. Determining which member of the Goddard and Townsend clan was responsible for the desk involved a lot of cross-referencing with other examples, but the case construction and the handling of the carved shells on the Gibbs piece really seemed to match best the two examples attributed to Edmund (both the eleven-lobed shell design and the way in which the top was attached were typical of his hand).

Within days of our visit to Ticonderoga (and following one long strategy session with Bill Stahl), I approached the owner with a formal proposal for the sale of the desk, bearing an estimate that fell between $350,000 and $450,000. At the time, it was the highest auction estimate ever quoted on a piece of American furniture, one that had taken into account the record-breaking $360,000 sale of the Robb chest of drawers the previous year. The fact that we nearly met that price with our low estimate indicated our extreme confidence in the piece.

I think the owner's decision to sell the desk was far more heart-wrenching than she had first imagined. The object had been in her family for a long time and she clearly delighted in her heritage. That said, I also know that she had both her sons' college tuitions to think about, and was simply delighted when the piece sailed past its high estimate in January 1983, before being knocked down to dealer Harold Sack for $687,500. I later learned that Sack had come to the sale with the intention of buying the piece for a young couple who had recently done well on Wall Street. The two had set a presale limit with Sack of $500,000, but when the bidding escalated beyond that price, they were thrown by the rapid pace of the sale and were unable to push their limit any further. Freed of his bond with the couple, Sack remained determined to win the piece, and he ended up setting a world record for American furniture. Weeks later, the husband and wife were so filled with regret and longing for the desk that they ended up purchasing it from Sack at a substantial markup, one that far surpassed the 10 percent commission he would have earned had they won it at auction. In other words, they paid a premium for their hesitation at the sale.

Within months of the sale of the Gibbs desk, Sotheby's American Furniture Department underwent some enormous changes. Bill Stahl moved into a higher position within the company, Tom Lloyd decided to leave the auction world altogether and pursue a career in architecture, and I, the junior member of the group, and not quite twenty-three, was elevated to department head.

5

A Philadelphia Story

DURING THE FIRST WEEK OF OCTOBER 1986, a number of phone messages began piling up on my desk at Sotheby's from a dealer named Chris Machmer. Chris is a big bear of a guy and has a steady, easygoing manner. Like Leigh and me, he grew up around antiques, since his father amassed over many years what is arguably one of the country's finest collections of Pennsylvania German folk art.

I hadn't found even a minute to get back to Chris. But when I finally did, he said in a less-than-veiled reference to my tardiness, "I think you'll be really glad you returned my calls."

He paused for a moment and then continued with evident glee. "What would you say if I told you I knew where you could find Gen. John Cadwalader's hairy-paw-foot armchair?"

What would I say? Gen. John Cadwalader (1742–1786) was one of the most prominent men in late-eighteenth-century Philadelphia, if not the colonies, and the details of the splendid Second Street town house that he shared with his wife, Elizabeth Lloyd (1742–1776), a Maryland heiress, are legendary. The Cadwaladers had bought the three-story Georgian house, located in the heart of the city's most fashionable district, in 1769. Immediately after the purchase, the new owners undertook a massive renovation of its interior. They raided Philadelphia's craft community to bring the reigning style of the day—the gorgeous and excessively elaborate rococo—to life in their home.

The Cadwaladers commissioned entire rooms that included interior paneling with carved ceiling cornices and friezes, extravagant new surrounds for the fireplaces, windows, and doorways, and molded ornamental stucco and gilt. The carving featured flowers, ribbons, egg-and-tongue moldings, birds, allegorical figures, and even a pair of dragons for the pediment above the parlor door. Then they filled these newly appointed rooms with elaborate avant-garde furnishings made to match the rich decor. By the time they were through, the Cadwaladers had spent well over £3,500 revamping the interior of their home and another £1,500 on furnishings—both astounding sums of money for that era.

Today, many people, including those of us in the auction business, often use the blanket term *Chippendale* to describe the ornate style that was put to great use in the Cadwalader home, but the name is really a misnomer. Thomas Chippendale was a London-based cabinetmaker, whose design book, *The Gentleman & Cabinet-Maker's Director,* first published in 1754, met with enormous popularity in both England and the United States. But Chippendale was far from alone in his influence on the age, and most historians now agree that the busy designs of the rococo have roots that reach back to antiquity.

But whatever the term used to describe this aesthetic, its beauty was not enough to preserve the Cadwalader place indefinitely. Sometime after the death of the general, the town house was rented out and eventually sold and the furniture dispersed among his five surviving children. By 1820, the house had been demolished and the site redeveloped.

Fortunately, many of the original bills and receipts for the Cadwalader renovations were preserved and are now housed at the Historical Society of Pennsylvania, which has allowed scholars to witness, in effect, the painstaking refurbishment of the house (Nicholas B. Wainwright's book *Colonial Grandeur in Philadelphia: The House and Furniture of General John Cadwalader* is the classic source on the renovations). It is now known, for example, that for its most important room—an elegant double parlor—Cadwalader and his wife commissioned an ornate set of furniture from the gifted craftsman Thomas Affleck (1740–1795). Like many in the elite crew who worked on the Cadwalader home, Affleck, a Scotsman, had trained in London before coming to Philadelphia, which meant he was well versed in the latest design trends. On October 13, 1770, Affleck billed the Cadwaladers £119.8 for goods, including a pair of commode card tables (*commode* is a period term used to describe a swayed or serpentine front), three large sofas, and a matching easy chair (valued at £4.10). Additional charges at the bottom of the bill from the carving firms of James Reynolds and the partners Nicholas Bernard and Martin Jugiez indicate that Affleck subcontracted the decorative carving for the suite. A separate receipt from the preeminent Philadelphia upholsterer Plunkett Fleeson shows that he stuffed the set as soon as that carving was completed, and supplied an accompanying set of blue-and-white-checked cotton slipcovers for use during the summer.

Since the Cadwalader household was disbanded, very few of its furnishings have resurfaced in the public arena. The largest disbursement of property probably occurred in 1904 at an auction held in Philadelphia of the property of John's great-grandson, Dr. Charles E. Cadwalader. Some copies of the catalog have survived and prove that the sale included a tantalizingly high number of items bearing descriptions that echoed those found in the Cadwalader receipts and inventories. (Oh, how I would have liked to have been there!) Soon after the auction, Dr. Cadwalader and his new wife (formerly the family's Irish maid) moved to her homeland, taking with them the few family pieces that they still owned.

In 1969, one of the serpentine-front card tables listed on Thomas Affleck's bill turned up in Canada and was found to match a second one that had a history of descent in the Cadwalader family (the two are now at the Philadelphia Museum). Both have elaborately carved undulating skirts and legs and rigorously carved hairy-paw feet, which resemble the paws of a lion. In 1983, another Cadwalader card table, this one with a less elaborate, straight front, surfaced in Pittsburgh and sold in our galleries. In 1974, five mahogany side chairs with hairy-paw feet sold at a Sotheby's sale in London; their skirt and leg pattern matched exactly the carving of the two card tables. As it turned out, the consignor had received the chairs from a friend, who had purchased them at an estate auction in Ireland during the 1930s, which meant they had probably arrived there in the company of Dr. Charles Cadwalader. Sotheby's ended up sending the chairs to New York, where they sold for a total of $207,500, an incredible sum at that time.

One of a pair of hairy-paw-foot card tables listed on cabinetmaker Thomas Affleck's original bill of sale to General Cadwalader.

Meanwhile, another chair from this well-traveled set descended in the Lewis family of Philadelphia. The Lewises had been neighbors of the Cadwaladers. Early in the twentieth century, that chair was taken to Florence, Italy, by its owners and was later bequeathed to an Italian house servant, in whose family the chair remained until it arrived at Sotheby's in 1982 (I was there on the loading dock to greet it), where it eventually sold for $275,000.

Since the few surviving Cadwalader pieces had ended up in such far-flung and often unlikely locales, if Chris Machmer could tell me the location of *any* piece of furniture from this renowned household—let alone an item from that fanciful parlor suite—it would be nothing short of a miracle. Knowing Chris, I wasn't sure if he was just getting back at me for not calling him sooner or if he was serious. But Chris was indeed serious, and as he began to explain what he knew of the chair's more recent history, I became serious, too.

As it turned out, Chris was calling on behalf of a man named Nate Wallace, who was the nephew of the present owners of the chair. Nate was a former antiques dealer but had left the field to attend business school and had since become a banker. Sometime after that career change, Nate's aunt and uncle, who lived just outside of Wilmington, Delaware, asked for his opinion on a large easy chair that they owned and had loaned to a local school, the Upland Country Day School. Apparently, the chair, which had found a home in the school's library, had caught the eye of another antiques dealer, Kenneth Lindsey, who had been called in by the school to evaluate recent loans and gifts to the institution. Lindsey suspected the piece was American, and he was particularly impressed by its hairy-paw feet. The character of the legs and feet on the chair reminded Lindsey of the Cadwalader card table by Thomas Affleck that he had seen at the Philadelphia Museum: It had similar distinctive hairy-paw feet. With the permission of the school and the owners, he was allowed to take the chair over to the nearby Winterthur Museum for a consultation. That seemed a smart idea, since Winterthur houses one of the country's most significant Americana collections (including a number of Cadwalader pieces).

But when Lindsey opened his van doors to the curator who greeted him, he was told not to bother unloading the chair. After eyeballing the piece in the dark confines of the vehicle, the curator had quickly concluded that the chair was not an eighteenth-century piece. Disappointed, but no less determined, Lindsey then enlisted the help of a well-connected local dealer, who in turn told him about a man who advised two of the most active collectors of Americana in the field at that time, George and Linda Kaufman. From him, Lindsey learned that the Kaufmans already owned two Cadwalader hairy-paw side chairs and a matching fire screen, which made them potential buyers for the easy chair. So following this convoluted series of introductions, the piece was brought into their home.

Seeing the easy chair sitting so close to the other Cadwalader furnishings in their living room convinced the Kaufmans that the piece was authentic. (George Kaufman would confess to me years later, "I should have grabbed that chair by the ankle and never let it go!") Their interest was conveyed to the chair's owners, but when the owners' nephew, Nate Wallace, heard of the Kaufmans' interest, he grew concerned. Nate figured that if the chair—which he had yet to see—intrigued these top-level collectors, despite its rejection by the Winterthur curator, there must be something more to it. Nate advised his aunt and uncle not to do a thing—yet.

It was a few months before Nate finally had an opportunity to visit his aunt and uncle's Delaware home and view the chair himself. When he did, his first thought was that it might be English. But as he began to look more closely, he recognized what he believed were American woods on the frame, and he began to suspect that he was standing before something of great importance. Like Kenneth Lindsay, Nate was familiar with the legend of the Cadwalader furnishings because of his background as a dealer. Still, the carving on the easy chair struck him as a bit too gutsy and dramatic and he decided the best way to resolve any lingering doubts about the piece was to take it to the Philadelphia Museum for an examination. So Nate, in the company of his aunt, took the piece to the museum, where presumably a number of pieces that had been made en suite with the chair were housed. Unbeknownst to the museum, the family had already decided that if the chair turned out to be historically significant, they would donate it to the museum's permanent collection. But such a donation was not meant to be, for once again the family's expectations were thwarted—this time by a museum curator who insisted that the chair was English and not American, and also out of period (meaning it postdated the style in which it was made).

Following this second rejection, the owners of the chair lost patience with the entire issue. Nate later told me that his family thought the chair was too valuable to be returned to the school but too ugly to be used anywhere in the house, so they placed it in a loft space above their unheated garage. Nate's aunt died within the year, but fairly soon after, his uncle asked him to renew his efforts with the chair and have it evaluated once again. This time, Nate decided, it was important to nail down the chair's provenance before proceeding any further, so he called upon his old friend Chris Machmer for some advice. Chris soon enlisted John J. Snyder, Jr., a scholar of Pennsylvania furniture, to document the chair's line of descent over the past two centuries. Amazingly, Snyder was able to trace the chair from Nate's relatives all the way back to Thomas Affleck's 1770 receipt of sale. He found that after General Cadwalader's death in 1786, the chair had descended through three generations of the family (one estate inventory of 1875 indicated it was kept in an attic and valued at fifteen dollars) before being taken north by one of the general's great-great-granddaughters, who married a New Yorker. The couple had one child, Beatrix Cadwalader Jones Farrand, who became a notable landscape architect. Mrs. Farrand took the chair to her home in Bar Harbor, Maine, but she eventually gave it to a friend, who later bequeathed it to her daughter, Nate's aunt. Armed with Snyder's research, Nate decided the time had come to consult with a New York auction house. With Chris acting as a liaison, the family contacted Sotheby's, which is how I came to have that astonishing phone conversation with Chris on that bright fall morning in 1986.

Within days of that talk, I met Nate Wallace for the first time at his uncle's Delaware home just outside of Wilmington. It was a large early-nineteenth-century white stucco

The 1770 Cadwalader bill of sale.

and stone house, filled with a number of significant pieces of modern art. After introducing me to his uncle, Nate led me out to the back porch, where the chair was being stored. My heart was racing. I had heard enough during my phone call with Chris to think that the object I was about to encounter had the potential to make auction history. The reading I had done prior to my trip further fueled my anticipation. I recalled the oft-quoted words of Silas Deane, a Connecticut member of the Continental Congress, who wrote on June 3, 1774, "I dined yesterday with Mr. Cadwallader [*sic*], whose furniture and house exceeds anything I have seen in this city or elsewhere." I also thought of the wording of Affleck's original bill, "to an easy chair . . . £4.10," and of the "1 large easy chair" listed in the general's estate inventory. As we pushed open the screen door to the porch, I felt as if I was about to throw the lid off a chest that I knew for certain was filled with gold.

As accustomed as I am to looking at American easy chairs, I was nevertheless struck by the massiveness of this particular example when I stepped through that door and saw it for the first time. It was nearly the size of a love seat and had been almost completely stripped of its upholstery and underupholstery due to the many examinations it had been subjected to over the past year or so. Traditionally, easy chairs, with their sheltering backs and coved side wings, were built to protect the sitter from chilling drafts and hopefully capture the radiant heat of a nearby fire. But my first impression of the chair brought none of those cozy qualities to mind, because most of its internal wooden framework had been laid bare, save for a few broad swatches of twentieth-century blue-and-white-striped mattress ticking wrapped along its arms and seat—all remnants of what was probably a 1950s reupholstery job.

Regardless, it was a thrilling sight. Take a walk across the preview floor at Sotheby's before any American furniture sale and you are bound to see a number of easy chairs in similar states of dishevelment. That is because removing the fabric of an easy chair allows collectors and dealers alike to analyze the wood of the frame and see what damage or repair, if any, the piece has sustained over time and, more important, whether or not the woods are American or English. Of course, if a chair maintains its original upholstery, then the fabric and internal stuffing must be preserved at all cost. But this was not the case with the easy chair before me; it sported multiple tack histories (a term used to describe the nail holes left by the upholsterer's work), which indicated it had been re-covered a number of times. Among those many holes, however, I was able to distinguish those that had been made by eighteenth-century nails. In a few instances, the shank of the iron nail had survived the wrenching tug of a later reupholstery stripping and was still visible, although deeply buried in the wood. Occasionally, the wood around these nail holes had acquired a dark halo, indicating that the metal had been embedded in the wood long enough to react with it. These clues were all vital to my analysis of the piece. Had the work not already been done for me, obviously I would have had to strip the chair myself in order to see the bones of the object and answer the family's burning question: Was this chair an authentic eighteenth-century American masterpiece or merely an English version or nineteenth-century American copy (as others before me had deemed it)? The question was a big one; if it was English, it was worth between eight and ten thousand dollars, but if it was American, it was worth significantly more. Why this huge discrepancy in price? Rarity is, of course, a tremendous factor; more than that, however, is the fact that Americana collectors think of Colonial furniture as a symbol of the uniqueness of the nation's experience. Such furniture was created as our country—the world's greatest democracy—was born.

With Nate's help, I carried the chair away from the shadowy recesses of the screened porch and set it down on a sunny patch of lawn. Finally, I was able to begin my hopeful examination. I began with a rapid rundown of the overall frame, which at first glance looked fine. The seat rails were crafted of oak, an obvious wood choice for this load-bearing section, given oak's renowned strength.

Originally, this area would have been filled first by interlaced strips of canvas webbing, then lined with sacking (or additional canvas), and subsequently stuffed with horsehair. The seat was probably then covered with two additional layers of canvas, a layer of linen, and the final decorative cover. This all would have been topped by a cushion or mattress.

Next, I turned my focus to the rolled arm supports, which gently angled upward and away from the seat frame before arching into a scrolled C shape. I was pleased to see these supports were cut from tulip poplar, a wood easily identifiable because of its creamy grain and slightly greenish tone. Poplar was indigenous to Pennsylvania and would have been a natural choice for the arms because it is a soft wood and thus easier to cut and shape.

Like an artist stretching his canvas across a newly assembled frame, the upholsterer would have covered the contours of the arms and high rectangular back with a network of fabric. But since no evidence of the original upholstery remained, it was easy to see the rough-hewn framework of yellow pine, another local wood. Yellow pine is easily identifiable because its dark medullar rings give it a prominent striped appearance.

Now came the heart of my examination—the lower half of the seat frame and legs. Unlike the structure of raw, unfinished woods above, this area was always meant to be seen. Made entirely of choice mahogany, the surface was elaborately carved and finished to perfection. The contrast between the upper and lower halves of the chair was made even greater because the lower mahogany show surface (or primary wood) bore the telltale signs of an untouched, original finish. On the serpentine-shaped front and side rails, for example, there was a wonderful pattern of lushly carved acanthus leaves, which appeared to spring downward from the point where the original fabric would have met the seat frame. Two centuries' worth of dirt had settled into the shellacked surface, offering added shading, nuance, and texture to the flips and curves of each veined leaf. At the front of the chair, the carving was particularly expressive because the carver had chosen to move the leaf pattern unencumbered toward the ground, rather than restricting it to the line of the rail. The elaborately carved pattern of leaves nearly obscured the bracing lines of the support structure lending an effect of asymmetry and exotic naturalism that propelled the design of the piece to exceptional heights.

Stripped bare, the Cadwalader chair reveals its oak, yellow pine, and poplar secondary woods—along with some circa 1950s mattress ticking.

Much of the chair's impact lay in the unusual hairy-paw front feet, so I chose to linger on them for quite some time. Hairy-paw feet, which had precedent in English and Irish furniture, were not an altogether unknown decorative device in America and had been used on some Colonial furniture from the third quarter of the eighteenth century. Still, they were never a common choice, which is what makes the all-encompassing hairy-paw statement of the Cadwalader suite such an anomaly (and perhaps contributed to earlier assessments of the piece as English). Each foot featured a four-toed spread that was awash in a tangle of wavy hair. Nearly buried within the tufts was a large ball that steadied the grasp. The calculated bold statement of this design gave the chair a thronelike presence that was anything but mainstream (especially in Quaker Philadelphia).

Just then, the wind picked up and noisily tossed the changing leaves overhead as I began to detect a slight misty rain starting to descend. "We'd better get this thing back on the porch," I said to Nate, who had already positioned himself behind the piece to move it indoors. We just made it back to the porch before the rain swept in.

When I concluded my examination, I was certain that the chair was indeed from Philadelphia, absolutely intact, and extraordinarily rare. What's more, it came with a well-researched and impressive provenance. Why did I have such confidence in a piece that others had so vehemently rejected? Quite simply, the object spoke to me on every level—and in an honest voice. The various woods used throughout the piece were exactly what I would have expected to see on a piece of Philadelphia furniture circa 1770. The wear patterns on both the primary and secondary woods were clearly authentic. And the design offered an incredibly well-fulfilled expression of eighteenth-century Philadelphia rococo style that well suited its hefty provenance and clearly related to the other Cadwalader pieces I had seen. As far as I was concerned, this was the real thing—the easy chair listed on Affleck's bill.

Within two weeks, after having sent the family a proposal for the chair's consignment bearing an auction estimate of $700,000 to $900,000, I returned to the house, this time in the company of Sotheby's then chairman, John L. Marion. John, who grew up in the auction world, is a towering man and possesses infinite charisma and a marvelously rich speaking voice. His father, Louis Marion, was one of Parke Bernet's founders, and from him, John inherited a keen eye for objects and enviable finesse. What's more, at the time of the chair's discovery, he was considered by many to be Sotheby's best auctioneer. Because the piece was potentially so significant, I had kept John apprised of my negotiations with the family (whom he knew from the auction rooms at Sotheby's, where they had been steady buyers of early-twentieth-century art, among other things). That friendship, coupled with John's personal interest in American furniture, brought him on the trip that day, for which John actually commandeered the Jeep Cherokee of Sotheby's president at the time, Diana Brooks. I was only twenty-eight and really got a big kick out of making the trip down to Delaware to seal the deal on the Cadwalader easy chair in the president's Jeep, accompanied by the company chairman.

Once we had a signed contract, John and I lingered a short time with the family and said our good-byes before quickly packing the chair into the Jeep and heading off. I always prefer to resolve these matters quickly because a deal is not done, quite simply, until it's done. In other words, I wouldn't want to lose a piece because the owners had a change of heart or tried to use the Sotheby's name as leverage to sell the piece privately. The Cadwalader easy chair was of such great importance that I had decided to oversee the pickup personally. The only other time I had taken such hand-holding precautions with an object was with the record-setting Gibbs desk, which I had driven down from Fort Ticonderoga myself.

As soon as John and I returned to the city (driving a cautious fifty miles an hour the entire way), the chair was sent up to his office, where big-ticket items were often displayed for top-level collectors and dealers. I then went straight to my desk and began calling both dealers and collectors who I thought might be contenders for the piece. The selling of the Cadwalader easy chair had begun.

A couple of hours ago, Leslie called to tell me that he just brought back the John Cadwalader hairy-paw wing chair. It is . . . quite simply, one of the most important pieces of furniture in the world. Undoubtedly, it will set the new world record for American furniture. I have a set of photographs of the chair, which I will send to Richard Dietrich tomorrow by overnight mail. I'll write the letters tonight. The chair belongs with the Cadwalader card table (that Richard owns). . . .

When I read over the passage above, written on October 29, 1986, it brings back the details of that day, and of the days and weeks that followed, with startling clarity. Leslie's news of the Cadwalader find was very exciting, not only because it spurred me as a young dealer to make connections and seek out a client but also because the chair was so extraordinary and the story of its discovery so enticing. It's not every day that a rare masterpiece of American furniture turns up at a country day school—particularly an object so renowned and well documented—and I was particularly proud that it was my brother who had helped reel it into the public arena. The double fiasco of its rejection by two museums (rather like taking a lost pyramid to Egypt, only to be told it doesn't belong there) only enhanced its status as a true survivor.

H. Richard Dietrich, Jr., the man about whom I had written in my diary, is an important client of mine and Leslie's (I first met him on the sales floor at Christie's, where we had established an instant rapport). He is a successful businessman and has spent the better part of the past four decades assembling one of the country's most important and well-rounded collections of American furniture. Richard is a gentleman in the truest sense of the word: a well-mannered, well-educated, and well-dressed individual. Picture Jimmy Stewart with an incredible passion for Americana. When I became a private dealer, Richard hired me to reappraise his extensive personal collection, as well as the holdings of the Dietrich American Foundation, an organization he founded in 1963 to educate the public about Colonial American decorative arts. My work for the foundation had even taken me to Ronald Reagan's White House, where some of Richard's furniture had been on loan since the Johnson administration. At one point, while I was examining a high chest of drawers in the Map Room, the one-thousand-watt quartz lamp that I was using to examine the furniture exploded. Flames and smoke were still spewing from the apparatus as a handful of alarmed assistants and Secret Service men came rushing into the room.

Richard's collecting taste runs from seventeenth-century to late-eighteenth-century furniture and related objects, but he definitely has a soft spot for Philadelphia pieces, because that is his hometown (he is very active with the Philadelphia Museum of Art). Richard actually owns one of the Cadwalader commode card tables on loan at the Philadelphia Museum (which I had examined at his behest only a few weeks previously), so I knew he would be ecstatic about the discovery of the matching easy chair. And I was not mistaken. As soon as he received the pictures, we immediately began discussing bidding strategies for the piece. Leslie had put a presale estimate of $700,000 to $900,000 on the chair (at the time, the highest printed presale estimate ever placed on a piece of American furniture), but there was no doubt in my mind that it would sell for much more—a point that I immediately stressed to Richard. I often advise clients not to bid above a certain price level on an object, because a similar one is sure to surface in the market, but I knew that the Cadwalader easy chair was a one-of-a-kind gem—and Richard knew it, too.

The morning of my phone conversation with Richard, I had gone to see the chair in John Marion's office. I already had great confidence in the piece because I implicitly trusted Leslie's instincts, but obviously, as a private dealer working for a client, I needed to render my own judgment. As soon as I began to go over the chair, however, I grew equally convinced of its authenticity. In terms of the four factors that we often use in the business to evaluate furniture—quality, rarity, condition, and provenance—this piece was a grand slam. Its quality was strikingly evident in its substantial proportions and elegant design, and there was a wonderful sense of balance among the various parts. In the front, the legs were bold and sinewy and well suited the generous massing of the framework above. The craftsman's handling of the rear legs, which raked back at an exaggerated cant and ended in swelled pad feet, particularly impressed me. Most easy chairs of this period were finished in the back with mildly backswept stump legs, simply angled toward the floor and uncarved at the feet. The design of the Cadwalader rear legs (closely based upon high-style London prototypes) added to the drama of the chair's profile by anchoring the form and emphasizing its animal-like energy.

The club-shaped ends of the raked back rear legs are rarely seen on Colonial American chairs.

Clearly, this object was not meant to be tucked in a corner, but viewed all around, a fact made clear by the eloquent treatment of the chair's carved detail, which was fluidly integrated into the overall form. The leaves spread in an organic way across the rails and around the sides and flowed into the S-shaped, or cabriole, legs, seamlessly uniting the elements. When I faced the chair head-on, I took careful note of the leg carving, which featured a large bellflower at the center of each knee, with a series of petals extending from its lower tip. Surrounding this elegant motif was a framework consisting of a pair of arching C-shaped scrolls flanked by additional leaf carving. Because a raking light can often bring out inconsistencies or patches in an older surface, I took a strong flashlight out of my bag and angled its beam across the knees. I was pleased to see that everything looked as it should—even under that harsh, unforgiving light—and the contrast between the raised areas and the smooth surrounds was dramatic.

The distinctive pattern of the carving was pivotal in establishing a relationship between the chair and the other objects in the Cadwalader suite. Indeed, I had just seen an identical design on Richard's Cadwalader card table at the Philadelphia Museum, adapted to the more attenuated proportions of the table form. The same held true for the powerful design of the hairy-paw feet, which were clearly brethren to the card table's feet. Sometime during the weeks that followed, I had a conversation about this work with Alan Miller, the man who conserved the Newport side chairs found in the chicken coop and who, because of his formidable skill as a craftsman, is an expert on the carving techniques of many eighteenth-century Philadelphia craftsmen. Alan thought that the long chiseled lines and strokes used throughout the design indicated that the carving had been done expertly but in haste—completely logical, given the scope of the Cadwalders' renovations and their eagerness to move into a newly appointed home. Soon after hearing Alan's observations, I ran into Luke Beckerdite, whose expertise had been instrumental in attributing the carving of Eddy Nicholson's $1 million piecrust tea table to Hercules Courtenay. Luke felt with growing certainty that the carving on the easy chair was by the firm of Bernard and Jugiez, one of the two firms listed on Thomas Affleck's original bill of sale, and he based his conclusion on other known examples of their work, including their architectural carving in the sumptuous Philadelphia home of Samuel Powel.

Rarity was also clearly working in this piece's favor: Only three other eighteenth-century American hairy-paw wing chairs have ever been found, and I could think of just one other example that even came close in its aggressive fulfillment of the gorgeous rococo aesthetic. That chair, now part of the permanent collection of the Philadelphia Museum, has long been attributed to the Philadelphia craftsman Benjamin Randolph because it has a solid history of descent in the family of his second wife. Randolph often worked in partnership with the carver Hercules Courtenay (to whom the carving on the Randolph chair is attributed), and both men were among the many leading Philadelphia artisans who contributed to the remodeling and refurbishing of the Cadwalader home. The Randolph chair was also the only other example I could recall that had similar back-raking legs and shaped feet.

Finally, in terms of condition, I had found no replaced parts on the Cadwalader chair, and only a handful of missing passages where the chair had suffered a bump or two. That, coupled with the chair's wonderful grungy original finish, meant that the piece was a winner. That left only the chair's provenance to factor into my overall analysis, and that was, of course, unbelievably satisfying in every way. When I spoke to Richard Dietrich later in the day, I was able to give him a rundown on the piece, including the name of the man who commissioned it (John Cadwalader), the chair-maker who created it (Thomas Affleck), the carvers who decorated it (the team of Bernard and Jugiez), the upholsterer who stuffed it (Plunkett Fleeson), and the room for which it was originally made (the front parlor). We even knew the color of the original upholstery (a blue damask), based upon the Cadwalader receipts. It all added up to a keenly personalized history of the object.

As the January sale date loomed closer, Richard and I continued to discuss the level of commitment it would take to win the chair, given the rising market for Americana and the buying capacity of such collectors as Eddy Nicholson, Richard and Gloria Manney of New York, or the Kaufmans, who, like Richard, already owned some Cadwalader furnishings. We considered auction prices both past and present for similar forms, including the only easy chair that came close to the design of the Cadwalader chair—the Randolph example at the Philadelphia Museum. That chair had sold back in 1929 at the famous sale of the Howard Reifsnyder Collection at New York's American Art Association for $33,000—a world record at the time. There was also the current world record for the form to think about, which had been set just a few months previously, in October 1986, when Eddy Nicholson purchased a Philadelphia easy chair with claw-and-ball feet at Sotheby's for $1.1 million.

I found that last statistic so important that I wrote in my diary not long before the sale:

The fact that Eddy Nicholson is in the action to such a major degree—buying whatever he wants—certainly affects this market in a major way. Eddy knows about the hairy-paw chair—and will definitely want it—probably at any cost. At this point, I feel that Richard could go up to $1.4 to $1.6 million—quite a jump on the recently set record (Nicholson of $1.1 on the . . . related chair). We'll see.

Well, on the morning of the sale, I did indeed have a bid in my pocket from Richard for $1.5 million, $400,000 more than the previous record for any piece of American furniture. That year, the January sale was a three-day event. The Cadwalader easy chair was scheduled for the afternoon session of the last day. Since I had no bids to place in the morning session (which was dominated by smaller decorative items and folk art), I had stayed at home on East Seventy-fifth Street, planning to arrive at Sotheby's just after lunch. However, my parents, who were in town, had attended the morning session (they always like to watch Leslie and me in action and hoped to bid on a few lots for themselves). During the lunch break, like many of the regulars in the crowd, they had gone to a pizza place on York Avenue, just two blocks from Sotheby's. I certainly hadn't given much thought to their lunch plans, so I was quite surprised when the phone rang as I was nearly out the door (the sale was scheduled to resume in less than an hour). It was Mom, calling from the pizza parlor.

"Hello, honey," she said in her warmhearted way.

"Yes, Mom?" I said, probably a bit tersely, since I was in a rush.

"Oh, I hate to bother you, dear, but I thought you might want to know that Dad and I are at the pizza parlor. . . ."

"Yes?"

"Well, I just heard a man telling some people seated near us that he was going to spend two and a half million dollars on that chair."

I couldn't believe what I was hearing. "Mom, well, who was it? Do you know who was talking?"

"No. Wait. Let me give you your father."

Mom passed the phone to Dad, who began a detailed physical description of the man whom they had overheard. "I'm sure he's a dealer, Leigh," he said in a low, conspiratorial tone (Dad always likes a bit of intrigue). "He said his clients were willing to go up to two and a half million." Based on Dad's account, I guessed that the speaker was Ron DeSilva. Ron is a good-hearted fellow, with an uninhibited enthusiasm for objects (he is also the only person to have ever headed the American furniture departments at both Sotheby's and Christie's, although obviously on separate occasions). At this point in his career, however, Ron was a private dealer, and I knew he often advised Richard and Gloria Manney, the pair of top collectors, who I had already suspected to be real contenders for the Cadwalader chair.

I glanced across the room at my desk clock—it was now half an hour before the afternoon session was set to begin. Hastily, I hung up with Dad and called Richard Dietrich, who was actually in London at the time. As quickly as I could, I outlined the chain of events for him. When I was through, I said, "Richard, you won't have a second opportunity to bid on this object. Ever. If you want that chair, you are going to have to stretch your limit—in a big way."

There was long silence on Richard's end. These were ridiculously high-pressured circumstances and I had just implied that he should increase his bid by over $1 million, and that was before the auction house's 10 percent buyer's premium. As I waited for his response, I knew that if this deal was going to work, I needed to make a gesture of

*For exhibition purposes, Sotheby's commissioned a
blue damask slipcover that was based upon a
description in the Cadwalader papers.*

self-sacrifice, as well. I had to show Richard that I was willing to go the extra distance
to get the object into the proper hands—his. So, for the first (and hopefully last) time
in my career, I decided to ask for a commission of only 1 percent of whatever the
chair brought.

"You would do that?" asked Richard somewhat incredulously.

"Yes, I would," I said steadily.

"Well then, you have a bid of two and a half million. Try to land on that amount."

I was exhilarated, but I also took his cautionary follow-up quite seriously. Richard
wanted me to land on the figure $2.5 million, which meant I had to calculate at what
point during the auction process I would jump in, so that I would end precisely on
that number. Since I knew the competition had the same cap of $2.5 million, it would
in essence be a duel for that single spot.

Now, I had never bid on an object over $1 million before, so during the taxi ride over to Sotheby's, I scrawled the figures of the rising bids in increments of $25,000 down the back of the sales catalog. Next to those numbers, I wrote a set of bidding cues for myself—"Him, me, him, me"—all the way down the length of the page, right up to $2.5 million.

But I never had a chance to look down at that page once the bidding for the chair actually started (and advanced in much larger increments than I had counted on). I had positioned myself as covertly as possible, next to a cement pole at the rear right of the auction room. John Marion was the auctioneer that day, with Leslie standing a few yards to his right, farther down on the stage.

As the bidding launched at $500,000, I glanced toward my brother, then quickly narrowed my focus to John Marion's commanding figure behind the podium. The bids rose in $50,000 increments and I put my green paddle, number 659, up at around $600,000, but when the numbers hit $1.1 million, I dropped back to assess the room. There seemed to be only one other person bidding from the rear center—Alexander Acevedo, the owner of Alexander Galleries and a sometime adviser to billionaire collector Richard Manoogian. Where was Ron DeSilva?

Leslie anxiously watches the bidding.

"$1.1 million," said John in his cool, clear voice. I kept the paddle braced low against my arm—I wanted Alex to feel as if he was going to get the chair at that price, the standing world record.

"$1.1 . . . $1.1 . . . $1.1 . . ." The figure hung out there for what seemed like an eternity.

I flashed my paddle again to John.

"$1.2 . . . $1.3 now . . . $1.4 million . . ." Now the bidding was jumping at a $100,000 clip. Standing directly next to me was a well-dressed, genteel woman, and I remember sensing the tension in her frame. I think she was afraid to move a centimeter, lest any gesture be misconstrued as a bid against me.

As we neared the $2 million mark, John paused for a moment to quip to the audience, "Don't walk out now." Some nervous titters rippled across the standing-room-only crowd, but it quickly died out as the auctioneer urged the sale along.

"$2.1 million . . ." I nodded my head.

"$2.2 now . . ." Alex met the bid.

"$2.3 . . ." I nodded firmly again.

"$2.4 now . . ." Alex affirmed again.

"$2.5 . . ." John seemed to stretch the number out across the crowd. This was it—I nodded one last time. The silence was deafening. "$2.5 million," John announced, followed by a fair warning. My single rival, Alex Acevedo, turned around and walked out of the room, signaling he was through.

Smack. John Marion brought his wooden auctioneer's gavel down on the podium. The room burst into thunderous applause. I had bought the Cadwalader easy chair for $2.5 million! With the auction house's 10 percent buyer's premium, that brought the total for the chair to $2.75 million. It was not just a record for American furniture but a record for *any* piece of furniture sold in the world.

I breathed a sigh of relief and looked toward my brother, who was smiling at me from across the room. The sale was a triumph for us both. Quickly, though, the crowd surged around me. Members of the press wanted quotes. Sotheby's wanted a picture. Other folks just wanted to offer their congratulations. I threw out a few words about what I thought of this incredible object and then beat a hasty retreat. I needed to protect the anonymity of my client and didn't want to be asked any leading questions. Furthermore, I needed to let him know that we had won the chair—this was, after all, the age before cell phones.

As I cut through the crowd, I wondered to myself, What ever happened to Ron DeSilva? I later learned that he had, in fact, been advising the Manneys, and that they, along with Richard Manoogian and his adviser, Alex Acevedo, had formed a consortium to buy the chair together as an investment. Alex was the chosen front man for the trio. I also found out that the comedian and Americana collector Bill Cosby, who had been in a private viewing room overlooking the sales floor, had thrown in a few bids, as well. He later joked to Robert H. Boyle, a reporter for *Barron's,* the business weekly, "The biggest disappointment was being an underbidder on that chair. I hope it's a fake."

Sotheby's chairman John Marion congratulates Leigh after the sale of the Cadwalader chair.
In recognition of the event, paddle 659 was permanently retired by the auction house.

6

Open Talons in the Hamptons

I ALWAYS MAKE IT MY BUSINESS to check out the lower-end sales at Christie's East, as well as at Sotheby's equivalent Arcade division (both devoted to items that are generally valued at less than twenty thousand dollars), because to this day, I am still on the lookout for sleepers. Even at the top auction houses, it is not unheard of for an exceptional object to occasionally slip through the cracks and land in a less important sale (just as Leslie's discovery of those mislabeled reproduction chairs on the Sotheby's loading dock proved the reverse). I've discovered sleepers several times at auction, including a Newport slipper-foot tea table and a fluidly carved child's armchair from Boston that dated to the second half of the eighteenth century. Both had been cataloged as reproductions, when they were clearly anything but. However, I still think there is nothing like those more elusive sleepers—the kind found in private homes, garages, or attics—that are uncovered only by a mere twist of fate.

One day in the spring of 1989, nearly two years after my purchase of the Cadwalader easy chair, I found myself at an Americana preview at Christie's East, where I ran into Morgan MacWhinnie, a Southampton dealer whom I had known for quite some time. Morgan had very good taste in Americana, but he tended to steer clear of high-style objects, gravitating instead toward things with a more "country" bent. Then in his mid-fifties, Morgan was a tall, handsome guy with a friendly face and a thick head of dark hair. He was born on Long Island and spent thirty years working for the phone company as a cable repairman before he turned to dealing in antiques full-time. He and his wife live in a historic house in Southampton that is packed with American furniture and decorative arts, and their adjacent barn holds a lot of the spillover. Morgan has a sizable collection of American pottery; old lighting devices, such as tin sconces; and quite a few furniture miniatures. In fact, some years back, he bought—actually, "stole"—a miniature blanket chest from my parents' booth at Brimfield (he paid $650, although it was probably worth closer to $2,500), which proves that Morgan has an eye for sleepers, too.

When I bumped into Morgan at Christie's East, he had been involved in the antiques business for about five years. As we chatted about the market, I mentioned that I had a prospective client, someone I had just met, who was actively looking for great Newport furniture, particularly pieces by the Goddards and Townsends. Would he let me know if he came across anything special? I asked. Morgan grinned. "You'd better be free for lunch, Leigh," he said, "because I've got a story for you."

Within ten minutes, Morgan and I had settled into a table at a small Irish pub just a hundred yards up the block from Christie's East, and over a beer and a burger, Morgan began to tell me an incredible tale. Nearly ten years earlier, when Morgan was still with the phone company, he explained, the village of East Hampton had been hit by a two-day-long snowfall, which cut off phone service to hundreds of residents. It was a busy time for Morgan and his crew, who had to work double shifts in order to patch the downed cables in the area. Like many of the towns on Long Island's East End, East Hampton is a quiet, somewhat isolated place for three seasons a year, with a full-time population of middle-class families, some with roots that date back to the seventeenth century. In summer, the town swells dramatically with moneyed summer home owners and renters.

I'd visited East Hampton on several occasions in the summer to stay with friends. A few years earlier, when I was still at Doyle's, Bill Doyle and his wife, Kathy, used to invite me out to the house they owned on Lily Pond Lane, a few driveways down from where Steven Spielberg now summers in his Charles Gwathmey–designed home. Bill and Kathy were members of the Maidstone, an old-guard beach club on the ocean with a golf course and grass tennis courts. As was typical of Bill's savvy sense of humor, he used to give his daughters and their friends dark green T-shirts printed with the William Doyle Galleries logo to wear to the beach. He figured it was good advertising to have all these fresh-faced young kids running around the Maidstone in Doyle T-shirts.

That snowy day, Morgan was just a few miles and many worlds away from the Maidstone, working with his crew in front of one of East Hampton's more modest homes. The two-story clapboard, now restored, sat to the right of the traffic light just before eastbound travelers on the Montauk Highway reach East Hampton's picturesque village green. "I was finishing up patching a cable under the lawn when this frail-looking old man came out of the house," Morgan told me. "He must have been about eighty, and even though it was less than twenty degrees out, he came shuffling through the snow in a bathrobe and slippers."

The man asked Morgan if he could check the phones in his house. "I tried to explain that I had just fixed the wire," Morgan said, "but the old guy was so insistent, I told him I'd be in just as soon as I put my tools in the truck."

The man waited for Morgan on the porch and then brought him into the house through the back door, which opened directly into the kitchen. With lingering amazement, Morgan described the bizarre landscape that greeted him: "The kitchen was stacked floor to ceiling on both sides with used aluminum TV-dinner trays. The old guy had left a small passage, maybe two feet wide, just big enough to walk through, and that was it."

A diamond in the rough.

Morgan made his way through this strange scene to the kitchen phone, which, no surprise to him, worked fine. The man insisted that Morgan check the bedroom extension—what if he needed to call for help in the middle of the night? He led Morgan through a room that was probably the house's original dining room, so neglected now, Morgan said, "that there were tumbleweed-size dustballs covering the floor."

The room was dark, save for one low table lamp, and as Morgan instinctively turned his head toward that light, he suddenly saw something that made him stop dead. "I couldn't believe it," he said, his face flushed with the memory, his big hands, callused from years of outdoor work, cutting excitedly through the air. "I saw a tea table and a bonnet-top highboy on cabriole legs. They were both definitely Newport pieces, Goddard and Townsend school. And once the old fellow led me out to the center hallway, I saw a drop-leaf dining table near the front door. No question—it was Newport, too." Curling the fingers of his right hand around an imaginary ball, Morgan continued. "All the furniture had claw-and-ball feet, but the feet on the tea table had open talons."

I looked at Morgan hard over my hamburger platter. This sounded too good to be true. As much as I respected his eye, I initially suspected Morgan had seen Colonial Revival copies, dating to the beginning of the twentieth century. He said the room was quite dark, and under such circumstances, he probably hadn't gotten a close-enough look. But Morgan can be pretty convincing when he wants to be, and the more he insisted that what he had seen was real, the more I wanted to believe him.

To begin with, a rectangular tea table with cabriole legs is one of the most desirable

forms in American furniture (it literally looks like a tray that has been set in a low stand). These tables are small and so elegantly shaped that they look as good in the middle of a room as they do against the wall. Specifically designed for tea drinking, the tables are wonderfully evocative of eighteenth-century custom and culture; you can easily imagine America's preeminent colonialists taking tea together, musing over the king's latest injustices to his increasingly short-tempered subjects. Today, collectors who are lucky enough to find a good example of such a table often place an eighteenth-century silver or porcelain tea service on its top.

Much of a rectangular tea table's character comes from the spring of its cabriole legs, which curve outward from the tabletop at each of the four corners before descending in a tapering reverse curve. Unlike the horizontally aligned versions seen on the round Philadelphia tilt-top tea table that I had bought from Eddy Nicholson, which sprang out from beneath the fluted support pillar, the cabriole legs of the table that Morgan described ran almost the entire height of the form. That meant they were much more attenuated and slender in appearance. But Morgan had described not simply a tea table but a Newport tea table with open-talon claw-and-ball feet, which are incredibly sculptural and compelling and tend to look like the feet of a large bird of prey. There are perhaps twelve eighteenth-century Newport examples of this form with claw-and-ball feet known in the world, fewer than six of which carry these most desirable open talons. To hear of one sitting undiscovered in a run-down house on East Hampton's main road—well, that was just incredible. I took a long swig, savoring the thought more than the beer.

To my further amazement, Morgan had also mentioned a Newport bonnet-top high chest in the house (often referred to as a highboy), a form that Americana collectors consider a true prize. American high chests of the 1760s and 1770s typically consist of a chest of drawers raised on a four-legged (usually cabriole) base that is also fitted with drawers. Although Morgan claimed to have spotted this one in a dining room, such chests were usually used in bedchambers to store linens and clothing, and they were often designed en suite with a low dressing table that resembled the base of the high chest in design.

I have often thought that eighteenth-century baroque and rococo furniture is the most collected American furniture and fetches the most money, because it was so clearly designed with the human form in mind. High chests are roughly the same height as the average person, and it is no coincidence that today we use words such as *legs, knees,* and *feet* to describe their various parts. The brass drawer pulls and escutcheons (the metal shields surrounding the keyholes) march up the facade of a chest like shiny buttons on a double-breasted jacket. In short, the proportions, the S curves of the sizable cabriole legs, the nooks and crannies of the carved detail—all appeal to us as if we are looking at another human being. The record price for a piece of Federal furniture, with its more restrictive, rectilinear designs, is a fraction of what major Queen Anne and Chippendale furniture has brought. I think that disparity arises because Federal pieces lack the curves, the anthropomorphic movement, and, quite frankly, the sex appeal of their earlier counterparts.

Original openwork brasses on the Tillinghast high chest.

The high chest Morgan had described had plenty of alluring curves, from its upswept bonnet top (which looks like a bell with a yawning break in the middle) to its racy cabriole legs. And like the tea table he had first mentioned, undiscovered full-blown high chests just don't turn up. As for the dining table spotted in the front hallway—well, that was like nuts on a hot-fudge sundae: two of the most desired, collectible forms around, and a bonus prize, too. The story alone was enough to ensure that I would be paying for lunch.

Obviously, if Morgan was right, he had found a virtual treasure trove of furniture made in Newport during the peak of its artistic prominence—the 1760s and 1770s. He had also attributed the pieces with a fair degree of confidence to the Goddards and Townsends, the town's most prominent craftsmen. That made the find an even greater coup. Indeed, the most expensive piece of American furniture ever sold at auction was a block-front secretary-bookcase (possibly made by John Goddard) for Nicholas Brown of Providence. That piece sold at Christie's for $12.1 million in 1989 to Israel Sack, Inc., buying on behalf of a private billionaire client. In fact, the Nicholas Brown secretary had sold just months before Morgan and I met, and the excitement of that sale further flavored our lunch as Morgan continued his story.

Before he left the East Hampton cottage, Morgan found out that the elderly man

My hands shook with excitement as I snapped this image of the chest's skirt shell.

was a longtime tenant; the furniture, in fact, belonged to his landlady, Caroline Tillinghast, who lived in a house at the end of the driveway, set farther back from the road. A few days later, Morgan returned to the property and knocked on her door to see if she was interested in selling any of the pieces. Mrs. Tillinghast, whom Morgan guessed to be in her early eighties, listened carefully as Morgan explained his interest in the furniture. She knew it had value—a local appraiser a few years back had valued the group at about $25,000—but she owed it to her tenant to provide him with a fully furnished house. She wasn't interested in selling. What's more, she told him, the furniture had been in her husband's family for some time, and when he died, he had willed it to her son Frank. In truth, it wasn't hers to sell.

Morgan knew Frank Tillinghast. He ran a prosperous deli in town, called the Chicken House, where Morgan frequently bought his lunch. So the next day, Morgan made a point of driving through the snow to buy his sandwich at the Chicken House. When he explained that he thought Frank owned some furniture of significant value, the deli owner, a man of few words, betrayed not the slightest expression of joy or amazement. "I might as well have been talking about the weather," Morgan said. "I figured he was asking himself, Now what does this guy know about antiques? He's a telephone repairman! I wasn't a dealer or a specialist. I had no credentials."

Frank sent Morgan back to his mother. Even if the furniture was technically his, any decisions about the pieces were really his mother's to make. Besides, his mother had a rental house that she needed to furnish. By the time Morgan ran into me at Christie's East, nearly ten years had passed since he had first seen the furniture, and neither Frank nor his mother were any closer to making a decision about the fate of their extraordinary heirlooms. Despite Morgan's occasional queries, Frank remained resolutely noncommittal.

Now I was completely hooked. My burger lay half-eaten and cold in front of me. I was far too excited to eat. What had started as another day scouting Christie's East in search of sleepers had turned into a potentially tremendous discovery sitting roughly a hundred miles away in a small East Hampton home. I wanted to see that furniture. "Morgan, you've got to talk to Frank Tillinghast one more time," I said.

Morgan smiled and agreed to try. This time, he hoped, maybe the presence of a New York antiques dealer with a profound interest in Newport furniture would alter the dynamic. And since I knew Morgan to be a man of his word, I felt confident that he wasn't going to approach another dealer with the same opportunity he'd given me. Before we separated after lunch, Morgan and I agreed that if a deal were ever made, we would split the profit equally, whether we bought the pieces outright or on a commission basis for a client. It was a standard agreement. Morgan found the pieces and I was going to place them—that is, if we could persuade Frank and his mother that the furniture was worth selling.

It couldn't have been more than a week or two after our lunch that I received a phone call from Morgan. He was pumped. Timing is everything in this business, and it seemed that by odd and sad coincidence, Mrs. Tillinghast's elderly tenant had died a few weeks earlier and the house was being cleaned out. She was going to let us in.

At this point, it was the start of summer, and as it turned out, Leslie and I, together with a few friends, had rented a house on Peconic Bay in Southampton, about fifteen

The Tillinghasts' East Hampton home.

miles west of East Hampton. The house was our antidote to dealing with antique American furniture all week long, because neither the house nor any of its contents was more than ten years old. We gave a lot of parties out there. One weekend, we hired a doorman and the deejay from Au Bar, a New York nightclub, and entertained some four or five hundred people. Freya, my girlfriend at the time, was a Californian who had come to New York to model. She was about five foot nine, with blond hair, blue eyes, and endless legs—really an American classic herself.

Freya's legs were so long, in fact, that she had trouble fitting into the 1967 dark green MGB-GT coupe that I drove on my way to my Saturday-morning appointment with the Tillinghasts and Morgan in East Hampton. The car was a loaner from my dad, whose passion for vintage cars Leslie and I both inherited. Even on the straight, well-maintained roads of the Hamptons, it was still a pleasure to drive. With the windows down, I could hear the engine purr, and I would recall many a windy drive with Dad as we climbed the curving hills above our house in Mohawk. Nowadays, Leslie and I drive vintage race cars, including a 1958 Lotus Eleven, a 1959 Lola Mark 1, and a 1979 Ferrari 512 BB/LM Silhouette, at track meets around the country. One of the main reasons the sport appeals to us, beyond the rush of moving fast in a machine designed specifically for that purpose, is that we are re-creating, in a sense, the excitement of an earlier era in motor racing. Each car on the track is like a rolling piece of sculpture, as precious as any American tea table or chest of drawers.

Leslie and I love racing vintage cars, especially this 1938 SS-100 3.5 liter Jaguar.

It was nearly eleven o'clock by the time Freya and I pulled up in front of the Tillinghasts' small clapboard home, just as Morgan arrived in his truck. He had stopped at the deli to give a ride to Frank Tillinghast, whose mother was standing on the back porch, waiting for us. We all trooped into the house after her: First came Freya, then Morgan and Frank (a large, burly guy), who was still wearing his deli apron. I brought up the rear, excitement gathering in my chest. Right before I see a new object for the first time, I feel a palpable rush of anticipation that hovers between elation and disappointment. Will it or won't it be something really great? In this case, Morgan had already sent my hopes soaring.

The house was dark inside, but it had been well cleaned since Morgan's first visit. There wasn't an aluminum tray or dust ball in sight. Breathing in that damp old wood smell so common in houses near the water, we all made our way from the kitchen to the dining room with its faded pink-flowered wallpaper, white wainscoting, and ceilings so low I could touch them with my arm half-bent. By now, my eyes were adjusting to the gloom of the house and I began to register the furniture. Everything else— the people, the voices—just faded away.

Directly in front of me, between the white-curtained windows, was a bonnet-top chest of drawers with a graceful broken-arch pediment that centered around two hollowed circles. The chest was set in a low frame with four meager-looking cabriole legs. In front of the chest, placed somewhat haphazardly toward the center of the room, stood the small rectangular tea table that Morgan had described, and to the left, against the wall, was a large low table with drawers, atop which sat a television.

At this point, I'm sure I must have started nodding my head, because that's something Leslie and I both do when we are excited about an object. And I was more than excited, but I was also trying to maintain an outward appearance of calm. Within seconds—if not instantaneously—I knew that the bonnet-top chest of drawers and the table with the television set belonged together. I don't mean they were designed to accompany each other; I mean that they were made as one piece—a two-part high chest of drawers that had at some point in its history been separated. Everything about the two pieces—the marvelous swirling wood grain that seemed to animate the facades, the matched proportions, the decorative hardware, and the quality of carving—pointed to their union. You see this sort of thing a lot at country auctions, when tops and bottoms have been separated for one reason or another. People slap a new top on the lower half and a set of legs on the upper half and create two new pieces.

As calamitous as this type of alteration sounds, it's often not a major issue, which was

The Tillinghast suite as I first saw it, with the high chest's top (right) mounted on a makeshift set of legs and the base sitting solo. The tea table stands between the divided piece.

the case with the Tillinghast pieces. To restore the high chest to its original form—which, judging from the room's low ceilings, wasn't going to be done here—the bonnet top simply needed to be lifted out of its current thin-legged frame and returned to its original base (which was covered with an easily removable single-board top). In short, the changes, which probably dated to the early twentieth century, were easily reversible. They didn't detract from the overall integrity of the piece.

When I look at furniture for the first time, I like to scan the piece and then zoom in on points of interest. Bells go off as I mentally go through a checklist of quality-related issues. When I began to examine the separated bonnet-top chest more closely, I marveled at the symmetrical arched S curves of the hood, an eloquent and more costly alternative to a flat top, which was a classic design favored by Newport cabinetmakers. The drawer fronts and case were crafted of a rich dark plum-pudding mahogany that glowed in the warmth of what little sun filtered through the curtained windows. This type of reddish purple mottled mahogany was, of course, a favorite with early Newport craftsmen. Punctuating the decorative surface was a lively progression of openwork brass pulls that marked each drawer front. My guess was that they had come from Birmingham, England, the industrial town that was home to many of the brass foundries that supplied the colonies.

Morgan watched approvingly while everyone else (excluding a rather bored-looking Freya) regarded me with considerable curiosity as I studied the construction details. I pulled out a drawer from the bonnet top and another from the separated base and began to make comparisons between them. What I found there was remarkable, and identical, workmanship that further confirmed that the two objects had begun life as one. In each instance, the drawer sides were thin and delicate, with rounded edges at the top. Both were constructed of poplar, the same wood Leslie had noticed in use on the drawer sides of the Gibbs block-front bureau that he found near Fort Ticonderoga. Next, I compared the openwork brass pulls on the front of the drawers, which also seemed to match. The posts that held the brasses in place had hand-cut threads (the spiraling grooves running down the length of the shaft) and were tapered, a sure sign that the posts were of the period. And like Leslie during his examination of the Gibbs piece, I was pleased to see there were no additional holes visible where the irregularly cut nuts that anchored the posts met the backs of the drawer, which suggested that they had probably never been removed or replaced.

I then turned the two drawers toward the sunlight to examine the wedge-shaped dovetails where the drawer sides met. Each joint was perfectly cut to a fine point and was spaced with the precision typical of the work of the Goddards and Townsends. Even the marks left by the kerfing saw used to cut the individual dovetail grooves (which could be seen on the inside of each drawer) were identical.

Characteristically refined and elegant Goddard dovetails.

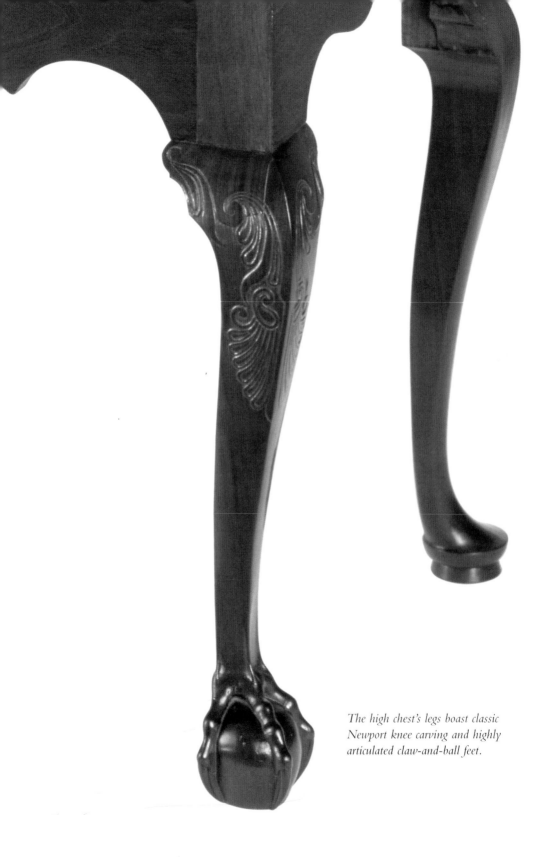

The high chest's legs boast classic Newport knee carving and highly articulated claw-and-ball feet.

I returned the drawers to their respective slots and turned my full attention to the details of the base. Morgan helped me lift the television set off the top and move the piece closer to the window, where Freya was now regarding our fierce attention to the furniture with perplexity and perhaps a little envy. Even by the window, however, the viewing light was poor, so I took a flashlight out of my bag before continuing with my work.

I began with the legs, which had wonderful peaked (or squared) knees that were covered in low-relief intaglio carving. The cabinetmaker squared the legs in order to continue the angled line of the chest's front corners into the legs below. It also provided him with two equal and distinct surfaces for decorative carving. When I raked my flashlight beam across each of the legs, the symmetrical palmetto-and-leaf pattern came alive. I was thrilled to see this particular design, because the style and execution of the carving were very familiar to me and pointed to one craftsman in particular, John Goddard of Newport. Goddard was, of course, the same man whose shop had produced the chairs found in the New Jersey chicken coop.

In fact, the carving on the legs of the high chest's base reminded me of a famous tea table that descended in the family of the wealthy Providence merchant Jabez Bowen (1739–1815). That tea table, which is now in the collection of the Winterthur Museum, features nearly identical squared cabriole legs with the same pattern of intaglio leaf carving. It is documented as having been made by John Goddard, and the particulars I recalled of its carved detail really strengthened my belief that the piece I was looking at was probably made by Goddard, as well. This type of comparison—that between previously unknown objects and other, documented examples—is the lifeblood of furniture research. It is why you can never look at enough furniture or pictures of furniture. The learning process always continues.

When the Tillinghast chest of drawers first came out of the shop in the 1760s or 1770s, the mahogany surface would have carried a number of coats of varnish, meant to give it a reflective quality. Now, as I examined the wood in a strong light, I could detect the small knots of the plum-pudding mahogany coming through the old darkened finish of the piece, just as it had on the bonnet top. As expected, two centuries' worth of dust and pollutants had settled onto the more horizontal elements of the structure and darkened them, while the vertical parts had stayed comparatively clean. It's rather like the face of a cliff—moss doesn't grow on the front; it grows in the nooks and crannies.

I took my hand and ran it along the large concave shell that filled the center of the skirt. It was a single, grandly proportioned version of the shells that Leslie had examined so closely on the Gibbs bureau. The shell's fluted body was bold and elegant and, like the Gibbs examples, featured a stop-fluted central intaglio detail at the base, designed in imitation of the muscles at a shell's base (the part that you rip when you pry it open). Recently, scholars have speculated that Newport craftsmen collectively used this distinctive, highly stylized version of a shell on their furniture designs (think of the smaller convex versions seen on the crest rails of the chairs from the chicken coop) as a form of brand identification or advertising (like the winged figural hood ornament on a Rolls-Royce). The reason for this is that eighteenth-century Newport (like many other Colonial ports) had a strong export economy that relied upon venture cargo or goods that were sent out on spec. Finished furniture constituted one such commodity, and a fair number of pieces built by the Goddards and Townsends were designed for sale in other ports. It may have been the cabinetmakers' hope that their superior designs would come to be recognized and associated with that unusual signature shell. It had certainly worked on Morgan more than two hundred years after the Tillinghast furniture was made.

Stepping back for a moment, I tried to visualize the two halves of the high chest as they would look when they were reunited. I quickly discounted the two urn-shaped finials mounted on the upper ends of the bonnet top, as well as the third one, which marked the center. They were no doubt later additions, because their Neoclassical Revival style postdated the rest of the design by at least twenty years. These were details that had probably been added at the time the chest was divided in the late nineteenth or early twentieth century, and their presence was minor and reversible.

As excited as I was about the high chest, however, it was the tea table that really blew me away. Just as Morgan had told me, the eloquent cabriole legs of the table ended in rare open-talon claw-and-ball feet. They stood in stark contrast to the closed-talon variety I'd just seen on the legs of the high chest's base, which were emphatically beautiful, although slightly less sculptural. The talons on the tea table were so open that I could almost slip a small pencil between the claw and the ball. They also called to mind Jabez Bowen's tea table at Winterthur, with its open-taloned feet. There as here, the carver (by now, I was certain he was John Goddard) had played up the tension of the form by pairing delicate, slender ankles with sharply articulated tendons and animal-like swollen-jointed toes. The juxtaposition of these elements was powerful and evocative. Goddard's gift was his ability to pour life into his carved work. Looking at the feet, I felt as if I could take the pulse of the creature that clasped the balls.

A few of the talons were actually missing from the Tillinghast table, which I took as a good sign. Freestanding talons are fairly fragile, and some damage is nearly inevitable over the years. Seeing this, however, made me think we should look around for a broom to sweep the floors in case any of the pieces were still about. But when I examined the feet more closely, I saw the wood had darkened and oxidized at the breakage points, which meant the fractures were old.

By now, Morgan had a relaxed smile on his face (his good eye had been confirmed), Freya was clearly yearning for the beach, and the Tillinghasts seemed impressed that I was paying such extended attention to their furniture. I picked up the table and marveled at its extreme weight. The very best pieces from the Goddard and Townsend cabinet shops were constructed from only the highest-quality mahogany, which tends to be unusually dense. I flipped the table over and set it down on the carpet. As I aimed the flashlight, the beam flickered across the unmistakable channel marks of an eighteenth-century planing tool, which ran perpendicular to the wood grain. Meanwhile, along the perimeter of the board, where it met the top of the skirt, was a more agitated lined pattern, like the surface of a ruffled potato chip, left by a toothing plane. The cabinetmaker texturized the wood this way, roughening the surface to give the glue a better grip between the top and frame. If any similar tooling marks had been left visible on the show surfaces of the piece, the craftsman would have sanded it away with a piece of shagreen, a material that comes from the rough skin of certain sharks or stingrays.

Also caught in the beam of my flashlight as I shone it on the underside of the table was a scrawled chalk inscription of the initials W.T., written in an eighteenth-century hand. I looked over at Frank and his mother. "Do you have any ancestors who had the initials W.T.?" I asked.

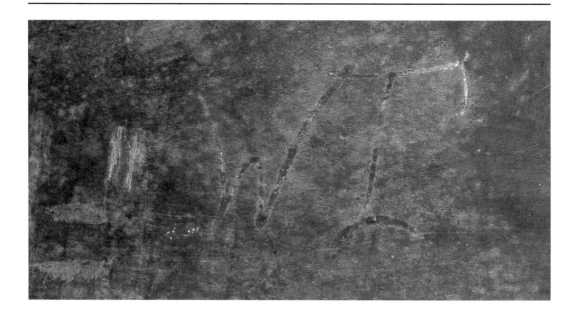

Frank shrugged and glanced at his mother. "William was a popular name in my husband's family for many generations," she told me.

I straightened up and turned off my flashlight. It was incredible to realize that after looking at those two magnificent pieces—both real stars—there was still a dining table sitting in the front hall. The table was set against the staircase wall between a pair of Victorian-looking chairs. Its two semicircular leaves were folded down. Standing on its narrow rectangular exposed top was a large stoneware jug with an incised blue bird that had been turned into a lamp. I placed my hand on the lamp to steady it and picked up one of the folded ends to feel the heft of the piece. Cut from solid, dense mahogany wood, it felt like it weighed a ton. I looked underneath the table at the frame and saw supportive cross braces made of maple, which were typical of Newport construction. But it was the feet of the table, with their closed-talon claw-and-ball design that matched the feet displayed on the high chest, that confirmed what I already suspected: Here was yet a third object by John Goddard.

I drew a sigh, closed my eyes for a moment, and then turned to the assembled group. Mrs. Tillinghast had taken a seat on one of the small Victorian chairs in the hallway, Frank and Morgan were quietly leaning against a wall, and Freya was impatiently looking out a window by the front door, wondering what had happened to her Hamptons weekend. Filtered through the window, the steady stream of Montauk Highway traffic passing by not thirty yards from the house could be clearly heard. How many had passed by over the years, unaware of the great treasures just a stone's throw away? How many other houses have I driven by that contain similar undiscovered treasures?

Because I didn't want to overwhelm the Tillinghasts with a lot of technical talk, I began by telling them how privileged I felt I was to have seen the furniture. These were some of the most amazing pieces I had encountered in my career, I said, and I

very much wanted to handle them. I interpreted each object for them in fairly general terms and then I began to talk about the market for Americana, which by 1989 was still steadily gaining momentum. The auction world can be an intimidating place for many people, even those who are quite savvy about furniture, and I tried to play that issue to my advantage. Morgan and I would offer a "sure thing," with no risk at all. Of course, he and I did not immediately name a price for the group because we needed to assess our own resources. I was still a young dealer with limited finances and Morgan had never dealt with this caliber of merchandise before. It was going to be a stretch for us both. We asked for a little more time.

Within twenty-four hours, however, Morgan went to see Frank at the Chicken House with an offer that was upward of $600,000. "You should have seen his face," he reported back to me. "Frank looked as if I had just told him he had lost his home and he would have to sleep on the street. He was stunned."

Amazed as he was, however, Frank was actually far from making a decision. We later learned that the size of the offer made him nervous, so he had gone to his accountant for advice, who had recommended a local lawyer, who in turn suggested he get a second opinion. That is how a set of photographs of the Tillinghast suite of furniture ended up in the hands of my old boss at Christie's, Dean Failey.

For as long as I have known Dean, he has always had a keen interest in the history of his native Long Island. In fact, he wrote the definitive book on Long Island furniture and decorative arts back in the mid-1970s (recently revised), so when he heard about a group of furniture with a long history of local ownership, I'm sure he was intensely intrigued. Not surprisingly, after seeing the pieces, he set about trying to bring them to auction.

Once Frank had a proposal from Christie's in hand, he still wanted time to weigh his options—a sure sale with a fixed price to Morgan and me, or a less certain sale at Christie's. By now, Morgan was making regular stops at the Chicken House, thinking we were close to a deal. Imagine his surprise, then, when he learned from Frank that Dean Failey had entered the picture. He couldn't get to the nearest pay phone fast enough to let me know.

With the Tillinghasts entertaining other options, we knew we had to come up with more money if we expected to clinch the deal. The problem was that we didn't have the finances between us to float the sale alone. We decided it was time to connect directly with a buyer and see if we could broker a commissioned deal instead of an outright sale.

From the moment I heard Morgan's story, I had had one buyer in mind for these pieces: the longtime East Coast collector whose interest in Newport furniture had precipitated my conversation with Morgan at Christie's East. He was a man who was so consumed by his hobby that he retained a full-time curator to maintain his collection. I had been aware of the collector's reputation long before we first met, nearly a year earlier, on a flight from New York's La Guardia Airport (confusing me for Leslie, whom he already knew, he had given me a hearty greeting). Now I placed a call to him and explained how spectacular the pieces were and just where Morgan and I had left off in the negotiations. Knowing how much a historical context adds value to fine objects, I'd also done some additional research on the Tillinghasts to see if I could learn anything about their early ties to Newport or about the mysterious W.T. behind the initials on the tea table.

A look through the East Hampton town records revealed that both the Tillinghast and Townsend families had eighteenth-century roots in East Hampton and Newport and that for a time, members of the two families even owned ships together. This was just the type of connection that I was looking for—one that established that the Tillinghasts must have been aware of the furniture productions of the Townsends and further suggested that the Tillinghasts had the means to transport large furniture across Long Island Sound from one port town to the other. Unfortunately, though, I couldn't narrow down which of the many William Tillinghasts had scrawled his initials on the underside of that table.

Nonetheless, this history, along with the pictures that I had sent by overnight mail to my client and my professional assurances regarding the rarity and value of the furniture, convinced the collector that he could and *should* up the ante. He told me to make an offer on his behalf that exceeded the figure Morgan and I had last presented, information that I promptly passed on to Frank.

Time passed. Summer drew to a close. Freya moved to Paris to pursue her career as a model . . . but Frank Tillinghast did not respond to my latest offer. I couldn't understand the holdup. Finally, one evening, from my apartment in New York, I gave in to my frustration and called him.

When Frank heard my voice, he said with complete nonchalance, "Oh, Leigh, I should have let you know. Mother decided to put the furniture up for auction in New York. Christie's is coming tomorrow to pick it up." When I heard his words, I felt as if a tremendous iron door was slowly closing shut in front of me. All I could do was try one last time to wedge my foot back in.

"Frank, from the start I was honest with you and told you these were important pieces that I would be honored to handle," I said. "I still feel that way. As a dealer, I'm incredibly excited to work with furniture that has never been seen by others in the field. It's like uncovering a hidden treasure—and it's what I am about; it's what makes me tick. We've been working together for months now. What can I do to make this happen?"

"Well, Leigh, I don't know," Frank said tentatively.

But I did know. I asked Frank to give me an hour and then hung up the phone. I sat for a moment, took a deep breath, and then called my client.

Forty-five minutes later, I was on the phone again with the deli owner. My heart was racing as I made a final offer. "Frank," I asked in as even a tone as I could muster, "would we have a deal if I offered you one million dollars?"

"Well, I don't know, Leigh," Frank said after a short pause. "I'd have to ask Mother."

"Could you do that, Frank?" I asked gently. "Could you ask her?"

Frank put the phone down. I listened to the sound of his receding footsteps. I pressed the receiver hard into my ear and tried unsuccessfully to catch a fragment of their muffled conversation. A few moments later, Frank returned to the phone. "Mother said that will be fine, Leigh. If you come tomorrow with a check, you can have the furniture."

I hung up the phone, completely drained.

The next afternoon, I met my client's curator at the East Hampton airport and drove him to the Tillinghast house, where we completed the transaction. The following day, Morgan and I were back at the house, supervising the removal of the furniture with Frank. In an odd way, I felt sad watching the pieces go. Since they were heading straight to the home of the collector and his wife, I would never have the pleasure of seeing them sit, however briefly, in my shop. All the same, I was glad they would remain together. And it was right that they had found a place with people who would truly appreciate them. (In retrospect, they were a great investment. Today, the suite is worth more than four times what my client paid.)

As the movers enveloped each piece in bubble wrap and blankets, Frank offered Morgan and me each a memento of the long roller-coaster ride we had all shared. He gave Morgan the large stoneware jug lamp with the incised blue bird that had rested on the dining table all those years. (Leslie and I had owned a similar jug when we were kids.) I received a narrow mahogany pipe box with a single drawer that had hung on the dining room wall, near the divided high chest. It was an unexpected and generous gesture on Frank's part, and we promised him that we would never sell the pieces he had given us.

Moving day. Clockwise from far left:
Leigh with Frank Tillinghast and Morgan MacWhinnie;
two views of the high chest's base before the added top
board was removed; Frank with the Newport pipe box
that he gave to Leigh.

125

126

The last time I visited Morgan, I noticed the jug sitting on an eighteenth-century tavern table next to the kitchen fireplace of his Southampton house. Meanwhile, the eighteenth-century pipe box hangs by the window in my second-floor Madison Avenue shop. Every so often, a visitor will comment on its beautiful form. When they do, I like to pull out the drawer to show the fineness and exquisite quality of the dovetails. And as I turn the drawer over to marvel at its construction, I like to think it might have been made by John Goddard, the master, himself. While I'm not completely sure, I can't help but smile to myself and think that my hunch just might be right.

7

All That Glitters . . .

TO THIS DAY, I VIEW THE MORNING MAIL like a mountain stream at dawn, when the cool white mist covering the water is only just beginning to roll back and reveal the lapping surface to my expectant casts. What will the first catch be? As a specialist in Americana, I rarely receive queries from abroad, so on a warm summer day in 1988, I was quick to notice one sizable envelope on my desk at Sotheby's that bore airmail stamps from Milan. Inside was a handwritten letter written in imperfect English and a set of professional black-and-white photographs (all eight-by-ten glossies) of a spectacular-looking pier table with a long white marble top supported by a pair of gilded winged female figures.

My pulse sped up immediately. It was one of those moments where I instantly knew I had hooked something big. Quickly, I scanned the brief letter for information. I learned that the sender was an Italian antiques dealer who was writing on behalf of the table's present owner, an elderly Frenchwoman. Although the table had been in her family for nearly two centuries, the woman was considering having it brought to auction. In closing, the dealer mentioned that the table was both stamped and labeled by Charles-Honoré Lannuier.

I really *had* hooked a trophy! Charles-Honoré Lannuier (1779–1819) was a French-born cabinetmaker who immigrated to New York in 1803 and spent the better part of the next two decades producing some of the finest furniture ever made on American shores. As might be expected, Lannuier worked in America in the style he had learned in his native France, mainly the Classical Revival style of the French Directoire (1795–1799) and Consulate (1799–1804) periods. During the latter period in particular, contemporary French furniture had taken a turn toward the architectural and was beginning to showcase decorative motifs that were based upon classical antique models (a theme spurred in large part by recent archaeological excavations near Herculaneum and Pompeii). Early in the nineteenth century, Lannuier stayed up-to-date on the changes of style in France through design journals and pattern books (particularly Pierre de La Mésangère's *Collection de Meubles et Objets de Goût*) and was able to reinterpret the gilded monumentalism of the French Empire style to suit the more subdued taste of his American clientele. The Neoclassical taste practiced by Lannuier and his contemporaries met with great popularity in the United States and is usually assigned the blanket term, Classical style.

As part of his business plan in New York, Lannuier seems to have developed a number of signature forms, pier tables being one of them. In fact, when one thinks of Lannuier's known body of work, a high number of marble-top pier tables like the one pictured before me that day come to mind. Usually found in a dining room or parlor, they were often designed in pairs and used to fill the space between two windows, which is architecturally known as a pier. Since one side of a pier table always hugs a wall, its front view is most important, and this particular example, probably made around 1815, proved a perfect case in point.

To begin with, there were the sculpted caryatids, whose torsos arched outward from the table's canted (or angled) ends like a pair of matched ship's figureheads. Each had a set of large gilded wings that swept magnificently back from her shoulders in place of arms and then curved upward to meet the table's apron, or skirt. Meanwhile, their twin faces were the very essence of classical beauty—almond-shaped eyes, aquiline noses, sensuous pursed lips, and full bosoms—they could have been cousins to the Venus de Milo. Working in direct response to the forward thrust of these figures were the lifelike and life-size lion's-paw feet (with acanthus leaves unfurling from their ankles) that extended from the table's base, or lower shelf. Their movement and coloration (the leaves were gold, the paws an onyx black) was the reverse of the gesture of the female figures above.

According to leading Lannuier historian, Peter M. Kenny of New York's Metropolitan Museum, when the craftsman came to America, he almost certainly brought with him cases of assorted ornamental metalwork, including flat bands, or borders (like the tulip pattern that edged the table in the pictures), as well as gilded cast-brass ornaments, or ormolu mounts, as they are called today (like the lyres and medusa-headed central appliqués that decorated the skirt). Even in his premier advertisement of July 1803, he announced the "newest and latest French fashion . . . gilt and brass frames [and] borders of ornaments." As I examined the examples laid out

before me, I recalled those words. Given his status as a newcomer, having that gilded metalwork at his disposal no doubt gave Lannuier an advantage over the competition. Kenny has even suggested that the craftsman was arguably the first cabinetmaker in America to have incorporated French-style ormolu mounts into his designs.

As busy as I was admiring these details, I was concerned that the table was said to have descended in a French family. I knew that before he came to America, Lannuier had trained and worked in the Paris shop of his elder brother Nicolas, who produced furniture for various members of the French aristocracy. Pieces from the Paris Lannuier shop occasionally show up on the market today. If the table predated Lannuier's New York phase, then it was probably worth between forty and sixty thousand dollars, a fraction of what it could bring if it were American. Such is the peculiarity (and some might say absurdity) of the Americana market—that objects crafted by the same person but on different shores could vary so greatly in value.

I was relieved, therefore, to see that among the assortment of photos were a number of close-ups of the Lannuier markings that the Milanese dealer had mentioned in his letter. One shot, taken with the marble top removed, offered a bird's-eye view of the table's inner structure, or carcass. It showed the rectangular form of the table's framing rails, including the tight corner that formed directly above the heads of the two winged female figures—literally, the hidden area where their forms ceased to be decorative and melded into structure. Stamped in bold block letters across the length of this juncture on either side was the maker's mark: *H. Lannuier New-York.*

Judging from the photographs, the two brands looked authentic. The letters were deep, the typeface was appropriate for the period, and, as expected, the oxidation within the indented areas matched the color of the wood around it. If the stamps had been later additions, then the indented areas around each character would have been lighter, because those areas would have been exposed to the air for a shorter period of time than the rest of the wood.

I was also encouraged to see the words *New-York*—presumably the table's city of manufacture—paired with the cabinetmaker's name. Another photo of the table's engraved paper label (pasted on the back rail, which supported the top) featured a finely drawn image of a cheval looking glass with an American eagle in its pediment and a bilingual message that read:

Hre. Lannuier,
Cabinet Maker from Paris
Kips is Whare house of
new fashion fourniture, Broad Street No 60, New-York, Hre Lannuier,
Ebéniste de Paris,
Tient Fabrique &
Magasin de Meubles
les plus à la mode,
New-York

The Sotheby's table with its marble top, imported French ormolu mounts, and painted and gilded caryatids—an exuberant expression of classical taste in America.

The label was familiar to me from books because it is considered by many furniture historians to be among the finest ever designed. Lannuier's penchant for marking and labeling his work (a large portion of his furniture is signed or branded in some way) can probably be traced to his training abroad. In Paris, trade labels were de rigueur because the competition among artisans was fierce and labels offered a convenient means of self-advertising. Peter Kenny has pointed out that Lannuier's use of a bilingual label was probably intentional, because it reminded his clientele of his foreign training and background.

Because of the time difference between New York and Italy, I had to wait a full day before calling the antiques dealer in Milan directly. I arrived at the office early the next morning just to place that call. I had no trouble reaching the dealer, but by the time we had finished with our introductions, it was clear that his English was nearly as bad as both my French and Italian—in other words, it was practically nonexistent. With his school-aged daughter acting as translator, however, we were able to get by. I soon learned that the table was, in fact, part of a suite of furniture that had descended in the family of the present owner, including a pair of torchères, or tall candle stands; a large square center table; and a pair of pier tables. According to the dealer, all featured elaborate caryatids incorporated into their design and all were signed by Charles-Honoré Lannuier.

I was astounded. To begin with, I had never even *heard* of, let alone *seen*, a Lannuier torchère. Furthermore, I knew of only two other furniture suites that had ever been attributed to his hand. For a moment, I worried that some critical information was being lost in the translation and that we were perhaps discussing a related suite of European furniture. But the young girl assured me that what she was saying was true. Still, I couldn't allow my curiosity about these other pieces to get in the way of the matter at hand—the pier table. I told the dealer that, based upon the photographs (and pending a firsthand examination), I would value the tables in the range of $200,000 to $300,000. The dealer promised to convey that news to the table's owner, and with that, our conversation ended. Two weeks later, I heard back from the man: The owner was committed to selling the table. Arrangements were being made to have it sent to New York.

Soon after Labor Day, the table arrived in New York. Immediately, I went down to my old stomping grounds—the Sotheby's loading dock—to see it uncrated. Would it satisfy my many expectations? During the preliminary stages of organizing an auction catalog, I always keep in mind the rhythm and pace of the sale. Once I have a star lot (as I expected this table to be), it helps create a buzz about an upcoming sale. A truly exceptional piece has the potential to draw in other strong consignments. People want their furniture sold in good company.

By the time I reached the platform, the table and its marble top (the two had been packed separately) had been freed from their crates and reunited. The instant I saw them assembled, I knew I had a winner on my hands. The success of the table's design was vividly apparent when viewed in person. The reciprocal movement of the golden caryatids and the lion's-paw feet was breathtaking. I was at once lured closer by the

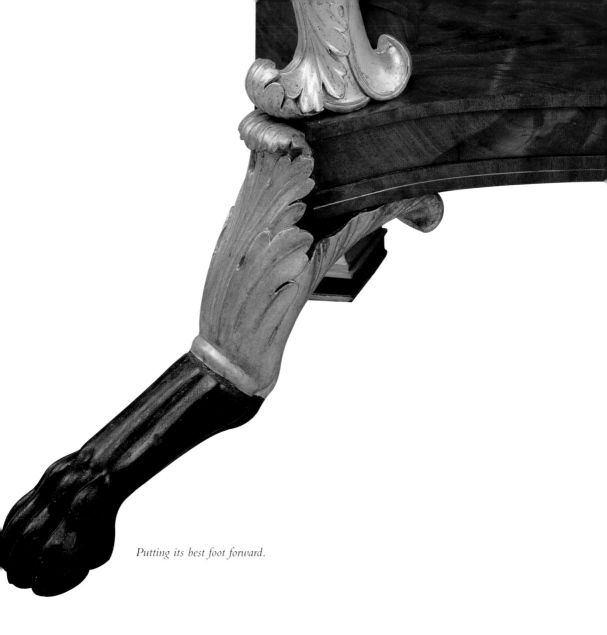

Putting its best foot forward.

intricacy of the design, but I forced myself to step back in order to continue appreciating the composition of the whole. Each and every part seemed in perfect balance with the others.

When I moved in for a closer inspection, though, I noticed that the gilding on the women's torsos and on the acanthus leaves above the front feet seemed thicker in places. It was the type of buildup that indicates some restoration work had been done. Likewise, the black-lacquered finish on the women's lower bodies and on the animal feet themselves was not the table's first coat. Underneath were traces of the original verdigris, or green painted surface, which was often used on classical furniture to simulate the look and patina of ancient bronze. Still, whoever had done the work had done so with a light touch, probably in the nineteenth century, and had not detracted from the value of the piece in any significant way.

Now that the table was at Sotheby's, I set about contacting some of the top collectors in the realm of New York classical furniture. High on my list was Stuart Feld, the president of Hirschl & Adler, a New York–based art gallery specializing in nineteenth-century art. I knew Stuart would be interested in the piece because he already owned a round marble-top center table by Lannuier with four similar winged figures and a cut brass tulip-pattern border that was identical to one that ran along the edge of the pier table's skirt. I also alerted Peter Terian, a Manhattan-based Rolls-Royce dealer who lived in a palatial Upper West Side apartment with sweeping views of Central Park. I could easily picture the table—a new jewel for his collection—set between the windows of his living room.

The October 22 sale fell on a Saturday. I had assigned the table lot 421, which was toward the end of the afternoon session. Bill Stahl was the auctioneer that day, and he opened the bidding on the piece at $100,000. From there, it briskly rose in twenty-thousand-dollar increments. As I suspected, Peter Terian was there, actively bidding from the rear center of the room. Early on, he had competition from New York dealer Dean Levy, but Dean dropped out when the numbers neared $200,000. After that, Peter found himself faced with a tenacious phone bidder. Soon, the numbers soared far beyond the range of the table's presale estimate of from $200,000 to $300,000. When the bidding reached $540,000, Bill and I and the rest of the entranced group in the salesroom looked to Peter one last time. He shook his head firmly—he was through. The table went to the phone bidder (who turned out to be Stuart Feld) for a total of $594,000, including the 10 percent buyer's premium. That figure was nearly twice the previous record for classical furniture ($303,000, paid in January 1987 at Sotheby's for a Lannuier-attributed secretary made in New York around 1815).

But the story did not end here. Almost two years after that momentous sale, in December 1990, I heard rumors to the effect that a Lannuier table that exactly matched the one Stuart had purchased was coming up for sale at Christie's. Like the table I had handled, it had been found in Paris, a coincidence that I found too strong for it not to have come from the same source. The news surprised me because I couldn't imagine that after the brilliant success of the first pier table at auction, the owner hadn't approached Sotheby's again. Since the sale of that table, there had been many a night that I had dreamed about handling the other pieces from that alleged suite. I called the dealer in Milan to investigate. As it turned out, the table at Christie's was indeed the mate to the one I had sold, but his clients had never owned it. Instead, the table had descended through another branch of the family.

I was relieved. My connection to the family was still safe. And sure enough, within a year of the Christie's sale (where the second table ended up selling to a fiercely deter- mined Peter Terian for $640,000), the agent in Milan contacted me again. The owner of the first table was interested in selling two more pieces from her Lannuier suite. This time, it was the matched set of pier tables that the dealer had mentioned years previously. The pair was now in his Milan shop. Was I interested?

Five days later, I was on a plane to Italy.

During our phone conversation, the dealer also said that he had some significant

The table that sold at Christie's in 1991.

early French pieces in his shop that he also wanted to have evaluated, so I asked Thierry Millerand, the New York head of Sotheby's French Furniture Department, to join me in Milan. Frankly, I was relieved to have Thierry on board, because I knew I could use his skills as a linguist. Furthermore, considering the quality level of the example I had sold, I thought Thierry would appreciate the pair we were about to see. So often I have watched Thierry, a handsome and always dashingly dressed Frenchman, stride through the previews of my Americana sales with his nose held high. He is, I think, continually astonished by the high prices this "brown furniture," as he calls it, continues to command at auction. When the Cadwalader easy chair set a new world record for furniture in 1987, I'm sure he was aghast (the previous record holder was a Louis XVI *secretaire* that sold in October 1986 for $2,090,000 at Sotheby's London). In fact, the only time Thierry has made a positive comment to me regarding the content of my sales was when he spotted the earlier Lannuier table on the selling floor in 1988. "Now that's a table," he said to me at the time, gesturing to its glistening gilded form, made by a fellow Frenchman on American shores.

Thierry and I rendezvoused with the dealer at his home on a bustling street in the heart of Milan and then walked down the block to his nearby shop. The dealer was a well-dressed, well-groomed man, probably in his late fifties, with graying hair and a small mustache. I remember that, despite my jet lag, I watched him with a feeling of great excitement as he fumbled about for his keys. (The last moments of a long journey to a new object are sometimes the longest.)

Once inside, I was surprised by the decidedly informal look of the shop. It felt more like a workplace than a private gallery that had been set up to make an impression on the public. The French furniture that Thierry had come to see was located in the front room, so the dealer and I left him there to examine the various pieces while we walked deeper into the shop, toward a smaller room in the rear. The lights were out, so I stood in the virtual darkness for a moment or two, waiting for the dealer to turn them on. Just ahead, I could barely make out some shadowy furniture forms. *Click.* The lights went on, and immediately my eyes settled upon the two objects I had flown across an ocean to see—the Lannuier pier tables.

First and foremost, I was struck by the resemblance of the pair, which stood side by side, to the first pier table I had handled. The similarity in design was extraordinary—from the white marble tops, to the golden caryatids, to the outstretched lion's-paw feet—and I had no doubt these pieces had been made en suite with the earlier table. I glanced over at the dealer, who was watching me carefully to read my reaction. I smiled my approval and then made a gesture toward the tables to signal that I was going to step in and evaluate them more closely.

One of the most compelling aspects of the pair was that they appeared to have survived with their original surface intact. Typically, Lannuier had used a combination of matte and burnished gilding to give subtle contrast to the gilded figures. Along the gilded wing tips and torsos of the women, the gold was burnished bright, kept that way, perhaps, by fastidious dusting with soft cloths through the years. Furthermore, each table had apparently withstood a fair share of spills, because there were water marks and stains noticeable on both the gilding and the wood. I thought these areas of discoloration lent a delightful aura of vulnerability and authenticity to the tables and pointed to the life they had lived.

Like the earlier table I had sold, these two examples each had a pane of mirrored plate glass at the back, flanked by a pair of half-round figured mahogany columns. I noticed on each that the plate-glass back was marked by small black spots where the silvering had peeled away from the mirror. Like the stains on the gilding and the wood, I took this as a good sign, because it meant the panes were probably old. Furthermore, when I glanced into each mirror, my reflection seemed slightly distorted. I tapped the glass on each table lightly with my fingers and saw that each shivered slightly from the impact. That meant that the glass was thin, just as a nineteenth-century mirror ought to be. To bolster this point, I glanced at the back of the tables and saw that the backboards had never been removed. Each was secured with nails topped by slightly irregular heads that had clearly never been tampered with.

Now I moved on to the lively mahogany veneers displayed on the tables' skirts, bases, and rear columns (veneering is a process by which a thin layer of a valuable figured wood is glued onto a cheaper structural wood to provide a more stylish surface). Everywhere, the thin crotch wood (sliced from the juncture where a large branch meets the trunk) felt just as it should—seamless and smooth.

Next I moved on to the ormolu mounts, which were positioned on the skirt exactly as they had been on the first table, at the center and at the front corners, although the patterns of the appliqués themselves were slightly different from the earlier piece. Because of that variation, I wanted to confirm that the metalwork was original to the tables. To do so, I needed to examine the wood beneath each mount to see if the shadows matched the shape of the decorative cast metal and if there were no additional entry holes or markings left from an earlier set. This was not difficult to do because each mount was held in position by only three or four short tapered prongs that protruded from its back. I easily lifted a few from each table and was pleased to see that in every case, the wood below was dark and not oxidized.

The marble tops were next on my agenda. At this point, Thierry had joined us in the room, having finished with the pieces in the front, which, from the look on his face, he had found disappointing. "Well, this is a good-looking pair," he said to me as we removed the top from each table. I peered down into the framework of each table and was relieved to see both were stamped twice—on the top of each of the two front corner blocks—with the now familiar mark *H. Lannuier New-York*. Neither table, however, bore a copy of the paper label seen on the earlier piece. I took a Polaroid camera out of my bag and shot a few pictures of the tables.

From the look of the shop, French furniture was clearly the dealer's forte. This made me somewhat nervous, because French furniture is collected under a completely different set of rules than American pieces. For one thing, there is no such worship of original patina. If anything, an old surface is considered a sign that a piece has been neglected by its previous owner. Even in the eighteenth century, not long after the furniture was first produced, French pieces were being refinished with polish and varnish to a much higher degree than their American counterparts. I wanted to make sure that the Italian dealer understood that American collectors view original surface as a strong indicator of authenticity. I turned to Thierry and asked him to explain in no uncertain terms that the furniture we were examining would greatly diminish in value if it were cleaned. Thierry translated my concern into French, and the dealer nodded his reply. He understood.

Not long after that, the three of us went out for a meal at a crowded restaurant nearby, where we were joined by the dealer's wife, a chic dark-haired Frenchwoman. Now removed from the furniture, my energy faded quickly. The time difference was really beginning to catch up with me and the conversation whirling around me in French and Italian certainly didn't help. At one point, though, I asked Thierry to query the dealer on the history of the tables. Was there anything more that he knew?

The dealer nodded quickly. Yes. Recently, he had learned that the elderly woman who owned the tables was a descendant of a woman named Eugénie de Bouchart. Bouchart was the mistress of the original owner of the furniture—a man named James Leray de Chaumont. According to the dealer, Leray was born into a titled family of French merchants but had spent many years in New York, married an heiress from New Jersey, and even became an American citizen, which gave him the right to purchase land there. (I later learned that at one point Leray owned upward of 600,000 acres in northern New York State.) Long after the death of his wife in 1812, Leray returned to Paris, where he apparently took up with Bouchart, an actress, to whom he willed all his personal property. Following his death in 1840, she inherited it (despite the fact that he had two surviving children by his American wife).

The tables' likely first home: the Leray mansion in Jefferson County, New York, built circa 1808.

Hearing this tale revived me. Finally, the presence of this exquisite group of New York furniture in France made sense—it had been commissioned by a Frenchman, from a Frenchman, while both were living on American shores. But on the flight back to New York, try as I might to rest and enjoy the memory of those beautiful tables standing side by side, I instead felt an overwhelming sense of unease. I couldn't shake the thought of the highly polished French furniture stacked around them. My concern was so great that on the journey home I drafted a letter to the dealer, in which I reiterated my position about the importance of original finish on American pieces. The next day, back at my desk at Sotheby's, I bolstered my written argument with photographs of a few actual examples plucked from my files, including two pairs of identical mid-eighteenth-century Boston side chairs that we had recently sold. The first pair had a crusty old finish and had brought $120,000 at auction, while the second set, which had been completely skinned, or cleaned, had sold for around $30,000. That nearly

James Leray de Chaumont.

$100,000 price difference was based upon surface alone.

I then had the letter translated into French, along with my formal proposal on the pair (giving each table a presale estimate of from $300,000 to $500,000), and I sent it and the photographs overnight to Milan. Within days, I received a brief response from the dealer. The tables were on their way to Sotheby's. When they arrived, I went down to the loading dock to see them uncrated, just as I had with the earlier table. But when the lid came off and the sides fell down on the first box, I was met by a shocking sight—a table I simply did not recognize. Although the piece displayed the same decorative elements of the pair I had seen in Italy—the marble top (wrapped separately), the gilded caryatids, the mirrored back—the resemblance stopped there. Quite simply, this looked like a brand-new table.

My first thought was that I had been duped, that the table I had evaluated in Milan had been replaced with a copy. But just as quickly, I was overcome with that sickening feeling that hits when your worst fears are about to be realized. Suddenly, I knew with great certainty that the Italian dealer, for whatever reason of his own, had chosen to disregard my advice about the furniture. I couldn't stop shaking my head as I watched the men on the loading dock uncrate the second table. It, too, had suffered the same fate.

I was so distressed, I started pacing around the pair, looking for any points of reference to their former state. There were none to be found. The mahogany wood had been heavily cleaned and polished, the gilding repainted a bright shade of yellow gold, and the original nut brown surface of the pine framework had been rubbed down with a reddish liquid stain that completely obscured the early surface. Even the lovely shadows beneath the brass ormolu mounts had been erased. To my mind, what the dealer had done was as bad as repainting and reoutfitting a vintage 1962 Ferrari GTO Team Car (the Mona Lisa of all cars) for a more modern look.

I couldn't get back to my desk fast enough to call the dealer in Milan and ask him what had happened. Why had he disregarded my warnings, particularly given Sotheby's track record with the earlier table, which had been only lightly touched up? He explained that the family would never have wanted to send the two tables to auction in the grungy state in which I had seen them. It was a matter of pride. I could barely contain my disappointment.

*Two of James Leray's tables, each unmistakably the work
of master cabinetmaker Charles-Honoré Lannuier.*

I managed to contain my anger, knowing that even though the tables had been stripped and dipped, they remained the work of master cabinetmaker Charles-Honoré Lannuier and it was my job to promote them as best I could. I advised the dealer that given the altered condition of the pair, it would be wise to adjust the presale estimate to broaden the pool of potential buyers, but he was unbending in his commitment to the reserve (the lowest price for which the owner would agree to sell). The previous pier table had set a record for classical furniture, and he was confident that this pair would do the same.

Later that day, I ran into Thierry in the hallway and told him what had happened. "Typical," he said with a slightly bemused look. "A striking example of what not to do with American furniture. I suppose we should have anticipated it, given all the French pieces in that shop. The rival aesthetics of our genres are just too deeply ingrained."

When I began showing the tables to collectors like Stuart Feld and Peter Terian, it was immediately clear that they were not going to sell. No one was willing to accept them in their refurbished state. Even the twenty or thirty photos that I had taken on my initial visit with the pair failed to bolster their case. Stuart told me point-blank that he thought the two were frauds. "These are the same tables," I explained, pointing to the swirled grain of the mahogany wood clearly evident in the photographs and still discernible through the thick gloss of the newly shellacked surface. "The brilliant striations of the grain essentially amount to the fingerprint of the wood. They are completely unique and cannot be copied." Still, this was not enough to convince him.

Needless to say, the tables did not find a buyer at the October 1992 sale. The general rule of thumb when important objects (like this pair) do not sell at auction is that they should be taken out of circulation for a while before being offered again. New buyers enter the market and hopefully the memory of their failure will fade or changes in the market will affect the way they are perceived. For three years, James Leray's beautiful pier tables sat in the Sotheby's warehouse. In January 1995, I notified the dealer that an acceptable amount of time had passed and that the pair could be offered again. I also recommended that he lower the estimate range to $150,000 to $200,000 each. This time, the tables ended up selling, to a southern collector with very eclectic taste (she freely mixes old-master paintings with Arts and Crafts and contemporary). Looking back on that sale now, I think she got a great buy. Despite their tragic refurbishment, the tables remain among the most ambitiously designed and extraordinarily well-made American tables I have ever seen.

In the fall of 1998, I once again heard from the dealer in Milan. He wanted me to go to the Christie's warehouse in Long Island City to examine a Lannuier center table that he had sent there (presumably in response to the poor showing of the paired pier tables at Sotheby's). Now he was unhappy because John Hays, my counterpart at Christie's, had told him the table was fake. News travels quickly in the auction world, and I had already heard rumors about the table, so I was curious to see it in person. A few days later, in the company of John Nye, then the senior cataloger for my department (he is now the director), I visited the Christie's warehouse (an occurrence that is not as unusual as it sounds).

It didn't take long for us to render an opinion on the marble-top center table with four winged female figures at its base. John Hays was absolutely correct: The piece was either a complete fake or one that had been built around a few older elements (I strongly suspected the latter). Having arguably sold more Lannuier furniture at auction than anyone else in the world, I was fairly certain that Lannuier had indeed made the four caryatids. The style and quality of the carving was undeniably superb. But on the rest of the table, the same high level of craftsmanship did not exist. The mahogany veneers were of poor quality, the brass inlay running around the table's edge was crude and imprecise, and the construction details of the base and frame simply didn't come close to matching the jewel-like precision for which Lannuier was known. I recalled for a moment the alleged pair of Lannuier torchères that the dealer had mentioned to me during our first phone call, a decade before. Could these caryatids have been lifted from those mysterious and still-unseen pieces? I could only hope not.

8

Catch and Release

ON A CHILLY NOVEMBER AFTERNOON IN 1994, I received a phone call at my shop from Morgan MacWhinnie, the Southampton antiques dealer who had led me to the Tillinghast suite of furniture. Seconds into the conversation, it was clear that he had some news for me.

"Yesterday I was up in Portsmouth visiting my old friend Ed Weissman," Morgan said, "and he told me a story that I think you'll want to hear." He paused for a moment and then added in a leading tone, "Although I almost didn't get it out of him!"

Well that got my attention. I was only marginally acquainted with Morgan's friend, a sturdy bulldog of a guy whose ads for his New Hampshire antiques business always begin "Discover the Source—Ed Weissman." But if Morgan said Ed was the source of a tantalizing story, I'd certainly hear him out.

"Go on," I urged Morgan, who clearly needed little encouragement.

Back in September, Morgan said, Ed and his wife, Margaret, were vacationing in Buenos Aires. On the day of their arrival in the Argentine capital, while Margaret rested in their hotel room, Ed went out to explore the neighborhood and stopped in a local bookstore. While there, he noticed a nice-looking bronze statue of a lion set on a marble plinth in a corner near the stacks. Ed asked the store's two young owners (a brother and sister) about it and learned that the statue was on loan from their parents, whose antiques shop was a short walk from the bookstore. A quarter of an hour later, Ed found himself in a narrow store that was well stocked with decorative European furnishings and Asian art, most of which didn't really interest him.

When he said as much to the woman minding the shop (the mother of the bookstore owners, who, as it turned out, spoke perfect English), she asked him what he did like. "American furniture," Ed replied. The woman paused thoughtfully for a moment and then said, "I think my husband knows of an American piece." The woman called her husband out of the back and spoke a few words to him in Spanish. He then proceeded to draw a quick sketch on a sheet of paper. When the man was through, Ed found himself staring at something that "looked like a bastardized nineteenth-century English Edwardian secretary," he told Morgan.

As Ed gazed down at the page rather skeptically, the woman explained that the secretary was owned by another pair of antiques dealers, who kept a shop in the nearby suburb of Acassuso. If Ed wanted to see it, she would call ahead. "She was pretty aggressive," Ed later reported to Morgan, "but in a nice way. And when she found out how I made my living, she seemed determined to help me."

At that point, Ed realized that he had been away from his wife longer than he had anticipated and that she might be getting worried. So he left the small shop without having committed to a trip to Acassuso and returned to the hotel. When he arrived back, he immediately told Margaret what had happened. "What should I do?" Ed asked her, knowing that they already had plans to visit a mountain village with a tour group the next day. "This could really be a wild-goose chase."

"We're antiques dealers," said Margaret, an eminently practical woman. "We *have* to take a look."

So the next day, Ed hired a car and driver and headed out to the shop in Acassuso with Margaret in the hope of seeing an American secretary. The two of them watched through the car window as the broad boulevards and high rises of Buenos Aires gave way to more sprawling neighborhoods and lower buildings. Forty minutes later, the car drew up in front of a two-story white stucco building at the end of the tidy commercial district of affluent Acassuso. Ed and his wife stepped out of the car and immediately walked over to the storefront to survey the scene. A thin beige curtain that hung across the shop's plate-glass window prevented any possibility of a sneak preview. Ed allowed himself a small degree of cautious optimism as he pushed open the front door, which he held open for Margaret.

The gallery's interior was far more formal and stylish than the shop Ed had visited the previous day in Buenos Aires. There was a large selection of attractive highly polished French and English furniture interspersed with some nice porcelain, carpets, and

Oriental art. Everything he saw was tasteful, although clearly geared to decorator-type clientele. In one corner toward the rear, two men were busy examining a large chest of drawers, but they quickly broke from their conversation at the sight of Ed and his wife. The men were, in fact, the store's proprietors, and as they came forward to greet the American couple, Ed spotted a tall secretary standing along the right-hand wall, which he was certain was the piece he had come to see.

The secretary-bookcase on display at a Buenos Aires antiques show.

As he later described to Morgan, "The owners were walking toward me with warm, welcoming smiles, but all I had eyes for was this piece of American Federal furniture that leapt out at me amid all those gleaming European things. Of course I didn't want to show my excitement, but there was no denying it was a wonderful thing. Streamlined, perfectly proportioned, mahogany veneers with a satinwood trim—simply a fantastic-looking object." And then he added, "Most incredibly, the secretary had an enormous amount of *églomisé* incorporated into its facade. I've been in the business a long time, but on first impression, this was the greatest piece of Baltimore furniture I had ever seen. Clearly no expense had been spared in its execution."

Ed jumped to the conclusion that the secretary was from Baltimore based upon the appearance of the *églomisé* panels he had mentioned. *Églomisé* is a method by which the back of a piece of glass is used as a surface for drawing decorative designs in paint or gilt. A coat of varnish or a piece of paper is then applied to protect the image before the entire package is set into the fabric of the furniture, much like a decorative veneer. The technique itself dates back to ancient Roman times but reached a heightened level of popularity in the United States during the Federal period (meaning the first few decades following the signing of the Constitution of the United States in 1787), particularly in the city of Baltimore, although it was certainly used elsewhere. Such was the logic behind Ed's rapid judgment call as to the origin of the secretary.

With all these issues swirling in his head, Ed managed to look away from the secretary long enough to introduce himself and his wife to the two antiques dealers, who immediately invited him to examine the piece more closely. So while Margaret chatted quietly with the men, Ed began to give the object a more careful run-through. He started at the slender pediment, which featured an arched *églomisé* panel in the center, flanked by two narrow rectangular panels, or plinths, with two smaller plinths at the ends. All four of these pediment plinths displayed a gilded pattern of a mask entwined with vines, set against a luminous pale blue ground. Ed marveled at the way the colored glass appeared to gleam from within like reflectors on a bicycle.

The pediment with its inset polychrome églomisé panels (the center one is a replacement).

Then he shifted his gaze down to the bookcase, which was fronted by two glazed doors. Ed hooked a forefinger into one of the two ivory keyholes at the center and pulled the door toward him (meanwhile, one of the two dealers broke from his conversation with Margaret to sift through a nearby desk for the original key). In the wake of that opening arc came the faint but distinct scent of red cedar, the wood used for the shelves. Ed stood still for a moment, breathing in the pungent aroma, and then gently began to test the swing of the door, which moved on its hinge without so much as a tremor. Eventually, he returned the door to its closed position and stepped back to admire the geometry imposed by the overlay of the glazing bars on the doors. There were two counterrhythms at work here: first, the dominant tone provided by the large rectangular panes of clear glass, and then the lighter, staccato beat of the small upended squares of *églomisé* that marked each of the cross sections. Every one of these hand-painted squares featured a vivid, highly stylized sunburst design painted in black, gold, and white.

Next, Ed's concentration shifted to the secretary proper, which was momentarily shielded by its retractable roll top. He grasped the two round brass pulls located on either end of the curved mahogany board and drew it back into its narrow sleeve. The entire unit moved smoothly and evenly out of the way, revealing a writing area lined with a series of pigeonholes and small drawers, each one bordered by a delicate inlaid pattern of alternating light and dark wood (called stringing), which shimmered brilliantly in the strong gallery light. The bright beam also bounced off the face of the prospect door located at the center of this small stage. It was marked by an oval-shaped *églomisé* medallion featuring the gold-painted figure of a woman in Greek dress playing a lyre, set against a rose-colored ground. Ed touched his hand briefly to the cool surface of the glass. When he pulled it back, the warmth of his palm left a light impression on the glazed exterior and then it slowly faded as his study shifted to the baize-covered writing surface.

That the rectangular swatch of aquamarine cloth that covered the top was a replacement was of little consequence to Ed. Had the baize been original, it would have made a fascinating addition to the piece, but the substitution did not detract from the beauty or value of the object as a whole. He was intrigued, however, by the ingenious mechanism of the desktop itself, which featured hinges at the front and collapsible legs at the back so that it could be raised and lowered to suit the user's needs. Ed tested the mechanism a few times, enjoying the way the slender legs unfurled like the legs of a newborn colt.

The secretary's lower doors display allegorical figures
of Justice and Truth, popular Federal period motifs.

Finally, he moved to what he considered the highlight of the piece: the lower cabinet with its splashy double doors. Within this tightly organized zone, there were so many grandiose decorative details that Ed had a hard time focusing his viewing. First, there were the slender *églomisé* bands that ran along the swing edges of the two doors. Each displayed a running pattern of entwined sheaths of golden wheat, drawn against a pale green ground. The richness of the green was a revelation to Ed, much like the pink used on the prospect door and the blue he had noted on the pediment plinths, because color is generally considered a rarity in *églomisé*. Black, white, and gold were far more commonly used, and there was something so late nineteenth century about the quality of these pastel shades—as if the tone had been inspired by a Monet painting.

Ed now turned his attention to the two enormous oval panels of *églomisé* that fronted each of the cabinet doors. Here, black, white, and gold were the colors of choice, but in a lifetime of looking at American furniture, he had never seen painted glass integrated so daringly into the facade of a piece. The time that it must have taken to paint and install them alone must have been tremendous. Ed admired the perfect geometry of the black-and-gold borders encircling both panels and then let his eye travel inward, across their matched milk white grounds to the nearly identical images of two women at their centers. Now he compared the two compositions, which were closely related, although not identical. The right door featured the image of a woman in Greek-inspired dress, gazing into a handheld mirror, while the left door displayed a similarly tunic-clad woman holding a set of scales in one hand and a sword in the other.

"They sound like allegorical figures for Truth and Justice," I said to Morgan in amazement, momentarily interrupting his narrative.

"That's what I thought, too," he replied.

I picked a pen up off my desk and began to draw a quick sketch on a scrap of paper of the secretary he had described thus far. Clearly, the piece made an incredible statement about the Federal period, to which it dated. Toward the close of the eighteenth century, the florid designs of the rococo were on their way out; a new taste for things Neoclassical was beginning to work its way into the mainstream of American culture. Having so recently cast aside the symbols of British rule, the nation was eager to embrace a new decorative style, one that might signal its independence, and yet the architects of the age had nowhere to look but back to Europe—particularly England and France—for inspiration and innovative style.

The Scottish-born architect and designer Robert Adam (1728–1792) is often credited with instigating this stylistic metamorphosis that signaled the end of the rococo. Adam had spent a number of years studying in Rome and eventually produced a book on architecture with his brother James that stressed the aesthetic unity of exterior and interior spaces. His designs for walls and furniture emphasized straight lines over curves, lightness, delicacy, and geometry informed by the measure of classical orders. By the 1760s and 1770s, Adam's designs were all the rage in the arts and crafts of England. Subsequent design books by George Hepplewhite and Thomas Shearer (both published in 1788) and Thomas Sheraton (published in four parts from 1791 to 1794) helped systematize the style for English and American cabinetmakers. The new style relied heavily upon inlaid motifs of things such as garlands, bellflowers, swags, and urns. Within a matter of years, this fascination with things antique would advance again into the more full-blown, "archaeologically correct" patterns of the Classical period, as exemplified by the work of Charles-Honoré Lannuier, which Leslie discussed in the previous chapter.

When Morgan resumed his story, he began by outlining Ed's take on the mechanics of the piece. Behind the doors of the lower case, he reported, there were three stacked columns of drawers. "Ed says they move in and out of their slots like pistons," Morgan explained. Today, because of modern technology and diamond cutting blades and lasers, it is not difficult to manufacture drawers with great tolerances, but amazingly, this secretary was completely handmade. Dominating the middle columns of drawers was one large removable document compartment with ledger-size partitions. After Ed had looked it over carefully, he told Morgan, "I slid it back into position and heard a gentle *whoosh* sound of the air being pushed out of the way as it glided perfectly closed."

By the time Ed was through examining the secretary, he was certain he was standing before a masterpiece of American Federal furniture. He did notice there had been some minor patchwork to the mahogany veneers and that the ivory knobs displayed on the interior drawers and the brass knobs of the roll top were probably replacements. The only significant change to the piece was that the central arched *églomisé* panel of the pediment was clearly done in the twentieth century. Ed quizzed the owners about the glass and they explained that it had been made by their own conservator in approximation of the original, which was missing when they acquired the piece.

And just how had they come to acquire the secretary? Ed asked.

Back in 1988, one of the dealers explained, the shop received a phone call from a used-furniture dealer, who said he had just purchased a nineteenth-century English apothecary cabinet that he thought might be of interest to them. He had gotten it off an old *estancia* (or a private ranch), where it had been stored in a barn.

"I was just on my way to a tennis match and didn't really want to break my game," the man explained with a laugh, "so I told my partner, 'It's your call,' grabbed my racket, and headed out the door."

The partner went to look at the "English" piece, which he ended up buying and driving back to the shop, traveling across many miles of cobblestone roads in a blue Ford Falcon station wagon, with half of the piece tied to the roof (a concept that made Ed cringe).

The dealers kept the secretary in storage until 1993, when they decided to restore it in preparation for an upcoming prominent Buenos Aires antiques show. While the piece was at the conservator's, he noticed one of the horizontal black-and-gold *églomisé* panels in the front pediment band had loosened. Naturally, he attempted to stabilize the panel, which was when he discovered a neatly folded strip of newspaper wedged behind the glass. Carefully, the conservator extracted the two-inch-wide scrap and unfolded it. What he found was a printed title banner that read *"Claypoole's American Daily Advertiser . . .* Saturday, July 26, 1800 . . . Philadelphia."

"Philadelphia?" said Ed with some surprise, turning to face the secretary again. He never would have pegged Philadelphia as the object's city of manufacture, simply because he didn't know of any examples of furniture with this much *églomisé* attributed to that city. It was clear, though, that whoever had produced this piece was a master at his craft. "Interesting," Ed commented.

The Argentine dealer continued with his story. Initially, he and his partner had little time to address the implications of an American attribution for the piece because their goal was simply to get it to the show in Buenos Aires. The secretary was easy on the eye and they were certain it would sell (it had been priced somewhere in the range of forty thousand dollars). But for some reason, it didn't sell. So soon after they took the secretary back to their shop, the dealers decided to investigate its value by sending photos of the piece to both Sotheby's and Christie's branch office in Buenos Aires. It was not long before the two auction houses got back to them, each with an estimate in the range of $150,000 to $250,000.

But even with that encouraging bit of news, the dealer explained, he and his partner were not particularly keen on sending the piece to New York. The fragility of the glass made shipping the secretary north an extremely risky and costly endeavor. If, for example, one of the large panels on the lower doors were to break, the value of the piece would plummet. (Leslie later told me that he remembered receiving the photos but that the owners' reluctance to ship it north had been a significant and eventually insurmountable hurdle to overcome.) Ed's pilgrimage to the shop in Acassuso occurred not long after that decision had been made.

"So has Ed done anything about the piece?" I asked Morgan, sensing his story was winding to a close.

"Well," he replied, "from the start, Ed's made it clear that he is interested in the piece, but the dealers quoted him a price in the range of the two auction house estimates, and at the moment he just doesn't have that kind of cash flow. He wants to see this piece come here, but he needs a partner to make it happen. Back in September, Ed contacted Albert Sack, because he'd worked with him in the past and he felt some loyalty. At first, Albert said he was concerned about the cost of shipping, but then he decided he might have a customer or possibly a decorator who had a customer, but nothing's panned out. Ed's been sitting on the whereabouts of this thing for nearly three months, all the while trying to stay in contact with the two dealers and maintain the impression that he's about to buy it. At this point, everyone's getting edgy, and from the way Ed described the shop, it's pretty busy. Someone could just walk in and snap it up any day."

Morgan paused for a moment and then he said, "Look, Leigh, I practically had to strong-arm Ed for pictures of the piece, because he's scared word of this thing will get out. I told him I would show them to only one person, someone I thought could place it quickly, and that's you. If you're not interested in the secretary, then I'm giving the pictures back and this conversation never happened."

But there was no question that I was interested in the piece. What's more, I thought I might have a buyer for it, a new client who, from my limited experience with him, seemed to have a voracious appetite for major American Federal and Classical pieces. The man I was thinking of was Jack Warner, the retired head of Gulf States Paper Corporation, one of the country's largest privately held forest-product companies. Then in his late sixties, Jack stood about six foot four, had broad shoulders and silver-gray hair, and spoke in a booming southern drawl. He was the type of man who, as my father would say, is as American as the American bald eagle. In addition to fine furniture, Jack also owned an outstanding collection of American paintings (a large part of which hung in his company's Tuscaloosa, Alabama, headquarters), including a fair share of work by Norman Rockwell, which should give an even stronger indication as to the extent of his good old-fashioned values. Federal furniture had great appeal to him because it was quite literally made just after the birth of the nation. Independence expressed through artisanship—that's how he viewed it.

"Send me the pictures, Morgan," I said. "I have someone in mind. He's coming to town tomorrow night and we're supposed to have dinner. If the piece is good, I'll discuss it with him then."

"Great," Morgan replied. "I'll send them by overnight mail. You won't be disappointed."

Within two days, I had good news for Morgan. "My client is excited," I told him. What's more, once Jack heard the piece had been found in Argentina, he posed a near-instantaneous theory as to why it might have been sent there. Apparently, soon after the Civil War, a sizable group of Confederate expatriates sought refuge in South America rather than live under Yankee rule. In Brazil, Jack said, there is a town called Vila Americana (American Town) that actually has a Confederate flag incorporated into its local coat of arms. Jack was convinced that the secretary had traveled to Argentina with one of these refugees from the Old South.

"If the secretary's the real thing, then I'm pretty sure I can sell it," I told Morgan. "But of course I have to see it first."

Morgan was thrilled, although he tried to convince me that a trip to Argentina wasn't necessary. "Ed's as good as anybody around," he said, "if not better. I would buy anything, sight unseen, on his say-so alone. That's how much faith I have in him."

But I didn't feel comfortable with that notion. As much as I trusted Morgan, I didn't know Ed very well, and I would never ask a client to buy something that I hadn't personally screened. "I have to go myself," I said to Morgan, then added with a laugh, "besides, December is the start of summer in Argentina. It's a great time for fly-fishing. I may try to tack on a short trip to Patagonia once I've sealed the deal."

"Fine, Leigh," Morgan said, "you and Ed can go, but there's no reason for me to tag along. It's just not my style."

By now, it was understood that this was a three-way deal. Ed had found the piece, Morgan and I would put up the money, and I would place it. Any profit that was generated would be split equally. Furthermore, I had already decided that if the secretary lived up to its description, I would take it to the Winter Antiques Show in New York. Probably the industry's oldest and most prestigious show, it is held every January and is timed to coincide with Americana Week, when collectors from around the country converge on the city for the extensive round of Americana sales put on by Sotheby's and Christie's. The confluence of all those key industry activities means that I can always count on January as being an exciting but chaotic month for me. Not only must I find time to cover the previews at the major auction houses thoroughly and prepare my booth for the Winter Antiques Show but I must also remain completely available to my clients.

I was excited about the Argentine secretary because it sounded right on the mark in terms of what I like to exhibit at the show—something completely fresh on the market and of major importance. I take special pride in the pieces I select for the show because it is one of the few opportunities a year that I have to present myself to the collecting public at large. That small handful of furniture needs to make a strong statement about my taste and the quality of my business. This secretary clearly had the potential to say all the right things. I might give Jack Warner a sneak preview of the piece, but if he wanted it, he would have to arrive early at my booth at the show.

It was already mid-December and the show was just weeks away. Ed and I would have to move quickly if this plan were to work. We made arrangements to fly to Argentina, and I even managed to convince Guy Roderick, a San Francisco-based client of mine, to join me for a few days of fishing at the end.

The last time I had been to South America was on a 1991 trip to Guyana that I had taken with Leslie, which was also meant to combine fishing and furniture hunting. The fish we were after was a rare freshwater breed, the *Arapaima gigas*. These bizarre-looking creatures—arguably the largest freshwater fish in the world—can grow upward of ten feet in length and two hundred pounds in weight and look like a cross between a fallen log and a prehistoric catfish. We expected our hunt for these fish to take us into the interior of the country, but we also planned to take a quick side trip to Suriname, which borders Guyana to the east. Suriname was a frequent eighteenth-century port of call for Newport-based sea captains, who often carried cargoes of finished furniture to sell in exchange for sugar and local mahogany. Leslie and I had it in our heads that perhaps some of that furniture had survived the notorious climate and insects and was ours to unearth.

We had read, for example, of a published correspondence between the Providence-based mercantile firm of Nicholas Brown & Company and the Newport cabinetmaker John Goddard, which alluded to the frequency of this type of trade (the originals are housed at the John Carter Brown Library in Providence). In May 1766, an officer of the firm requested that Goddard make a "Handsome Mahogany Arm Chair" for a "Gentelman in the West Indies [*sic*]." Goddard subsequently wrote back for some clarification as to the chair's design. He received prompt reply that "the Chear should be Very Neet & Handsum therfor Desire You'l make it with 3 claws & if Possible have it Dun in 10 Days otherwise as Soone as you can. . . ." When the chair was finished, it was sent to an appropriately named Captain Bogman in swampy "Surinam," who paid just under six pounds for the chair. The last time a true Goddard corner chair with ornately carved claw-and-ball feet sold at auction was in 1972 at Sotheby Parke Bernet for $85,000. So naturally, Leslie and I hoped that Suriname held promise of others.

Another source of inspiration for Leslie and me was a well-known picture by the Boston artist John Greenwood, now in the collection of the St. Louis Art Museum. The 1746 painting, titled *Sea Captains Carousing in Surinam* [*sic*], features a group of American mariners sprawled about a crowded, ill-lit tavern in varying states of intoxication. Imagining for just a moment the cargo that any one of those men might have delivered before stepping into that bar had always inspired Leslie and me to make the journey south someday.

However, my brother and I never made it beyond the fishing leg of our trip. Two days after our arrival in the capital city of Georgetown, after we had secured a license to fish in the interior and had queried the hotel desk clerk about access to the hinterland, we hired a pilot and a single-engine plane and traveled to the southwest. I remember having felt a morbid sense of unease as we flew out over Jonestown, the deserted site of the People's Temple and the ill-fated cult led by the Reverend Jim

Jones, which ended in the mass-suicide of over nine hundred people in 1978. Over the roar of the motor, our pilot, a broad-bellied, easygoing fellow named Taffy, told us that he had shuttled numerous people to the compound in the mid-1970s.

Nearly four hours later, after one stop to refuel, we landed on a runway of sorts (it really amounted to nothing more than a cow path), set in the hardscrabble grasslands of the northern Rupununi Savanna, somewhat near the Venezuelan border. Having heard the sound of the plane's approach, a small group of Amerindians had materialized out of the brush to meet the plane. Taffy brought the engine to a stop, and as the three of us slowly climbed down and stretched our legs, we noticed a tall, deeply tanned woman, probably in her mid-seventies, walking purposefully toward us from a nearby field. Strikingly dressed all in black, with a turban wrapped around her head, she easily cut a path through the small crowd of people that had formed around us.

"Taffy, darling, it's been too long," she said, startling Leslie and me with her clipped British accent. "What have you brought me?"

"Hello, Diane," said Taffy in a lazy, cowboy way. "These boys want to do some fishing. Can you put 'em up?"

"Twins," she said archly as she assessed us with her light blue eyes. "Of course I can."

Taffy flew out the next morning, but Leslie and I ended up spending a week with Diane McTurk at her home amid the termite mounds, forested hills, and freshwater creeks of the Rupununi Savanna. Despite the simplicity of the surroundings (the immediate property consisted of a couple of small thatched-roof buildings and one freestanding outdoor shower), the place was actually a working cow ranch called Karanambo, which had been founded by Diane's father, "Tiny" McTurk, back in the

With Diane McTurk at Karanambo Ranch.

161

1920s. Diane had been raised in England but had returned to this remote spot in the late 1970s to manage the ranch. According to Amerindian legend, somewhere on the property there was a cluster of large stones endowed with mystic properties that shielded the land from danger. For her part, Diane had made it her priority as an environmentalist to protect a rare breed of indigenous large freshwater otters that lived in the network of creeks and streams that threaded the property but which was under constant threat of extinction by local poachers. There were a few other, larger cattle ranches some miles away, but Diane's only real link to the outside world was an ancient shortwave radio that she kept in her kitchen.

That first night, as the finale to a delicious welcoming meal, Diane brought out an old silver tea service emblazoned with her family's Scottish coat of arms. Each piece was beautifully designed with an intricately chased (or tooled) foliate pattern. Naturally, Leslie and I commented upon the incredible workmanship of the set, which Diane explained had been made for her family by the famous British silversmith Paul Storr (1771–1844). Suddenly, an already-magical moment in our lives took a twist toward the fantastic. Leslie and I couldn't believe that we had flown for hours into the heart of the Guyanese interior, only to find ourselves drinking tea from a silver service designed by Storr, whose work was in tremendously high demand at the time it was made and is now showcased in museums throughout the world.

By week's end, although we had caught countless varieties of exotic local fish, neither Leslie nor I had hooked, nor even seen, the elusive *Arapaima,* and by the time Taffy had returned us to Georgetown, there wasn't enough time to visit Suriname in search of Newport furniture. Our search for those hidden treasures would have to wait for another trip.

All in a day's work.
Today, however, our fishing
is strictly catch and release.

However, on my subsequent journey to South America, this time in pursuit of the *églomisé* secretary, furniture was quite clearly my priority. Ed had flown into Buenos Aires a few days earlier than I, so we rendezvoused at the hotel before heading out to the shop in Acassuso. Like Ed, I was enormously impressed by the glamorous presence of this piece when I first saw it. The allegorical figures of Truth and Justice were so wonderfully drawn and richly symbolic that they struck a poignant chord with me. I was certain they would have great appeal to a die-hard patriot like Jack Warner. Recently, I had purchased an original 1788 edition of *The London Cabinet Book of Prices,* a book of furniture and room design typical of the kind that might have been available in Philadelphia during the Federal period. When Ed sent me early photos of the secretary, the images on the *églomisé* panels had reminded me of a pair of engraved medallions shown on that book's title page; they featured two women (clothed in ancient Greek dress) posed as Unanimity and Justice. Standing

before the secretary that day, I felt certain that its anonymous maker had carefully studied, if not owned, that London price guide.

I spent most of the afternoon going over the piece, and when I was through, I was completely convinced as to its condition and authenticity. In addition to the alterations that Ed had already pointed out, I noticed that the shop's conservator had treated both the interior and exterior of the secretary with a thin wax finish (the dealers called it "*cera Suiza*"), typically used on furniture in Latin American countries because, it is believed, that it helps seal the wood and protect it from the humidity. Wax is the last thing you want to see on the interior of an American case piece, because it obscures the time-earned signs of wear, which are used to establish authenticity. Fortunately, the overall consistency in the mechanics and construction techniques used on this piece was sufficient enough to waylay any doubts. The appearance of the wax coating on the outside of the secretary concerned me even less because so much of the drama of this piece lay in the vivid contrast of the wood veneers and in its unusual handling of the many *églomisé* panels. Veneering is by its very nature a two-dimensional effect. Therefore, it is less dependent upon the residue of time to enhance its character than is, say, the highly carved surface of a rococo piece. Nevertheless, I used the issue of the refinishing to my advantage, for I negotiated the secretary's final price in the low six figures. Considering the fragility of the piece, it was critical to keep the final price as conservative as possible.

Now the challenge was to get the piece properly packed in time for the New York Winter Antiques Show. The crates and protective material used on this job would all have to be custom-designed. In anticipation of this dilemma, Ed had already done some preliminary research on local shippers who were well versed in the transport of antique furniture by air freight. We probably interviewed about four different packers before settling on one company that regularly did work for both Sotheby's and Christie's. The outfit we chose planned to separate the secretary into three parts—the cornice, the bookcase, and the base—which would be individually packed and then floated within a larger box. In all, it took about four days to construct the entire container, and I stayed in town long enough to see the last nails hammered into the crate before leaving on a three-day fly-fishing excursion with Guy Roderick.

Ed Weissman oversees the preparations for transport.

As part of the deal, Ed had agreed to stay in town until the piece had made it safely through customs. He took this aspect of his job quite seriously and actually ended up accompanying the piece to the airport, disguised as one of the packers. He later told me that he lingered in the restricted cargo area as long as he could, a baseball cap pulled down low over his face and a crowbar held in one hand, just to keep an eye on the crate. Eventually, though, Ed left the airport and returned to his hotel to relax. His long-held dream of buying the secretary had been realized, and in a matter of hours, the piece would arrive in New York.

Sometime around midnight, Ed, who had fallen into a light doze in front of his hotel television, was startled awake by the phone. It was Morgan MacWhinnie calling from New York, where he was stationed to retrieve the secretary as soon as it cleared customs at Kennedy Airport.

"Ed," Morgan said urgently, "the secretary didn't make it. It was taken off the airplane in Buenos Aires."

"What?" said Ed, sitting bolt upright on his bed.

"It's not here, buddy. I just got a call from someone in U.S. customs because my name was on the manifest as a local contact. He said the secretary had been placed on a commercial flight but that it was bumped for passenger luggage. Apparently, passenger bags take precedent over freight."

Now, Morgan is a bit of a jokester, and it actually took him ten minutes to convince Ed that he wasn't pulling his leg. But once Ed was persuaded, he hung up with Morgan and began a frantic twenty-four-hour search for the crate (which finally turned up in a domestic storage zone at the airport in Buenos Aires). It then took him nearly another full day to secure a space for it on a subsequent flight to New York.

The second time around, the crate made it onto the aircraft. Morgan once again drove out to JFK to retrieve it. Now he was presented with a new problem: The loading docks at Kennedy's cargo terminals were built to accommodate tractor-trailers, not stocky cube trucks like the one Morgan was driving that day. "The floor of my truck was a good foot and a half lower than the loading dock," he later told me. "So when the crate was brought out on a forklift, the machine operator couldn't just ease it into the van. Instead, he had to work the container off the steel prongs by tilting them down and then backing up so that the thing would slowly slide off on its own. "Unfortunately, the whole thing dropped into the van with a loud *ba-boom!*" said Morgan. "I was dying. The entire drive into Manhattan, I kept shaking my head because I was sure that we had lost a lot of glass with that fall."

At this point, I, too, had returned from Argentina, having actually beaten the secretary back to New York. So when Morgan arrived at the loading dock of my gallery building, I was there to greet him. The expression on his face when he stepped down from the cab spoke volumes. We were both pretty nervous as we moved the crate out of the truck and upstairs into the shop, where we then proceeded to unpack it. But by some miracle, only one pane of glass had broken throughout the course of that transcontinental journey—one of the less important panes, a clear glass one fronting the bookcase doors—but the more precious *églomisé* had remained intact. With characteristic efficiency, Clifford Harvard, my gallery manager of nearly twelve years, had it replaced in time for the opening of the show, now less than a week away.

The most frenzied moments of the Winter Antiques Show are no doubt the opening minutes of the gala preview, which traditionally consists of back-to-back cocktail parties (the earlier the party, the more expensive the ticket) and benefits a local charity, the East Side House Settlement. Many people, including top-level collectors and museum staffers, buy tickets to the earliest of these parties to guarantee a shot at the fresh-to-the-market offerings of the show's participating dealers. (Of course other people buy tickets to the first round of viewing, simply to enjoy the glamour of the event, which tends to attract a lot of socialites and assorted glitterati.) Since Mom and Dad are often in town during Americana Week, I usually ask Dad to help me out during the frenetic last few hours of preparation before the show.

In 1995, the year I exhibited the Argentine secretary, I was, as usual, so crunched for time that I had a little less than half an hour to run home and change into a suit before the show's official start. As I cut a hasty path out through the front door, I noticed that a significant number of people had already gathered outside the entrance to the show. I knew that Jack Warner had flown into New York earlier in the day on his private jet, and I assumed that he was somewhere in that early crowd. In anticipation of his arrival and the near certainty that he—a man who was not accustomed to waiting—would be asked to wait on line, I enlisted my father to keep an eye out for the tall multimillionaire. "Just listen for his voice; you can't miss it," I said.

Dad had no trouble hearing or spotting Jack, who arrived at the show within moments of my departure, his private curator in tow.

"I've come for the secretary," he said to my father, who walked up and introduced himself.

"So I've been told, Mr. Warner," Dad responded.

"I didn't realize I would have to wait on a line," Jack said with obvious impatience.

But having already been forewarned as to Jack's character and knowing how important this sale was to me, Dad carefully disarmed him with a few words. "Mr. Warner," he said, "not even General Patton and all his legions could get past this entrance before the opening signal."

Jack cocked his head sideways for a moment and looked hard at my dad. "Damn it," he said with a sudden broad grin, "if Patton couldn't get in, then I guess I can't either. I'll wait here." With that, Jack and his curator stepped into place near the front of the line.

When the show opened at 5:00 P.M., Jack and his curator walked swiftly into my booth, where the well-traveled secretary—with a $440,000 asking price—stood front and center. And I, who had managed to change my clothes and then make it back to the show with a minute or two to spare, was standing proudly by its side. Jack looked the piece up and down for approximately twelve seconds and then turned to face me.

"I'll take it," he said, beaming. "It looks even better than in the pictures." He then pointed to a wonderful pair of Classical New York card tables that I had displayed on either side of the secretary. Each featured an inlaid brass star on the front edge of the skirt, and a five-figure price tag. "Throw those on the bill, too," he said.

I've never sold three pieces of furniture more quickly in my life.

My booth on opening night of the New York Winter Antiques Show, 1995.

167

9

Two for the Road

AS I JUMPED INTO A TAXI outside of Sotheby's York Avenue headquarters not too long ago, I was surprised by the greeting from the driver, a heavyset fellow with a turban and a dark beard. "So how's the family up in Mohawk?" he asked, peering at me through the rearview mirror. "How are Ron and Norma?"

For a brief moment, I was stunned. How did this perfect stranger know my hometown and parents' names? Was this a prank? Was that Allen Funt beneath the turban? I half-turned in my seat, looking for a hidden camera, but then suddenly I knew: The driver was a fan of the *Antiques Roadshow,* the PBS television series that takes a team of antiques appraisers on a city-to-city tour of the United States to evaluate objects brought in by local residents. Leigh and I have both served as guest experts on the show since its inception in 1996, which means that by now, our faces and stories (as well as those of our fellow evaluators) have grown familiar to the almost 15 million viewers who tune in to each show. The program has been a huge success: Within its second year, it quietly eclipsed such perennial favorites as *Masterpiece Theatre* and *This Old House,* becoming PBS's top-rated prime-time series. As a result, incidents such as the one in the cab are beginning to happen to Leigh and me and the rest of the *Roadshow* appraisers with increased regularity.

For instance, recently I was grabbing a quick bite to eat at a restaurant up near Sotheby's cavernous warehouse in the heart of New York's Spanish Harlem. Salsa music was pouring in through the loudspeakers overhead as I settled into a booth near the back and began my meal. Suddenly, the front door of the restaurant swung open and a burly dark-haired man lunged into the place, pushing a handcart stacked high with cases of beer. Slowly, he began to make his way toward the kitchen, but then he abruptly changed course and brought his cart to a halt right next to my table.

"Say, aren't you one of those brothers from the *Antiques Roadshow*?" he asked in a Spanish-accented voice.

I looked up from my plate, hastily swallowed my food, and answered, "Yes."

"That story about the Boston highboy," he said, "*de veras me afectó*. I felt for those people."

I smiled and nodded in agreement, knowing that he was referring to a segment taped during the show's premier season (it was our very first on-air appearance), in which Leigh and I appraised a circa 1740 bonnet-top high chest of drawers that had been brought in by a young couple from Concord, Massachusetts. Though crafted primarily of walnut, the piece also featured vivid crossbanding (or thin strips of veneer cut across the grain) on the front and star-shaped compass inlays on the sides (so called because the form was layed out with a compass tool). In addition, both the central upper and lower drawers featured magnificent inlaid fan motifs.

Fairly recently, the piece had been cleaned, save a small section of molding that had fallen off the upper cornice. Leigh and I had found the molding in an upper drawer (along with a small stack of old Valentine's Day cards).

"We forgot to take those out," said the wife, coloring slightly as Leigh drew them out for the camera.

"That's okay. I think they really add to the interest of the chest," said Leigh. Then he held up the broken shard of molding and said, "This piece actually has the original grungy finish that was on the chest before it was cleaned. The interesting thing—and the sad thing in a way—is that if the entire item still had this kind of old crackled finish, it would be worth in the neighborhood of one hundred thousand to one hundred and twenty thousand dollars."

Turning to me, he asked, "Les, what would you say this would be worth as a cleaned piece?"

"About fifty thousand dollars," I said carefully, casting a sympathetic glance toward the owners. It was an edifying television moment—unfortunately, at the expense of the owners—and really hammered home to viewers the notion that original finish is highly prized among Americana collectors.

And that is, of course, the essence of the *Antiques Roadshow*—educating people and helping them figure out whether or not they have that proverbial winning lottery ticket stashed away in their attic or garage. The premise is simple but thoroughly intoxicating, probably because collecting is a universal impulse. Who hasn't collected something at some point in his or her life—be it baseball cards or comic books or simply shells on the beach? Even seasoned professionals such as Leigh and I, who are accustomed to looking at beautiful objects, are genuinely moved by the show's conceit. Why? Because at every taping, without fail, a genuine treasure is always unearthed. And when it is found, the news sends a charge around the appraisal room that is comparable to an electric shock. For me, the experience correlates directly with the adventures Leigh and I had as children, browsing the open fields of Brimfield. The main difference (camera overviews and spotlights aside) is that now the treasures are being brought to us.

The success of the *Roadshow* is due in no small part to the energy and commitment of Peter Cook, the show's talented executive producer, and Aida Moreno, a petite powerhouse of a woman, who was the show's original executive producer. After WGBH bought the rights to the show from the visionary Dan Farrell in 1995 (its concept is based upon an identically named program produced by the BBC in England), Aida basically took the ball and ran. I met her the following year, in January 1996, when she came to Sotheby's to meet with a number of department heads whom she wanted to audition for her panel of on-air personalities.

(left to right) Leslie, Aida Moreno, and Leigh.

On the day of her visit, I had just launched the preview exhibition for one of the most important single-owner sales of my career—that of the Americana collection of Mr. and Mrs. Adolph H. Meyer of Birmingham, Michigan. The Meyers had spent over forty years, beginning in the 1930s, assembling a well-chosen group of furniture under the guiding hand of a local dealer named Jess Pavey. Wisely, Pavey had cautioned his clients *not* to refinish their furniture—a reflection of his pioneering good taste, rather than of the pervasive connoisseurship mantra it has become today. As a result, the collection was a real gem, and I had taken particular care in displaying it to its best advantage within the brown-carpeted, blue-walled interior of what was, at the time, Sotheby's primary exhibition space—the south gallery on the second floor. (It has since been demolished and replaced by a ten-thousand-square-foot glass-walled high-tech exhibition area eight floors up.)

I was standing at what amounted to the center of the Meyer exhibition when Aida walked into the gallery. We did a quick tour of the Meyers' property and then came to a stop virtually where we had started, in front of a magnificent block-and-shell mahogany bureau that was without a doubt the sale's star lot (it ended up selling to Leigh, bidding on behalf of a private collector, for a record-breaking $3.6 million). There, Aida turned to me and said with characteristic efficiency, "Tell me everything I should know about this desk. You have two minutes."

Although it was a dress rehearsal of sorts, I couldn't help but smile. The bureau was my favorite object in the entire Meyer estate and I could have talked about it in my sleep (which, as my wife, Emily, will attest, wouldn't be an altogether-unusual occurrence). It was the sort of piece that caused true lovers of eighteenth-century furniture who visited the gallery that week literally to drop to their knees in awe. Once owned by a powerful Newport merchant, Capt. Samuel Whitehorne, Jr., the desk was attributed to the master craftsman Edmund Townsend, based upon its similarity to another example bearing Townsend's label. (*That* bureau is now the crown jewel of the M. and M. Karolik Collection at the Museum of Fine Arts, Boston.)

But more than its impressive provenance and distinguished maker's attribution, the Whitehorne desk seemed to possess a sense of dignity and grace that I had never seen before in an object. The depth and richness of its aged reddish brown mahogany (which shone through the darkened surface in the areas of highest wear) was utterly alluring and the wonderful golden halos that had formed in the wood surrounding the original brass handles served as eloquent testimony to its use over time. It was clearly an object that had stood in silent witness to a great deal since its creation in the mid-1780s.

Leslie's "screen test" for the Antiques Roadshow *entailed describing the most important attributes of this Edmund Townsend desk in under two minutes.*

So within my allotted two minutes, I tried to touch upon the most obvious high points of the piece. When I was through, Aida quizzed me on a second item in the Meyer sale—a stately walnut secretary-bookcase that had been made in Boston, probably in the early 1740s. The secretary featured a wonderful pair of original arch-shaped mirrored and beveled glass doors in the upper case that were flanked by a set of engaged pilasters. Each featured a foliate-carved Corinthian capital sculpted of gesso and gilt that was so lushly rendered, it seemed to blossom out of the wood itself. For a number of years, the Meyers had lent the secretary to the Diplomatic Reception Rooms of the United States Department of State, where it no doubt impressed countless foreign dignitaries as to the greatness of early American craftsmanship and design.

By the time Aida and I parted ways, I was very excited about the concept of the *Roadshow.* (She was sufficiently impressed with my passion for furniture that an hour or so later, when I happened to run into her in the elevator, she snapped at me playfully, "Why are you following me around? You've already got the job!") Primarily, I thought the program could do a lot toward deflating the notion that the antiques world was a place only for the elite. I am well aware of the fact that auctions intimidate many people, so anything that could demystify the language of antiques by bringing it into America's homes was bound to be a good thing. What could be better than educating people about the furniture I so love and helping to identify some previously undiscovered American treasures in the process? When Aida and her team approached Leigh for the show, he, too, had been instantly swayed by its potential. As he said to me at the time, just about everyone we meet has an antique at home that he or she would love to have examined by an expert.

My brother and I have just finished taping our fifth season with the show. By now, we are used to the hectic shooting schedule, which takes up nearly every weekend of the summer (taking us away from our respective families, unfortunately). Regardless of the city, the format is always the same: Local residents are invited to bring in no more than two antiques or collectibles for a free verbal evaluation, usually at a local convention center. Since we often stay in hotels that are adjacent to the taping site, it's not unusual to awaken to the sight of a long line of antique hopefuls stretching around the block. There's been many an early morning when I've worked my way through a quick room-service breakfast while peering out the window and fantasizing about the treasures that might be brought to the table that day. And invariably, I find that if I run into Leigh in the lobby en route to the show, he, too, will confess to having spent the morning in a similar fashion.

Once the doors to the week's designated site are officially opened and the property owners begin to remove their assorted heirlooms and flea market finds from paper bags, laundry baskets, and even old toaster boxes, spirits really begin to soar. What will the next carton reveal? For us, the setup presents a rare opportunity to work as a team with people whom we might ordinarily view as competitors. For example, I can't think of another situation in which I might find myself standing shoulder-to-shoulder with John Hays of Christie's analyzing furniture. (To protect the program's integrity, the *Roadshow* maintains a strict policy against soliciting business from visitors, though we are allowed to leave our business cards at a table by the exit.)

Judging from the feedback we've received from the property owners, the wait on the appraisal line has become a key component of the *Roadshow* experience. Since nearly everyone in the room holds a significant conversation piece in their arms, the snaking line quickly evolves into an animated talkfest of exchanged history, fable, and family lore. Last season, when the *Roadshow* made a stop in Tampa, Leigh and I left some tickets at the front desk for a pair of top-level Americana collectors who were curious to see a taping in progress. But when the couple arrived at the Tampa Convention Center, they somehow missed the VIP table and ended up joining the end of the query line. Five hours into the event, long after Leigh and I had given them up as no-shows, the two materialized before us with huge smiles on their faces.

"But you could have bypassed the line," I told the two, aghast that they had waited so long to meet us.

"We wouldn't have missed it for the world," said the wife, brushing aside my concern. "In the past few hours, we've heard so many great stories—and learned so much about the collecting history of Florida. It's been fascinating!"

Roughly six thousand people are admitted to a single *Roadshow* event, which means each expert may view upward of two hundred items per taping. The sheer volume alone prevents most objects from being videotaped. Instead, a piece comes to television if and when an appraiser senses that it was acquired for too much or too little, if its history makes a good story, if it stands as a great educational tool, or if it provides a strong combination of the above. I'd say about 80 percent of what is brought to *Roadshow* events is exactly what it appears to be. In other words, if an owner paid fifty dollars for a painting, it's generally worth fifty dollars. The program's drama lies in that remaining 20 percent.

I also think viewers respond to the way the show gives art and antiques a homespun, human face. For example, at a stop in Albuquerque during the first season, I evaluated a bassinet made from the shell of an armadillo. The animal's scaled tail had been looped above the body of the piece to form a handle, while its prehistoric-looking claws jutted out over the rim (in full view of the baby).

A tattered pink fabric lining the interior of the shell was the only indication of its intended and thoroughly unusual use. The owner of the piece, a slender dark-haired woman wearing a lot of silver jewelry, explained that her grandmother, whom she described as "a strange character," had slept in the shell as an infant. I looked at the woman in amazement and said only half in jest, "No wonder, this looks like something out of *Rosemary's Baby*!"

Luckily, the woman had a good sense of humor and we both laughed. I ended up appraising the piece at between seventy-five and one hundred dollars, mainly for its novel conversational value.

Less novel are the seemingly endless examples of elaborate late-nineteenth-century and early-twentieth-century Renaissance Revival furniture, inspired by fifteenth- and sixteenth-century European pieces. Because these pieces are grandly proportioned and highly carved (elaborate leafage, chubby-faced putti, and gargoyle masks are all common motifs), owners think they are in possession of something quite rare. In fact, many of these pieces are partially machine-made and not all that valuable (other than in a sentimental way). I am also amazed at the number of primitive high chairs that continue to surface on the show, probably because no one wants to throw away a chair from a child's youth. We must see about five or ten per city. (With these again, sentiment weighs in far heavier than dollar value.)

But—chalk it up to the law of averages—great treasures *are* always uncovered in every city, and I feel blessed that I can still get as excited about a new object now as I did when I was fourteen. There was, for instance, a rare Federal sewing table, probably made between 1805 and 1815 by the New York cabinetmaker Duncan Phyfe, that surfaced during a stop in Southfield, Michigan. Initially, the owner, a fragile white-haired woman, probably in her seventies, had simply approached me at the evaluations table with a description of the piece. She said she owned a small mahogany table with a lift top that opened to a retractable writing surface (complete with silver-capped inkwells and blotter compartments). Below the writing compartment was a narrow drawer outfitted with a trapezoidal case for holding sewing materials.

I was so intrigued by her account (she also described slender S-shaped legs ending in hairy-paw feet and Regency-style lion's-head brass pulls on the drawer) that I asked her if she would be willing to drive home and retrieve the piece. She agreed, but when she returned at the end of the day, Leigh was on duty alone at the furniture-appraisal table. Thinking he was I, she asked for his help carrying the table into the hall. Leigh quickly realized her confusion, but he offered to help with the piece. When he reached the woman's van and saw what was inside, he nearly fell over at the sight. Despite the substantial weight of the table's dense mahogany wood, he later told me, "I carried it into the hall like it was made of feathers. I was that excited." Less than an hour later, Leigh and I appraised the piece with the cameras rolling and "Mary from Michigan" soon learned that her table could reach $120,000 on the open market.

Inspecting the Duncan Phyfe sewing table just minutes after it arrived on the set.

The segment grew all the more moving after the table's owner explained to us the importance of antiques in her life. "I had cancer of the cervix twenty-three years ago, and if I hadn't had the hobby of antiquing, I think I would be gone now," she said in a quivering voice. "But antiques have kept me . . . the running and looking for them, the finding and researching, reading through the papers and magazines. . . . Sharing with other people your finds, your treasures—it just carries you and lifts you. You have no time to get sick or die." By the time she was through speaking, we were all on the verge of tears.

To date, our most exciting *Roadshow* discovery occurred in September 1997 during a taping filmed at the Meadowlands Exposition Center, a huge stadium arena in Secaucus, New Jersey. It was after 11:00 A.M., but Leigh and I and the rest of the *Roadshow* crew were already well into our third hour of appraisals. I had just placed a value of one hundred dollars on a late-nineteenth-century oak rocking chair (another form that surfaces a lot on the show), while nearby, Leigh was winding down his analysis of a circa 1830 spinning wheel (another frequently seen object, also worth about one hundred dollars). Next in line was a blond woman, probably in her late sixties, wearing royal blue slacks and a white blouse, with a small folded semicircular, or demilune, tabletop (consisting of two hinged half-moon-shaped boards) braced against her side like a stack of books. Accompanying her was another woman, who had what was clearly the matching four-legged frame slung over one shoulder.

Despite its dismantled state, I could already see that this object was vastly different in quality from the dozens of items I had already examined that day. I was still a few yards away as the woman with the table frame slid the piece off her shoulder and onto the floor, while her companion stood by, preparing to position the brown mahogany top. Each of the table's straight, tapering legs featured a brilliant band of satinwood inlay, used to accentuate its narrowing slope. Even without the top in place, it was easy to appreciate the geometric interplay between the light wood framed by the dark. At the bottom of each leg was an elongated four-sided foot that resembled a pedestal (usually referred to as a term or spade foot). The form is common on English furniture of the late eighteenth century but it is uncommon to find it on American pieces. The front rail of the table arched outward in a luxurious sweep (designed to echo the curved shape of the demilune top) and was decorated with a delicate pattern of inlaid satin-wood swags of husks draped from a series of bowknots. In short, the entire package was so striking and distinctive that it immediately called to my mind the work of the father and son cabinetmaking team of John and Thomas Seymour.

Today, the furniture of the Seymours—who emigrated from Devonshire, England, to Portland, Maine, in 1784 and later settled in Boston, where they worked together from 1794 until 1804—is revered for its supreme level of craftsmanship and sophisticated style. They are known to have made furniture for a number of wealthy, style-conscious clients, including, most significantly, Elizabeth Derby West, the daughter of Elias Hasket Derby of Salem, who is said to be New England's first millionaire. Unfortunately, though, there were not enough millionaires in the Boston market to support their meticulous (and costly) craft adequately. In 1818, John died penniless in the Boston

The table's term foot, with an inlaid husk above.

Almshouse, while his son suffered two failed cabinetry businesses before becoming the foreman for a former competitor. I have always been intrigued by the story of these men, particularly since I have the luxury of placing some twentieth-century perspective on their tremendous yet underappreciated talent.

Needless to say, when I guessed that day in Secaucus that I was likely looking at an undiscovered treasure by the Seymours of Boston, my heart began to race. I glanced over at Leigh—whose intense focus upon the piece, I had already sensed—and his wide-eyed expression told me that he, too, had drawn the same rapid conclusion.

Within seconds, Leigh and I were flanking the two women, eager to confirm our suspicions. Before we could even introduce ourselves, the woman in the blue slacks, who had been holding the table's top (which was now resting on the frame), identified herself as the owner. Then she abruptly reached down and peeled off a roughly twelve-inch square of bright green-and-gold Christmas paper that was attached, rather inexplicably, to the exposed underside of the table's top. As soon as she lifted it, we understood why it had been placed there—to protect a well-worn rectangular strip of paper adhered to the surface below, which I instantly recognized as a cabinetmaker's label.

"Is it?" I said to Leigh under my breath as we both stooped closer to decipher the faint wording.

"It is," he answered softly as we read the inscription: *John Seymour & Son Cabinet Makers Creek Square Boston.* Offhand, I could think of perhaps five known examples of labeled Seymour furniture, which meant that this table's appearance before us was nothing short of a miracle.

But as excited as Leigh and I were, it was important for us, as appraisers on the *Roadshow,* to maintain a facade of calm so as not to undermine any potential on-screen excitement. We needed to sound out the table's owner regarding the history of the piece while keeping our own feelings under wraps. So in the most straightforward tone I could muster, I asked the woman, who introduced herself as Claire (*Roadshow* guests are asked to refer to themselves on a first-name basis only in order to maintain their anonymity), how she had acquired the table.

"I bought it at a lawn sale about thirty years ago," she said. "I bargained the owner down from thirty dollars to twenty-five because it was all I had in my purse at the time."

Now I could hardly contain myself. A masterpiece of American Federal furniture found at a yard sale, bought for a few dollars. It was the stuff of dreams—really so far-fetched that it reminded me of an outrageous prank that Leigh played back in 1979 while he was pursuing a postgraduate fellowship program in American decorative arts at Historic Deerfield in Massachusetts. (I had graduated from the same program the previous summer.) One night, he and a friend stayed up late to place hand-painted signs around the grounds of the historic village museum, announcing a (mock) clearance sale. One read: TAG SALE—TODAY ONLY. HIGHBOYS! LOW-BOYS! QUEEN ANNE AND CHIPPENDALE! YOU NAME IT WE'VE GOT IT. Another said EVERYTHING HERE PRICED TO SELL. ALL STYLES REPRESENTED FROM PILGRIM TO CLASSICAL, INCLUDING YOUR FAVORITES, QUEEN ANNE AND CHIPPENDALE.

Within a few hours, that sleepy museum town (famed for its out-

Leigh, age twenty-three, with a Windsor armchair, at Historic Deerfield.

standing collection of Americana) awoke to the sound of the switchboard ringing off the hook. The callers had seen the signs from the road and wanted to know all kinds of things. "What time is the sale starting?" "Will they ship to Boston?"

Claire's discovery of the elegant Seymour card table sounded just about as unlikely. Leigh and I needed to find Aida quickly.

"Well where is she?" was Aida's rapid response when we presented her with a quick description of what had just unfolded. Within seconds, we were all back with Claire.

After introducing herself, Aida asked gently, "Would you feel comfortable going on television with your table?"

"Of course," Claire responded with a ready smile. "That's why I'm here."

Once a property owner like Claire is tapped for an on-air interview, he or she is then ushered into a small waiting area, otherwise known as the greenroom. There the owner will find coffee and snacks and a few television monitors set up where it is possible to watch other segments in the process of being taped. Guests may have to wait anywhere from thirty minutes to three hours for their segment to be taped, which doesn't always give the appraisers much time to prep for the enlightening object lesson that they will be expected to deliver when the cameras start rolling. Although much of what we say on-screen stems from our professional expertise, it helps if the explanation contains a couple of hard dates or facts (such as the work dates for the Seymours) culled from the *Roadshow*'s traveling research library.

Usually, Leigh and I don't do our on-screen evaluations together, but in the case of the Seymour table, which we had spotted simultaneously and were equally enamored with, it seemed like the best (and most equitable) thing to do. I began the on-air interview by asking Claire, who we learned was a retired elementary school teacher and divorcée, to recap how she had come to own the table.

Claire's table in use at home.

"I had moved into a new house and I knew I needed a diminutive table," she explained carefully. "I thought I knew the shape and size. When I saw this one at a local yard sale, I thought it was a great thing—even though it was pitch-black and a moldy mess."

Claire had gone to the yard sale with a friend, who cautioned her against buying the piece because the top was slightly unstable. "It will never hold a lamp" was her advice. When Leigh and I examined the piece prior to the taping, we, too, noticed that the table was a bit shaky. But that was because it was attached to the frame with a set of original eighteenth-century screws. The table had been designed to convert from a semi-circular pier table into a round-top gaming table (the half-moon leaf simply unfolded and was supported by the two swing legs).

Despite her friend's warning, Claire seized the initiative and purchased the table for the bargained-down price of twenty-five dollars. It was only after she took the table home and down to her basement workshop (where she attempted to tighten the few loose screws) that she spotted the Seymour label. She copied down the names, and a few days later, she visited her local library and investigated the Seymour name. In a

1959 book titled *John and Thomas Seymour: Cabinetmakers in Boston, 1794–1816,* by Vernon C. Stoneman (which, despite considerable advances in scholarship, remains the most thorough book on their work), she learned a little bit more about the men who had made her table. She then decided that her yard sale find might have some historic weight after all.

I wanted to introduce a little bit of the history into the dialogue, so I pointed to the Seymours' label, affixed to the underside of the table's top. "With most pieces of furniture from the Federal period, we make attributions on the basis of inlay, style, and secondary woods," I explained to Claire. "With your particular table, we are very fortunate to have the actual maker's label. It's a little bit deteriorated, but we can still read it, and that is really just extraordinary."

I could sense by the body language of Leigh, who was standing close by my side, that he was eager to share his own excited appraisal of the piece, so I took a discreet step back.

"Claire," he said, moving in toward the table. "Even if this wasn't a labeled piece, everything about it says John and Thomas Seymour. The quality is just incredible." Leaning over excitedly, he skimmed his hand along the curved edge of the top, where an intricate inlaid design of oblong seed husks interspersed by small dots could be seen. "This pattern," Leigh explained, "was actually sand-burnt, which means hot grains of sand were used to scorch the wood and give the inlay a shaded, three-dimensional effect."

The inlaid skirt pattern of Claire's table featured delicate swags of husks suspended by tied bow knots.

Next, his hand moved to the inlaid pattern of continuous swags of three-petaled wheat husks displayed across the sweeping arc of the table's front. "So many of this table's decorative elements came out of late-eighteenth-century English design books by cabinetmakers like George Hepplewhite or Thomas Sheraton," he said, referring to two of the most influential sources of the Federal era. "The inlaid swag pattern, the demilune form, the tapering legs with the spade feet . . . but the Seymours took these references to the highest level."

Pacing is always a factor in these interviews, so Leigh paused only for a breath before asking, "Now, Claire, did you ever try to clean this table?"

"Linseed oil and turpentine," she answered quickly. "But then I saw this," she said, pointing to the inlaid pattern along the front, "and I thought, Well, I'll just wait."

"Well, luckily, Claire, you are not a very good refinisher," Leigh quipped.

"But I am . . . I am," she earnestly protested.

"No, I'm joking," he said with a smile. "Because if you had cleaned it any more, you would have taken off a lot of the value. Luckily, the table still has a nice old color." Pointing to the tapering slope of the rectangular-shaped term feet, he added, "You see all the dirt at the bottom? I love that."

Now, Leigh began to wind down the interview. "When we first saw your table, my heart went thump, thump, thump," he told Claire, hammering a fist to his chest. "Feel it right now," he said, impulsively grabbing her hand and holding it to the front of his double-breasted gray pinstripe suit. "It was one of the most exciting moments in our lives."

Next came the classic *Roadshow* question (as familiar to viewers as "Heeeere's Johnny!" or "Is that your final answer?"). Did Claire have any idea of what the table was worth?

"Probably about twenty thousand dollars," Claire answered, quoting a figure she had been offered once, back in the 1970s, after she showed the table to a Connecticut antiques dealer. "But I'm just saying that."

Leigh tapped his hands lightly against the table's dark surface and then said with a grin, "I think the estimate we are going to give you is going to top that." He paused

Inspecting the label.

dramatically and then continued. "Les and I both feel that because this table is a ten in all the right areas—quality, rarity, condition—on the open market, the piece could bring in the range of two hundred thousand to two hundred and twenty-five thousand dollars. But on a really good day—now I don't want to get your hopes up—it has a possibility of bringing three hundred thousand."

Claire blinked her eyes slowly in the bright television lights. "That's not bad," she said in a voice that broke ever so slightly. She then added pragmatically, "Are you writing this all down so that I can remember?"

The interview ended there, and all too quickly it was time for us to say good-bye to Claire and her wonderful table. Knowing that I worked at Sotheby's, she mentioned to me in parting that she had visited the preview exhibition for the estate of Jacqueline Kennedy Onassis. "It was very exciting," she told me, a gleam in her eyes.

The moment of truth.

Though I was forbidden by *Roadshow* policy from speaking with Claire any longer about the table, I was nonetheless thrilled that of all the sales for her to have visited at Sotheby's, she had gone to a blockbuster like the Onassis sale. It gave me hope that, given the newfound value of her table, she might, on her own accord, decide to bring the piece to auction. Perhaps the relationship we had forged in the studio would be enough to attract her to Sotheby's.

Leigh and I stood for a moment and watched Claire leave the hall with her table, its two parts once again separated between her and her friend. I was sure that Leigh, too, was nursing similar thoughts of handling the piece. In a sense, we represented the two best options for a property owner like Claire. At auction, with the right buyers in the room or on the phone, Claire was assured of getting a competitive price for the piece. But if she consigned the table to a private dealer like Leigh, who advises many of the best collectors in the field, she could also get a top-dollar price, but without the same level of exposure. Some sellers and buyers prefer the anonymity of a private sale because it offers a way of sidestepping the curious (relatives, for example), while others wouldn't think of missing the excitement of the auction room. All my brother and I could do was hope that on her way out the door, Claire might stop at the courtesy table to pick up one of our respective business cards.

Friday of the following week, I walked into my office and was greeted by the sight of a pink telephone message slip lying on my desk. It said "Claire" and there was a phone number with a New Jersey area code. I let out a holler. A few days later, I drove down to Mahwah, New Jersey, to the home of the woman, whose full name I finally knew: Claire Wiegand-Beckmann. Also with me that day was senior cataloger John Nye. As we pulled into Claire's driveway in John's dark green Ford Explorer, we saw a man standing on the front steps, holding a video camera. As it turned out, the man was Claire's ex-husband, there to record the event for posterity sake. Seeing him reminded me of a time almost two decades earlier: I had driven out to a modest home on Long Island to pick up a masterful Chippendale marble-top pier table that had a long history in an old New York family. As I carried that table out to my car, the owner snapped a number of pictures of me with the table. I thought it was a sweet gesture, but I later learned that the photos had been taken as a precautionary measure to document the fact that I was removing the heirloom from the house.

Claire's table was just so exceptionally beautiful and untouched, it really could have sold itself. Still, to highlight its finer points, I hired Robert Mussey, certainly the field's preeminent scholar on the work of the Seymours, to write the sale catalog entry for the piece. John Nye and I had already discovered that Claire's table was identical to another labeled Seymour gaming table owned by the collectors George and Linda Kaufman, which to my mind only enhanced its value. Thanks to Robert's research, we learned that the two were exact mates and that the stationary top on Claire's table appeared to have been cut from the same plank of mahogany as the folding leaf on the Kaufman example. This made the two tables the only known pair of labeled Seymour furniture of any type at the time.

The morning of the sale, Claire and I were invited to do a segment with the table on *Good Morning America.* Upon our return to Sotheby's with the piece, we were faced with another camera crew from the *Roadshow,* there to record the end of the story, so to speak. When the sale began, Claire opted not to sit in one of the private sky boxes that overlook the selling floor, but in the first row on the auctioneer's right (some clients prefer to watch the proceedings from a discreet distance, out of the public eye). Seated just a few chairs away was Albert Sack, one of the main contenders for the piece. Also in the front row, directly in front of the auctioneer's podium, was Leigh, flanked by our father and older brother, Mitchell.

"I have a $100,000 bid to start it. Now bidding at $100,000," Bill Stahl began, then quickly began ticking through the rising bids. "$120,000, $130,000, $140,000, $150,000 . . . in the back now . . . $200,000, $210,000 . . ."

I could see the Connecticut-based dealer Wayne Pratt in the far left of the room, nodding his bids to Bill. Within seconds, the bidding surged past the estimate Leigh and I had given to Claire on the *Roadshow.* From my position on the dais, I could see her excitedly clutching the hand of a friend seated next to her. The numbers continued to rise.

"$290,000, $300,000, $310,000, $320,000, $330,000 . . ."

At $350,000, Wayne dropped out of the bidding.

"$360,000, $370,000, $380,000 . . ."

Now, Leigh raised his paddle and jumped in. Having taken careful note of the stir caused by the table during the exhibition preview, he had already warned the client for whom he was bidding that it was sure to go for a record price.

"$390,000, $400,000, $410,000 . . ."

The room had grown noticeably more quiet. Suddenly, the contest for the Seymour table seemed to be a duel between my brother and Albert Sack.

"$420,000, $430,000, $440,000 . . ."

As was his custom, Albert was signaling his bids with a flick of the wrist at Al Bristol, Sotheby's beloved octogenarian exhibition coordinator, who for decades has stood at a lectern to the right of the auctioneer's podium, helping to spot bids. My wife, Emily, who used to work at Sotheby's, calls Al "a real morale booster" because he is never without a few kind words and a butterscotch candy to hand to a weary staffer or loyal client.

"$450,000, $460,000, $470,000 . . ." The last number hovered above the crowd and then Leigh called out to Bill from the front row that he wanted to go up a half increment of five thousand dollars.

"Why not?" Bill said playfully. "$475,000 . . . do I hear $480,000?"

Albert gestured with his hand in Al Bristol's direction. "$480,000," Al called.

"The bid is right front at $480,000," said Bill, acknowledging the offer. "At $480,000, then . . ."

Leigh lifted his paddle again.

"I have $485,000," said Bill, but then Albert quickly countered at $490,000. Bill shot Leigh a questioning look. Was he still in the game? Leigh shook his head. He was through.

"At $490,000, still on the right side at $490,000," Bill warned the room before—*smack*—he brought his gavel down on the podium. "Sold for $490,000."

Claire with Leslie after the auction.

Clair congratulates Albert Sack.

There were some happy shrieks from Claire's corner as the entire room erupted in applause. (With the buyer's premium included, the sale figure would be $540,000.)

The Seymour gaming table had a new owner. As it turned out, Albert Sack had been bidding on behalf of Peter M. Brant, the polo-playing businessman, who bought the table as a present for his wife, the supermodel Stephanie Seymour. (No, she is not a descendant of the Boston cabinetmakers, but, yes, their common name was a partial motivating factor in the purchase.)

After the sale, Leigh and I invited Claire to join us for a celebratory bottle of champagne at Petaluma, an Italian restaurant just two blocks from Sotheby's. I guess she was feeling pretty cheeky by then, because when she arrived at the restaurant, she walked straight up to our father and said, "Young man, I've just sold a table for five hundred and forty thousand dollars. How would you like to take a trip around the world with me?"

Leigh, Mitch, and I, who overheard the exchange, were standing nearby, wearing looks of mock horror. "Claire, that's our father," I warned. "Stay away. He's a happily married man!"

189

10

Hidden in Plain Sight

WITH ITS CRENELLATED REDBRICK FACADE and fortresslike solidity, the Seventh Regiment Armory, which takes up a full city block on Park Avenue between Sixty-sixth and Sixty-seventh streets in New York, stands as an anachronism amid the proper limestone apartment buildings that rise around it. But as we have already seen with the case of the Federal secretary found in Argentina, the Armory is very much a part of the social fabric of this posh neighborhood, because every January its cavernous interior drill space is transformed into the giant collector's carousel known as the Winter Antiques Show.

At around two o'clock in the afternoon of January 16, 1998, nearly two and a half hours before the start of the show that year, a furniture conservator named Robert Fileti climbed the twenty or so well-worn stone steps leading to the entrance of the Armory. In his pocket was a one-thousand-dollar ticket to the earliest of the numerous gala preview parties that were to occur throughout the night. Bob is a slight man with a wiry frame, whose face bears the quiet intensity of someone who has spent a lifetime studying things close at hand. He is, by his own admission, the type of person who is always early. So when a client of mine asked him to stand on line for him to purchase a particular piece of furniture that I was taking to the show, he wasn't about to alter his track record. As a matter of course, Bob intended to be first on line for the gala—and he was.

For nearly an hour, Bob sat alone in the huge entrance corridor preceding the show space, watching the steady stream of caterers and dealers scurrying back and forth in last-minute preparation for the opening. In time, a small line of other early ticket holders began to grow behind him. When there was less than half an hour to go, the line numbered close to one hundred people. In the front were the hard-core collectors and museum people who, like Bob, had come to the Armory in pursuit of big-ticket items. Behind them snaked a crowd of people—many bedecked in black tie and diamonds—who were there simply to enjoy the glamorous scene. From behind the pages of his copy of *The New York Times,* Bob quietly assessed the group. Most of the faces were unknown to him. Could any in this crew be after the same object as he?

Dealers like to keep the content of their booths somewhat cloaked in mystery until the start of the show, to enhance the buyers' sense of expectation. But as soon as the vetting phase of the show is completed—when every piece must be shown to a committee of industry experts for preevaluation—the metaphorical sheet begins to lift. That means there is always the possibility that more than one of the early ticket holders will arrive with their sights set on the same object. Then, too, sharp-eyed collectors have been known to spend large sums on impulse because they feel confident knowing the objects have all passed muster with the various vetting committees. (A few years ago, a prominent Midwest collector dropped $115,000 on a gate-leg table in my booth within a few minutes of seeing it for the first time at the opening.) But nothing is ever a certainty in the world of antiques, which is why Bob Fileti carefully guarded his place at the head of the line.

It must have been late October of the previous year that I received a phone call from Daniel Putnam Brown, Jr., a furniture scholar and occasional collector, whom everyone calls "Put." Put called because he wanted my advice about an important Newport tea table that was then on loan to the Yale University Art Gallery in New Haven, Connecticut—at least Put thought it was important, for lately the table's authenticity had come under some dispute. The table, he explained, had been bequeathed to some friends of his—two brothers and a sister—by their mother, who died in 1992.

When the three had initially inherited the piece, it had been evaluated for estate purposes at $250,000. Presently, Put explained, the trio was exploring the possibility of permanently transferring the table to Yale as a combined gift and purchase. (A below-market sale would accomplish a number of objectives: It would allow the three to recoup the original estate taxes, incorporate a modest appreciation, and still have the table count as a charitable gift.) Peter, the youngest of the three siblings, had gone to Yale, and he felt good about sending the tea table to his alma mater, particularly since the museum's magnificent Mabel Brady Garvan Collection is already such a draw to Americana groupies. Furthermore, the heirs wanted the table to stay in New Haven, where it had resided for so many years (they felt it would be in keeping with their mother's bequest). With all this in mind, the three owners had given Yale the right of first refusal on the table, should it ever be offered for sale.

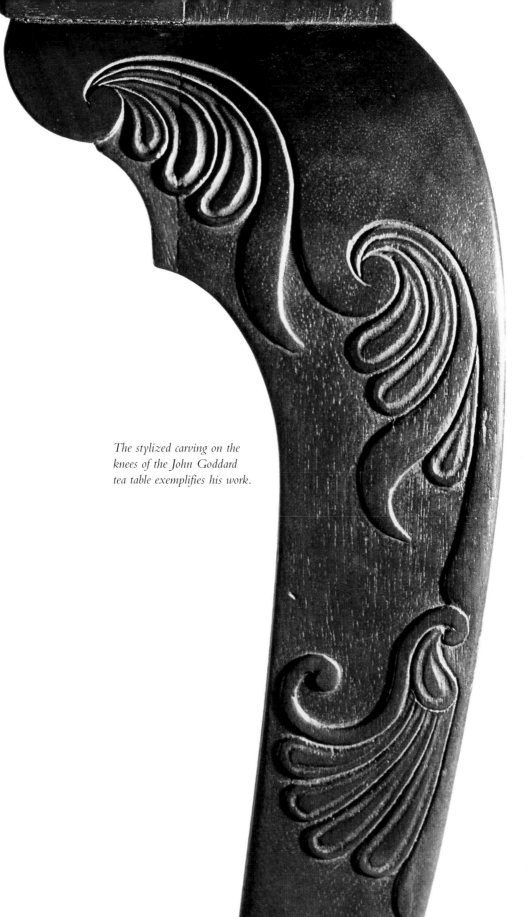

The stylized carving on the knees of the John Goddard tea table exemplifies his work.

Put thought the table was worth more than the $250,000, considering the obvious good looks of the piece and the fact that the table was attributed to the Newport master craftsman John Goddard. On the other hand, the museum's staff had told his friends rather recently that there was a possibility that the table's top was a replacement. In light of those issues, Put had advised the three that before they forever relinquished the piece, it would be wise to get a second opinion, as well as an appraisal for presentation to the university, and he suggested me for the job. He called that day to ask me to schedule an appointment with Peter, who was the designated point person with regard to the table, since he lived closest to the museum in New Haven.

Appraisal work is something that I do maybe five or six times a year. It is a good way for me to meet and nurture new clients and broaden my knowledge of what is out in the market in terms of objects and taste. You may remember that well before I purchased the Cadwalader easy chair on behalf of Richard Dietrich, I had thoroughly assessed a large portion of his private collection, as well as the holdings of the Dietrich American Foundation, which loans furniture and other objects to many institutions, including the Philadelphia Museum of Art, the State Department, and the White House. My firsthand knowledge of those objects meant that Richard's name had been first in my mind as a possible buyer for the Cadwalader easy chair. Only weeks prior to Leslie's receiving the chair, I had meticulously examined two Cadwalader side tables and a fire screen that Richard owned. That said, when Put Brown, a man whose taste I eminently respected, asked me to do an appraisal on his friends' table—particularly one that was considered strong enough to be on display at the Yale University Art Gallery—I didn't think twice about making the call.

Over the phone, Peter and I quickly made arrangements to meet up at Yale by week's end, and he was easy to spot a few days later when we met at the museum. An elegant man in his late fifties, with his tweed jacket and pleated cords, he well suited the kindly voice I had heard on the phone. Also present at our first meeting were two people from the museum's staff, Patricia Kane, the well-published head of the American Decorative Arts Department, and David Barquist, a lanky, professorial-looking man in his early forties, who is the associate curator. Together, the four of us walked to the third-floor exhibition space, where the table I was to evaluate was on display.

When I first caught a glimpse of its sculptural form against the whitewashed walls of the gallery, I was truly moved by its beauty. The spring of the table's four delicate cabriole legs, the dramatic tension of the claw-and-ball feet, and the glossy allure of its rectangular tray top were a powerful combination. The table was crafted completely of highly figured mahogany, and right off I could see that the wood used for the legs was deeper in tone than that of the sides or the top. This sort of interplay between the inherent color values in the wood was a device I had seen on other Newport furniture by the Goddards and Townsends. It gave a subtle sense of vertical lift to the piece. I glanced over at the exhibition card on the wall and noticed that the owners' three names were clearly displayed on a museum placard beneath the table. Immediately, the dealer in me wondered why someone hadn't tried to contact the family directly. The wording of the placard made it clear that the table—an obvious masterpiece—was there on loan but was not a promised gift.

In the most general terms, the tea table was similar to the one by John Goddard that I had seen in the East Hampton home of the Tillinghasts. But with the present object, the craftsman—who I never even doubted was anyone other than Goddard—had pushed the envelope of his ability many degrees further. To begin with, there was the astoundingly sculptural treatment of the table's apron, or sides. Unlike the Tillinghast piece, which had straight sides all around, this table actually featured an apron that swelled outward and inward, like waves breaking against the sand. The effect seemed to defy the very property of the wood itself. The movement was so carefully choreographed that even the brilliant striations in the mahogany grain had been selected to enhance this visual effect. The craftsman even went one step further by carrying the contours of the rolled sides through to the top and its molding. Dished (or hewn)

from a single one-inch-thick board of mahogany, the top's fluid edge was the table's ultimate declaration of restrained opulence. The graphic simplicity of the molded edge itself brought the entire movement to vivid conclusion. This was the only Newport tea table that I had ever seen with such a simple edge. Usually, the rim is devised with a series of subrims, or steps, that descend from the uppermost part of the edge down into the table's flat top.

As I stood marveling at these details, Pat Kane interrupted my thoughts to offer the use of a well-equipped studio next to the gallery to examine the piece more carefully. Within minutes, the table was lying upended on a blanket-draped table (looking somewhat like a beetle trapped on its back), with a couple of high-beam spotlights trained on its frame. Even in this unflattering position, with the swirled reddish surface of the dense mahogany top now buried against the blanket, the table continued to dazzle. Now I was literally on an eye level with the overturned claw feet, and their animalistic beauty electrified me. Goddard had not only left space at the bend of the talons at the bottom of each ball (as he had on the Tillinghast tea table) but also opened the space at the top of each ball. You could actually see daylight between them.

The rich grain of the solid mahogany skirt enhances the table's undulant form.

*The remarkable foot carving includes
open talons and—most incredibly—
a space above the ball.*

I had seen the cabinetmaker attempt such a scheme only a few times before—on, for example, a wonderful card table at the Metropolitan Museum of Art, and on a marble-top slab table that had been used as an altar at the Cathedral of St. John in Providence before it sold at Sotheby's in June 1986 to the heiress Doris Duke. (It was the only visit that Leslie had ever been on where the consignor was a man of the cloth. And before he could offer the table at auction, it had to be deconsecrated by the Bishop of Rhode Island.)

I turned to my client and the two curators and remarked that out of the six other tea tables of this type that I knew of in either private or public hands (five by Goddard and one by John Townsend that was owned by George and Linda Kaufman), I couldn't name one that attempted this ambitious feature. Pat mentioned that she knew of one other table, which she had never seen firsthand (to her knowledge, its picture had never been published), owned by the Rhode Island Historical Society. Apparently, the table had been willed to that society's John Brown House by a local family, but ever since its arrival in the early 1980s, there had been issues as to its authenticity. I was amazed by her news of another Goddard tea table, and I immediately made a mental note to follow up on the object.

Pat paused for a moment, glanced kindly at the owner of the present table, and then mentioned the fact that, recently, issues had been raised about its authenticity, as well. A large part of that confusion, she said, was rooted in the fact that there simply wasn't another known table by Goddard that was quite like it. There was, for example, the clean, uncomplicated rendering of the table's edge (which I had already noticed and, in fact, admired). And there was also the fact that the craftsman had left space above the ball of each foot (again a characteristic that I had viewed positively). A third issue that she mentioned was a faint reddish stain that appeared to cover the underside of the top. I had noticed the stain as soon as we had overturned the table in the small studio, but because furniture analysis is a methodical process (and so many other aspects of the table on first sight rang true), I had decided to hold off assessing the stain until I had carefully gone over the rest of the piece.

Now it was my turn to glance kindly at Peter. He appeared unfazed by Pat Kane's words, but at that moment, I was struck by the fact that, to him, the whole evaluation process must feel very much like a doctor's exam. He just wanted some expert to tell him the truth about the table. I moved forward with my examination with even greater vigor. Although I always temper my analysis of any object with a hefty dose of caution, I wanted the beautiful object before me to be proven authentic because, quite frankly, it had already struck a chord. I took note of the fact that the bottoms of the feet were slightly hollowed at the center, as if to receive a caster. All four displayed a hole configuration (with three screw holes centering the central caster post), as well as tool marks and an even wood tone that suggested wheels had been original to the design. This was not surprising, given the fact that tea tables were designed to facilitate entertaining with grace and efficiency. Raised on small metal casters, the piece could easily be drawn before a couch for tea, or pushed to the side when not in use.

I repositioned a spotlight so that its beam hit one of the table's upended cabriole legs

A detail of the table's underside shows replaced glue blocks. Note the finished backsides of the two knee brackets (top), typical of Goddard's work.

just where the knee began to swell outward from the top. The white rays bounced off the wood's velvety finish, highlighting a neat arrangement of stylized intaglio leaf carving that symmetrically covered the two outer sides of the squared leg. The pattern was similar to the one I had seen on the legs of the Tillinghast high chest (which had, in turn, reminded me of the carving on Jabez Bowen's tea table at Winterthur). Here, however, the carver had widened the spacing among the three leaves, a detail that enhanced the design's inherent sense of weightlessness. Their fluid shapes appeared to cascade freely downward, in perfect harmony with the leg itself.

I walked around the table and examined the carving on each leg. On one of the knee brackets, which both decoratively and structurally bound the uppermost part of the leg to the skirt rail, I detected a slight irregularity in the carving, as if the carver's tool had momentarily strayed from its path. I could imagine his exasperation when, having already glued the bracket in place and shaped the volute (or scroll-like formation that curved along its inner edge), his chisel slipped ever so slightly. Since the decorative leaf pattern bridged the seam where the bracket met the leg stock, it would have been agonizingly difficult for him to replace the bracket to correct this small imperfection. Instead, he probably heaved a sigh, shook his head, and continued on with his painstaking work.

Still, to reassure myself that the bracket was original to the piece and not a later replacement part, I peered into the dark pocket that formed on the inside of each leg where the skirt's side rails converged. The wood tone and oxidation looked consistent among the parts. Furthermore, the tool markings on the back of the bracket were identical to those seen on the table's other brackets. Although hidden from view and never meant to be seen, all were sanded smooth. It was the sort of fastidious attention to detail that is typical of the best Newport work and is rarely seen on furniture from other cities.

Now that I had positively reviewed the outer show surface and the carving, I was finally ready to assess the smoking gun, so to speak—the faint reddish stain that covered the underside of the top and had triggered concern from the staff at Yale. To begin with, the light-handed application of the wash was far different in nature from the well-saturated red stain that had forever masked the original surface of the refurbished Lannuier side tables sold by Leslie a few years back. Instead, it appeared to be the sort of wash—called pinking—that eighteenth-century cabinetmakers sometimes used in an effort to "sanitize" the wood to protect it from insects—much like the thin layer of wax that had been applied to the interior surfaces of the *églomisé* secretary found in Argentina. The color had been applied in a flagrant, slapdash manner, atypical of a faker's work, and several large patches of the mahogany underside had been missed. As expected, the wood in those areas left exposed to the air had oxidized to a dark chestnut brown tone. Nonetheless, staining and overpainting are the classic tools of a forger because they can help mask or disguise added sections of wood.

It was clear from the concerned looks of the two curators standing next to me that there had been some lively debates as to the nature of that stain. If the top was not original, then the $250,000 value that had been assigned to it a few years previously

*A bird's-eye view of the table's top shows
the shaped edge carved from a solid plank.*

The table's
underside prior to
removing the top.

The oblong, light-colored witness marks from
the now-lost original glue blocks are revealed
when the top is removed.

was probably right on target, but if the top was original and true, then that figure could be off by millions. I think it is critical for great pieces of American furniture to remain accessible to the public in museum collections, where they can be admired and studied. That said, I nevertheless strongly suspected that if I could prove beyond a shadow of a doubt that the table before me was completely authentic, then the fair-market value, even with a significant gift component, would take it way out of the range of Yale's acquisition budget. If that were to happen, it would be a great loss for the museum, which I knew did not own an example of comparable design.

Witness marks from glue blocks past and present match between the top and inner skirt.

So it was with considerable gravity that I moved in closer to examine the treatment of the underside more carefully. I noticed that the wash had been applied when the table still carried its now-missing original glue blocks (the small rectangular-shaped pieces of wood used to secure the juncture where the table's top meets the sides). A few of those blocks had been replaced with obvious machine-cut twentieth-century versions. This didn't concern me, because changing the glue blocks on a table is rather like changing the tires on a vintage auto—it doesn't detract from the overall importance or value of the piece.

What did interest me, however, was that the rectangular patches of exposed wood left by the missing glue blocks on the underside of the top and the marks along the upper inside of the skirt exactly corresponded in their placement. All the markings were significantly lighter in color than the wood around them because, having been protected from the air for so long, they had oxidized at a slower rate. Like the shadows left behind when the original brass mounts were removed from the Gibbs bureau (or the ormolu mounts were examined on the Lannuier pier tables in Milan), these witness marks, as they are called, helped me place the stain in the time line of the piece. Their appearance made it clear that the wash had been applied very early in the life span of the table, when the first set of glue blocks was still new and in place.

It was then that I noticed beneath the wash, a chalk inscription O on the inner side of the skirt rail on one end of the table and a corresponding O drawn by the same hand on the underside of the top, just near the juncture of that rail. There was no doubt in my mind that these were the original markings used by the cabinetmaker to align the top with the bottom when he assembled the table in his shop. Whenever I uncover original layout marks such as these, I am thrilled, because, like the irregularity in the leg bracket I had spotted earlier, they furnish the form with a history of its creation. I turned toward Peter, who had been quietly observing me as I bent over the piece, and asked if the table bore any significant history in his family. Peter's face brightened noticeably at the query and he began to tell me all that he knew. Given the details he provided, it was instantly clear that he and his siblings all took a lively interest in their family's history.

Sometime before 1959, Peter said, his mother bought the piece for somewhere in the range of five hundred to five thousand dollars (neither he nor his siblings could remember the exact amount) from her brother, who had inherited the table from their father a few years earlier. The family could trace their roots back to a New Haven sea captain named Buckminster Brintnall (c. 1731–1789), who was traditionally thought to be the table's first owner. Peter and his siblings had spent time researching the estate inventories of his ancestors in the Connecticut State Archives, among other places, and had found a number of references (such as an 1850 inventory that listed "(1) mahog. table. Old—$5.00" and another one dating to 1928 that named "the mahogany table with claw feet"), all of which he believed referred to the object before us that day.

Peter said that he and his siblings long remembered Captain Brintnall's table standing in the living room of their childhood home. Then, sometime in the 1970s, a young neighbor, who happened to be studying American decorative arts at Winterthur, stopped in for a visit. When she spotted the table (as Peter recalled, it sat next to his mother's couch perhaps a little too close to the fireplace), she excitedly told the family that it was a rare Newport piece. She said that the Delaware-based museum owned a nearly identical example (the Jabez Bowen table), which was a star of the museum's collection.

In time, Peter's parents made a pilgrimage to Winterthur to see Jabez Bowen's former tea table and returned to Connecticut satisfied, in his words, "that their piece was even more beautiful and alive than the Winterthur example." Thereafter, whenever parties were thrown, the table was moved to an upstairs room for safekeeping. When Peter and his siblings learned that their mother had left them equal partnership in the table—obviously a difficult thing to share—they decided to place it on loan at Yale.

I was enthralled by Peter's story and thought the extended family provenance added yet another layer of history to what I already viewed as a historic piece. I gave the table a last hard look and turned to leave. Once outside the museum, Peter and I spoke briefly and I promised to get back to him with a written assessment of the piece within a week or so. "It's an important table," I reassured him as we parted, although I did not elaborate any further.

Days later, I was putting the finishing touches on that report, which took up an astonishing nine pages. I could not stop writing about the piece, wanting to cover everything from the singular eloquence of the table's design to a detailed comparison of the object with the five other known tables by Goddard (inclusive of the tool work, wood quality, and oxidation evidence). All that remained was the value of the table—an issue that I had turned over in my head again and again, ever since I left it behind in New Haven. What dollar amount could I assign to this object, which I viewed as an unquestionable masterpiece?

The last Goddard tea table to enter the market was the Tillinghast one, which I had sold, but that had been nearly a decade earlier, and to compare that table to this one was like measuring apples against oranges (so dramatically different were the two in overall appearance). Furthermore, the market in general had surged significantly since that time. To my knowledge, the only other Goddard tea table of similar design to come to auction in the past century was the Jabez Bowen table at Winterthur. When Henry du Pont bought that table for $29,000 in 1930, it was the third-most-expensive piece of American furniture ever sold. (To help put that figure in perspective, realize that in 1930, the average annual per capita income in the United States was approximately $750 and that a Duesenberg SJ, by far the grandest car of the era, was priced in the neighborhood of $25,000.) Other than that, the tea table form had come up privately only once, in 1984, when George and Linda Kaufman bought the John Townsend example from the Sacks for $675,000. My determinations also led me to think of the Nicholas Brown secretary that Israel Sack, Inc., had bought for $12.1 million in 1989, and even of the Philadelphia tea table that I had purchased at the Eddy Nicholson sale for just under $2.5 million in 1995. In truth, there was scant material for me to draw upon, which is why, more than anything, I had to go with my gut instincts about the value of this unique object before settling on a final number.

Once I calculated that figure, I thought it would be wise to prepare the owners for my conclusions, rather than send them the report without preface, so I gave Peter a call. When I reached him, I briefly explained that I had completed my evaluation and that I thought he would enjoy reading it. I told him that regardless of the table's earlier analysis, I would stake my reputation on what I thought the table's true value should be. My heart began to race as I led up to the climax of my call. I felt as if I were about to tell Peter that he and his siblings had won the lottery. All that was missing was the drumroll. "Are you sitting down?" I asked.

"Yes. Why?" Peter asked cautiously.

I took a deep breath and continued. "Given the exquisite level of craftsmanship and absolute rarity of the table, not to mention its wonderful provenance, I feel comfortable valuing your table at three and a half million dollars."

My excited announcement was greeted with complete silence.

"Hello?" I said nervously.

"I'm still here, Leigh," Peter said softly before pausing to clear his throat. "Well, you've certainly gotten my attention."

To lessen the obvious shock of the moment and to allow my client to collect himself, I began speaking about the piece in the broadest, most conversational of tones. It was clear, though, that he needed to confer with his sister, who lived in London, and his brother in Massachusetts right away, so within a few minutes, we hung up.

I leaned back in my chair and gazed out my shop window in a moment of reverie. Just outside the plate-glass pane, there was a large American flag hanging from a brass pole that projected from the building's facade. As I watched that flag flapping about in the cold autumn wind, I remembered a day back in 1994, when I first moved to my current gallery space. Dad had stopped by to see the new shop and had commented on the close proximity of the flag. He liked the idea that I had staked a spot on the site of the old Parke Bernet building—a place that had symbolized so much to Leslie and me when we were young—with that patriotic banner flying so close by. At the time, busy with the work at hand, I had brushed away Dad's comment with a nod, but now, for some reason, I was touched by the memory. I thought about the table I had just appraised and of how that single object, made as our nation stood on the brink of independence, was about to affect the lives of its current owners, all descendants of a Colonial sea captain. I probably shook my head to break away from those cornball thoughts, but for days to come, I continued to wonder what action the table's three owners would ultimately take.

Nearly two weeks later, Peter called to say that he and his siblings were still wrestling with the future of the piece. "At the previous appraisal of two hundred and fifty thousand dollars, we felt comfortable donating the table to the museum, which we consider a worthy cause," he explained. "But at this new level, I think we have to look at other possibilities." Clearly, my speculation at Yale as to the table's future had not been unfounded.

Then Peter asked, "Would you be interested in finding a good home for it, Leigh, should we choose to take that course?"

"Absolutely," I replied. "I could find it a very good home."

"And can you really find a buyer at the price you've named?" he asked.

"Absolutely," I firmly repeated as I began to scroll through a mental checklist of possible clients.

Peter took that promise back to his family. When he called back, he reminded me that I had mentioned an upcoming trip to London. "Would you be able to stop in and see my sister while you are there?" he asked.

Understandably, his sister, who had been living in London since the 1950s, was feeling too far removed from the process to make a final decision about this family heirloom. So on a mid-November afternoon, less than a week after that call, I found myself climbing the steps to the elegant Chelsea town house that she shared with her husband, a British writer.

My hostess, an animated, chicly dressed woman, whose well-drawn features closely resembled those of her brother, greeted me at the door. We were still in the process of exchanging our introductions when I noticed, not ten feet away, a small, cherry-wood dressing table with a scallop top (the front and side edges were cut in a series of repetitive cyma, or wave-shaped curves) and cabriole legs that was clearly a Colonial American work. Immediately, I recognized the table as a Connecticut River Valley piece, probably made in or near the town of Wethersfield during the mid- to late-eighteenth century and probably worth upward of $200,000. Not wanting to seem like an overbearing New York dealer, I remarked upon its beauty, suggested its potential value, and then followed her into her warm, pleasant living room. There we were joined by her husband and spent a few good hours discussing her family's history and the Newport table.

At week's end, I was back in my New York office, awaiting the arrival of the table from Yale. I had passed the sister's inspection and the Brintnall tea table was mine to sell on consignment. I was ecstatic and had already decided I would take it to the Winter Antiques Show at the Armory. Over and over in my mind's eye, I pictured the table front and center in my booth. For a short while, I even toyed with the idea of making the table the only thing in my booth. That's how magnificent it was.

When the table arrived near day's end, I immediately secreted it under a blanket in my interior office so that it would remain shielded from the buying public until the show. It was virtually impossible for me to do any work, however, knowing that this animal of a piece was sitting beside me. All I wanted to do was stare at it, so as soon as my assistants had left for the night and the shop had grown soothingly quiet, I cleared the blanket off the table and began to go over it again.

As I moved deeper into my reexamination of the piece, I found myself becoming transfixed again by the consistency and quality of that red stain. Now that I was in the quiet confines of my shop, I decided that it might be wise to remove the top to find out if the stain continued on to the side rails. If the color also appeared on the rails, then it would further support the notion that the wash was old and honestly applied; after all, the authenticity of the skirt had never been questioned. As cochairman of the vetting committees for the show that year, I knew the type of scrutiny the table was sure to undergo (of course I would excuse myself from evaluating any of the pieces in my booth), and I wanted to be able to address any questions that were raised.

Carefully, I removed the top from the base by releasing the few screws that anchored it to the table's skirt. Then I laid the top, back side up, on the floor and set the table's frame down next to it on one of its two longer side rails. Now I could compare the inner wood of that longer rail with the wood of the top. I raked a strong light evenly across the two boards. I saw there in the sharp beam what I was looking for—color applied to both the inside of the side rail and the underside of the top. I made the same comparison against the other three rails, and by the time I had worked my way around the table, I was more certain than ever that the color was as old as it was honest. It had definitely not been brushed on to mask the marriage of a newer top with an older frame, as earlier appraisers had once suggested. Furthermore, with the top now removed, I could see that the four original screws and their corresponding holes aligned exactly. There were no extraneous holes on the top or frame left by a later alteration.

By the time I rejoined the top with the base, I was more convinced than ever of the authenticity of this extraordinary piece, for which there seemed to be no exact precedent. So imagine my surprise the next morning, while browsing through a new book by cabinetmaker Jeffrey P. Greene called *American Furniture of the 18th Century,* when I came across a photograph of a table that looked to be identical to the Brintnall piece. (I like books by cabinetmakers because they often use exploded views or diagrams of the furniture to explain construction techniques.) To my great excitement, the table featured a top handled identically to the one on the Brintnall example and also featured claw-and-ball feet with openings above the balls—two of the key issues raised by the curators at Yale. From the caption, I learned that the table pictured was the one from the John Brown House in Providence—the one that Pat Kane had mentioned to me but which she had never seen.

Knowing that Pat had intimated that there had been issues in the past as to the authenticity of the table in Providence, I called Linda Eppich, the curator at the John Brown House, to learn more about the piece directly. The next day, I flew up to Providence to meet with her and see the table for myself. It was then that I discovered that the table bore a line of descent in the Herreshoff-Sperry family, the members of which were the direct descendants of the wealthy Providence merchant John Brown (1736–1803) and generous donors to the Rhode Island Historical Society. For the piece to have a Herreshoff provenance was spectacular, because some of the most important and best-preserved Goddard-Townsend objects known had descended in that family. It made me curious to learn what kind of problems the table allegedly had.

As it turned out, those "problems" really had to do with the learning curve of furniture research. There simply hadn't been enough information available to the curatorial staff when the table was evaluated in 1983 (initially, they thought it was a *nineteenth-century* piece). Just like the Brintnall example at Yale, this table had been misunderstood because there was nothing else exactly like it known. The existence of the Herreshoff-Sperry piece, recently authenticated as a John Goddard piece, bolstered the strength of the Brintnall table because it supplied the type of stylistic comparison upon which American furniture research thrives. In that way, the rediscovery of each table helped confirm the authenticity of the other.

Needless to say, my spirits were high as the show date loomed. I knew that an object this masterful would always sell—it was simply too rare and special to remain in limbo for long. But given the table's hefty price tag, I knew it would be smart to introduce the piece discretely to at least one key player before it went to the Armory, just to boost the odds. The collector I ended up contacting was someone who, I knew, had for years yearned to find a superb Newport tea table—a person, who, in my opinion, would be prepared to go all the way. One evening, we clocked a number of hours with the piece, surrounded by what amounted to a virtual picture gallery of related examples, because he was the type of client who thrived on that sort of careful form-by-form comparison.

I had just ushered him out of the gallery at the end of our session, having received his assurance that he would in all probability make every attempt to be first in my booth on opening night, or send someone else in his stead. I had just returned the tea table to its hiding place beneath a blanket in my inner office when the phone rang. It was Leslie. He and Albert Sack had just had a drink across the street at the Carlyle Hotel. He wanted to know if they could stop by.

"Come on over," I said.

Minutes later, I welcomed them in with a bottle of Scotch and some eighteenth-century port glasses. As I poured the liquor all around, I realized that Leslie was trying to signal me. He pointed his head toward the double wood doors of my office. Being a twin, I instantly knew the message he was trying to convey. Leslie wanted me to show Albert the Newport tea table, which he assumed was hidden in my office.

Now, Albert may be a professional rival, but he is first and foremost a friend, not to mention a legend in the field, one whose love of Americana knows no bounds. Leslie was right: It would be a shame for him to leave my shop, never knowing he had been feet away from that incredible piece.

"Albert," I said, as he settled into a large eighteenth-century Boston easy chair, "I want to show you something."

I walked into my office and returned a minute later grasping the table with both hands, then set it upon the carpeted floor in front of Albert. Leslie and I then stood to the side (both grinning from ear to ear) and watched Albert assess the table from his seat. Starting at the gleaming top, he worked his way from the sinuous edge to the wavy skirt and down to the powerful legs and feet. "Well now," he said in a low, deep voice, "that's incredible."

Within a few days, though, I was finally able to take the Brintnall tea table officially out of hiding and present it to the public at large in my booth at the Winter Antiques Show. Although I couldn't really fulfill my fantasy of showing the table solo— imagine how disconcerted potential customers would be by a single object for sale with a price tag in the range of $4 million—I had surrounded the piece with a variety of objects that were beautiful in their own right.

The Britnall tea table on display at the 1998 New York Winter Antiques Show.

There was, for example, an outstanding early Philadelphia rococo tall-case clock that stood just under ten feet in height—nearly the farthest depth of a swimming pool—which had already generated a buzz because I had advertised it in *The Magazine Antiques.* Every year, I have the first booth to the right of the entrance to the show. My close proximity to the gate means that as the opening hour nears, I am keenly aware of the growing buzz out in the hall of buyers waiting to enter.

A few minutes after four o'clock, a pair of security guards ushered the swelling crowd into a large room, satellite to the show space, replete with windows designed by Louis Comfort Tiffany. Here, champagne and hors d'oeuvres were being served before the event's official 4:30 start. Bob Fileti, the mild-mannered furniture conservator, who had been standing patiently at the head of that group on behalf of my client, was first to enter that room. He stopped momentarily to grab a drink, bypassed the food, and then stationed himself near a doorway on the far side of the room that was cordoned off by a velvet rope. There he remained for the next half hour, until the crimson cord was lifted, whereupon he and the dozens behind him finally moved forward into the main exhibition space at a pace that he later described as like being in Grand Central Station during rush hour.

I had just turned to face the doors as they were thrown open at 4:30 P.M. and the well-heeled crowd of early ticket holders began to stream into the show, so it was hard to miss Bob Fileti quickly bearing down upon my booth. He had the confident look on his face of someone about to complete a job well done. Bob walked purposefully up to the tea table at the center of the booth, placed one hand upon the gleaming surface of its cool mahogany top, and turned to face me. Tapping the table lightly with his palm, Bob announced, "I'll take it."

The selling price for the table? $3.65 million.

Bob then pointed to the tall-case clock, which had a price tag of $365,000. "I'll take that, too."

The words had just left his lips when Wendy Cooper and Michael Podmaninsky, the senior curator of American Furniture and the director of conservation, respectively, at Winterthur, came briskly into the booth. They had seen my ad for the clock in *The Magazine Antiques* and were anxious to examine the piece, but as holders of the twentieth spot on the line, they were literally seconds too late.

Bob and I sealed the deal with a handshake, and as he turned to leave, I placed a red sticker on the table's description card, indicating the object had been sold. I knew that news of the sale, which instantly set an opening-night record for the show, would spread quickly across the selling floor. However, since my client wanted to remain anonymous, I was never able to answer the evening's burning question: "Who bought the table?"

Later in the evening, Yale's Pat Kane, who was also in attendance that night, stopped by my booth to visit her former charge. Silently, she regarded the table, which dazzled in the glare of the hot exhibition lights. "Doesn't it look great?" I said to her gently.

"It's quite a piece," she replied softly, nodding her head. "It will be missed."

11

Double Take

IT WAS A FAIRLY TYPICAL MONDAY MORNING in the American Furniture Department at Sotheby's in early October 1998. The phones were reawakening after the quiet of the weekend, a few pieces of furniture had just arrived to be photographed for an upcoming catalog, and the all-important mail (the lifeblood of the department) had already been distributed. I was sitting in my office scanning some catalog proofs when John Nye, the young, smart, mild-mannered, and invariably bow-tied senior cataloger for the department, walked in holding a photograph.

"Leslie, you've got to take a look at this table!" John is rarely given to histrionics, so when I heard the urgency in his voice, I braced myself for something truly extraordinary.

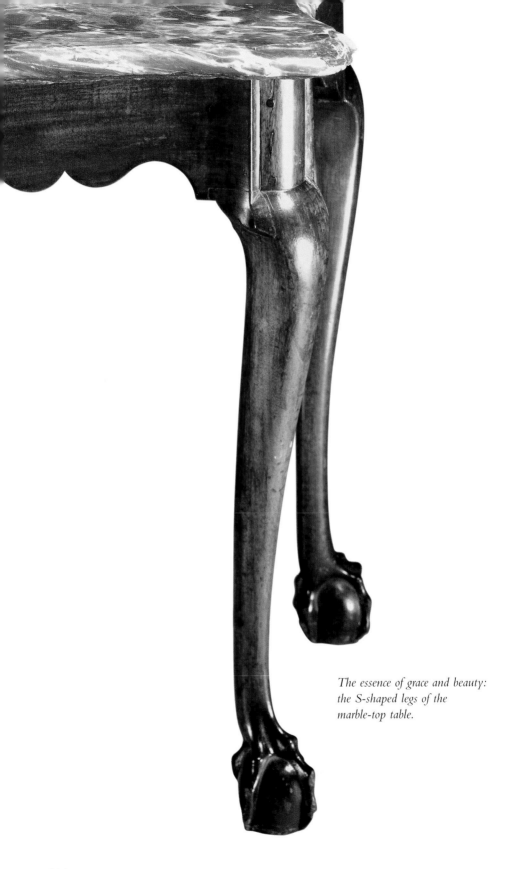

The essence of grace and beauty: the S-shaped legs of the marble-top table.

I was not disappointed. The photo he extended toward me featured a magnificent-looking pier table with a gray-veined white marble slab top and a trim mahogany cabriole-legged frame. I marveled at the understated S shape of the legs and the fluid handling of the skirt, which was edged in a rippling pattern of cyma and ogee curves on three of the table's four sides. The powerful claws that gripped the round ball feet were formal and stylized—utterly in keeping with the cool beauty of the entire form. The mahogany frame was so gracefully rendered, it seemed to belie the fact that it was designed to support the massive weight of the solid marble top (which, judging from the size of the slab, easily weighed close to two hundred pounds). Based upon the distinctive shape of the skirt and treatment of the legs, I thought the table was probably made in Boston around 1755.

"This is fantastic," I said to John. "What's the story?"

"I just got off the phone with the owner," John replied. "He's a San Francisco–based antiques dealer. I think his specialty is estate jewelry and silver—things like that—but definitely not furniture. He found the table in a consignment shop, suspected it might be American, and wanted to know if it might be *worthy* of one of our sales."

"*Worthy*," I said to John. "We'd put it on the cover!"

"No kidding," he replied. "Out of curiosity, I asked him what he thought the table might bring at auction, but he really didn't want to answer. Finally, I said to him, 'I can see that you're not going to name a figure.' Only then did he reluctantly say, 'Well, I guess about thirty thousand dollars—maybe fifty thousand on a good day.'"

"So what did you tell him?"

"I said that it could be worth more than twenty times that," John replied. "Then, after some considerable silence, he asked me how I could be so sure."

John had then explained to the man that even from a photograph—and a poor one at that—it was easy to see the electrifying beauty of the form. "When you see something by a master craftsman, it just sings out," he had said. "You get a hunch, a feeling—it's nothing that can be calibrated."

I nodded in agreement. People often find it hard to understand that appraisers can glean so much information from a handful of photographs. They forget that our days are often spent looking at furniture and saying, "This is a fake" or "That has been repaired." Over time, we've developed a sixth sense about such matters. Furthermore, the sheer volume of inquiries received by Sotheby's—or even a private dealer such as Leigh—from far-flung corners of the country makes it impossible for us to visit every object. We had better be skilled at reading photographs; otherwise, we'd constantly risk losing objects to competitors.

Of course, when a truly great piece such as the slab table reveals itself, it is vital that we see it firsthand and promptly attempt to establish a rapport with the owners so they'd feel comfortable about consigning it to Sotheby's. I knew that by fortunate coincidence, John was already scheduled to fly to San Francisco within two days' time to give a talk to a local branch of the Daughters of the American Revolution, so it would be easy for him to arrange a visit with the table's owner.

"I already have an appointment scheduled for Thursday," he told me with a grin as he turned to leave my office.

After a day of anxious waiting, I finally received a call from John, just through with his visit, who had this to report: Robert Backlund, the table's owner, lived in a 1960s ranch-style house perched on a steep hilltop overlooking San Francisco Bay. The living room was furnished with mostly nondescript contemporary pieces, except for a couple of baroque-looking side chairs missing their seats, a pair that Backlund also wanted John to examine (they turned out to be New England in origin, heavily repaired, and worth no more than the few hundred dollars he had paid for them), and, of course, the extraordinary slab table tucked in a corner next to the sofa.

"When I first saw the table, my jaw nearly hit the ground," John said to me over the phone. "It just seemed so out of place—and it was such an absolute knockout, completely honest. I never had any doubts about it."

Still, John had a job to do, so with the help of the owner, a heavyset silver-haired man in his early fifties, he removed the table's heavy marble top and leaned it against the sofa. Then, because the light in the living room was not ideal for viewing furniture, he carried the mahogany frame out onto the sun-drenched deck.

"I probably spent half an hour going over the piece," he reported, "to be reassured that it was as good as I first believed." John didn't need to look beyond the table's surface for confirmation: The mahogany wood boasted an exceptional swirled grain that was predominantly deep purplish brown, enlivened by reddish undertones that simmered beneath the surface like molten lava. The cabinetmaker had expertly used the figured wood to enhance dramatically the serpentine, convex swell of the table's front rail.

The table's old finish was, of course, another plus. As expected, dirt and grime had settled in all its nooks and crannies, including the crevices above the serpentine corners of the frieze, the swelled knees, and the furrows surrounding the ankles and jointed talons. There was, however, a faint glossiness to the wood, indicating that at some point in the table's history—possibly in the nineteenth century—it had been treated with a thin coat of shellac or varnish, which had settled in the table's original finish. But enough time had passed since the application of that once-shiny coating that it had begun to develop a crackled, dark patina of its own, evoking the canvas of an old master painting. (If the sealant had been applied in the twentieth century and had had less time to mellow and age, the surface value would have been brash and far less compelling.

While John examined the table, Backlund filled him in on some of the details of its discovery in the consignment shop. He said the place had been filled with some terrific things and that he had nearly purchased a tall baroque cabinet before homing in on the slab table. While he was studying the piece, he learned from the woman who oversaw the place that most of the furniture had been evaluated by an outside appraiser. That appraiser had deemed the table a nineteenth-century English piece with a replaced marble top and had valued it at $4,500—a price that was later reduced to $1,500 because one of the leg joints was slightly loose and the back of the marble slab had sustained some minor damage.

The consignment shop.   *The table in Robert Backlund's living room.*

John shook his head in disbelief. "So you paid almost nothing for it?" he said incredulously.

"Well, not exactly nothing," Backlund replied. "But at first, my name was simply placed on a waiting list, because two other people had placed holds on the piece. For whatever reason, those folks decided not to buy it, so the shop gave me a call."

Toward the end of John's visit, the table's owner announced that he was prepared to consign the piece to Sotheby's. Right there in the living room, he signed the contract John had brought along with him. But minutes later, while he and John were saying their good-byes out in the driveway, Backlund said quite casually, "I think I'd better call Christie's."

John was momentarily flustered. "But we just shook hands and you happily signed a contract."

"No, no, not like that," the consignor said quickly, seeking to allay John's fears. "You see, in addition to Sotheby's, I also sent pictures of the table to Christie's. I think I should call them and let them know that the piece has been accounted for."

John relaxed. "Don't worry, they'll call you," he said with a smile. "Believe me, when they open your letter and see the pictures, they'll call you."

Five days later, the marble-top table had been crated and shipped to Sotheby's vast warehouse in New York, where I went to see it almost immediately. It was easy to spot amid the shadowy maze of mahogany, walnut, and maple furnishings that always piles up before our January sales. Despite the harsh, uneven lights of the warehouse, the blue-gray marble was luminous. It was not hard to imagine the table standing against the wall of a mid-eighteenth-century Boston parlor, perhaps richly appointed with silver or glassware or laden with platters brimming with savory foods. (Like its predecessor, the slate-top table, marble-top tables were commonly used as servers or sideboards because the stone was nearly impervious to heat and spills.) Since marble was expensive and hard to come by in Colonial New England, it was sometimes the well-connected merchant who commissioned the table—rather than the cabinet-maker—who found the stone. Once the marble was selected, it was submitted to a stonecutter for shaping.

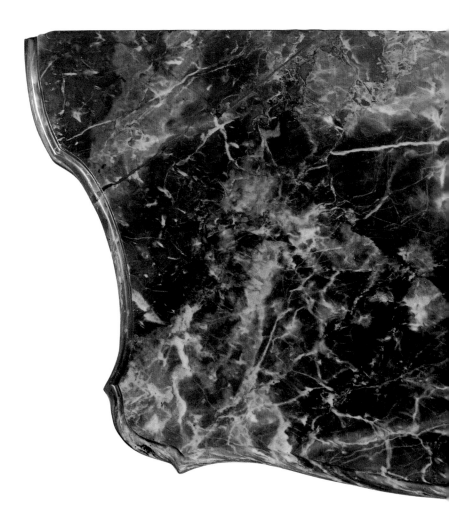

Whoever had cut the marble on the table in the Sotheby's warehouse had done a perfect job of matching the serpentine contours of the base (which curved in at the sides and swelled out at the front) to the top. The overall movement also worked in perfect concert with the profiled series of S curves marking the lower edge of the table's front rail. I had seen that same scalloped pattern on the skirts of many Boston tea tables and it was the reason that, when I had initially eyeballed the piece, I thought it was made in Boston. The treatment of the claw-and-ball feet—with ovoid balls that were wider than they were tall, clutched by talons that raked back slightly—was also typical of Boston furniture of that period. A quick glance beneath the top revealed some more Boston features, including the choice of secondary woods. There were two white-pine corner blocks at the top of each leg (used to brace the sides), while the rear rail was made of maple, rather than of expensive mahogany (since it was meant to remain out of sight, against a wall).

Not long after my visit to the warehouse, John received a phone call from Robert Backlund. "You were right," he said. "The folks at Christie's did get back to me. They told me that my table was an exact mate to one that they'd sold in the Joynt sale in 1990."

"The Joynt sale, really?" John said, immediately turning in his chair to grab a copy

of the catalog off a nearby bookshelf. Howard and May Joynt were two well-known Americana collectors, and they had spent nearly fifty years filling their historic Alexandria, Virginia, town house with unique examples of seventeenth- and eighteenth-century furniture and decorative arts. Not long after Mr. Joynt's death in 1989, his wife and children sold the collection in a milestone sale at Christie's. John skimmed the catalog until he came to the image of their slab table. Its resemblance to the table stored in the Sotheby's warehouse was astounding. From the flitch (or cut) of wood displayed on the skirt to the veining in the marble, they looked to be nearly identical. It crossed his mind that the likelihood of reuniting a pair of long-separated tables of this quality was almost—though perhaps not completely—unimaginable.

When John shared this latest twist in the tale of the pier table—that there might be an exact mate—I immediately thought back to the spring of 1983, weeks after I had been made head of Sotheby's American Furniture Department. I had just decided to make a project out of combing the department's old client files for property. Very often, people query us on the value of an item but never follow up on the appraisal letter they are sent. Those letters are kept in boxed files that literally stretch back for

The shape of the table's skirt, with a central rounded pendant drop flanked by cyma curves, can be found on other Boston furniture. The raked back side talons on the feet are also typical of eastern Massachusetts.

decades. From my perspective, that meant that each file contained valuable leads to hidden treasures around the country. Perhaps a gentle, friendly follow-up call would result in a fresh consignment, I thought. Sometimes, I'd stay at my desk late into the night, elbows deep in the files, hoping that a great piece of Americana was just moments away from being rediscovered.

One day, fairly early in this methodical process (the boxes were arranged alphabetically by owner's name, and I was no further than *C*), I opened up a folder and found a faded Polaroid of a brilliant Federal card table (probably circa 1805) sitting on the crumbling sidewalk outside of a Baltimore-area home. The table featured a folded oblong top that opened to a square baize-covered playing surface. Beneath the top was a magnificent pedestal, carved in the shape of a sharp-eyed eagle with its wings spread, crouched above a smooth half-sphere, or orb, that merged into a hairy lion's mask. Four down-curved legs with acanthus carving sprang out beneath this sculpted form, each ending in carved animal-paw feet raised on brass casters.

I loved the dramatically patriotic sentiment of the American eagle perched in dominance above that sad-faced symbol of the British monarchy. I scanned the appraisal letter, dated 1976, and saw that we had estimated the table's value at $15,000 to $25,000. But the market had grown stronger in the ensuing seven years, so I knew I could give the owner (who, according to the letter, was a minister) a stronger quote. I immediately turned to the phone, hoping that the table was still in the minister's possession.

I reached him right away and, after briefly explaining the purpose of my call, asked him, "Do you still own the table?"

The minister answered in a voice that was clearly accustomed to public speaking. "Yes. In fact, I am looking at it right now," he said.

My heart began to race, but I was determined that my voice not betray my excitement. I began my measured pitch by saying, "Sir, do you realize that the market for Americana has changed dramatically since you first wrote to us in 1976? Back then, we estimated your table in the range of twenty-five thousand dollars. Today, it could be worth somewhere in the range of eighty thousand to one hundred and twenty thousand dollars, maybe more."

No, he wasn't aware of that, he told me. Then he told me what he did know. "The table has been in my family for many generations," he said. "We're originally from New York, and we always assumed that the piece was from there, too."

"I'm thrilled to hear you say that," I told the minister, "because I'm almost certain the table was made by Duncan Phyfe, a Scottish-born cabinetmaker who worked independently in New York from around 1792 to 1847. The intricacy of the design and the quality of the carving both seem characteristic of his style. Your family history only supports that notion."

The minister and I talked for some time about the shifting market for Americana and the details of sending furniture to auction. After agreeing to give the matter some careful thought, he hung up. He called back within a few days to say that he had decided to consign the table to Sotheby's. I was ecstatic. We would sell the piece the following June.

The eagle has landed.

In late April, right before the catalog deadline, I gave the table's owner a quick courtesy call to discuss the reserve and let him know how things were progressing. As the conversation wound to a close, the consignor suddenly said, "By the way, I heard you were an identical twin."

"Yes," I said politely, although I wasn't really in the mood for yet another twin conversation.

"Well, I'm an identical twin, too," he said, jolting me out of my cynicism.

We spent a few twin-bonding moments, and then he said, "You know, Leslie, my twin owns the mate to the card table you're selling, and when the two pieces are together, the eagles appear to be looking at each other."

The adrenaline surge was instantaneous. The idea of two eagle-based card tables by Duncan Phyfe staring each other down across a doorway or window was fantastic. It

would be incredible to offer the pair at auction. I asked the minister if he thought his brother might be interested in putting his table up for auction, as well.

From his response, I sensed they were not close. "We don't see a lot of each other because he lives out west," he said. Knowing they were twins, I was saddened to hear that. (I could never imagine living on the other side of the country from Leigh—we see each other nearly every day.) Still, the minister said he would call his brother and explain the situation.

By the time the minister reached his brother, the final galleys for the June sale catalog were literally hours away from being shipped. I hate to pressure clients, but in order to capitalize upon the twin beauty of the tables—I was certain that as a pair, the value of the two would be far greater than the value of each piece separately— I needed an immediate answer. Fortunately, the brother was able to give me one.

Identical twins—long separated, at last happily reunited.

Minutes before the page proofs left my desk, I was able to alter the boldface description of the lot to reflect the change from one table to a pair.

On the day of the sale, the minister showed up, with his entire family in tow. As expected, there was a frenzy of bidding, and when the dust settled, Berry Tracy, a Goshen, New York, dealer who was bidding on behalf of the New York collectors Richard and Gloria Manney, had won the tables for $275,000. It was a record price for Federal furniture at the time, which gave the market for furniture of that era a significant boost. (Remember that in 1983, the record price for any form of American furniture was $360,000, set in 1980 for the Newport three-shell chest of drawers once owned by Mr. and Mrs. Walter B. Robb.) I remember glancing over at the minister when the hammer fell and seeing that he had tears in his eyes. Although his brother was not by his side, their identical tables had been reunited.

As John Nye compared the contours of the Joynt table to the one he had seen in San Francisco, he was beginning to rethink the strategy for selling the slab table. We started bouncing ideas off of each other. Perhaps the buyer of the Joynt table would be interested in owning a pair. Or better yet, considering the recent surge in the art market, perhaps that person would be interested in selling his or her table (which had brought, in 1990, a hammer price of $170,000). We agreed that offering the two as a pair could only enhance their desirability to top-level collectors and dealers.

To set either of these schemes in motion, we needed to track down the present owner of the Joynt table. Obviously, we couldn't call our chief competitor, Christie's, for such confidential information, so instead, I placed a call to Martin Wunsch, a savvy, eminently well-connected collector of Americana (among other things). I was pretty sure that Martin would be intrigued by the idea of helping reunite a long-separated pair of rare rococo tables.

"Give me a few days and I'll get back to you," he said once he had heard my story.

True to his word, Martin called within forty-eight hours, with this to report: "Leslie, you don't have the mate to the Joynt table in your warehouse—you *have* the Joynt table."

"*What?*" I replied, completely astonished.

"The Joynt table sold to a buyer from the West Coast," he said. "You told me the table that you have in your warehouse was found in a California consignment shop. The coincidence of finding two identical marble-top tables on the West Coast is next to impossible. It's the same piece."

Martin was right, of course. The chances of finding two identical versions of the same circa 1755 Boston slab table in California was infinitesimal (I could think of only one other pair of comparable high-style examples in existence, and that pair was now split between two separate museum collections).

But if the table in the Sotheby's warehouse was the Joynt piece, how had it ended up in a consignment shop? Could it have been stolen? A table with a two-hundred-pound top didn't sound like the obvious choice for a robber, just as a consignment shop didn't sound like the most discreet way to launder it. Still, to play it safe, John and I alerted the legal department at Sotheby's. We didn't want the auction house to be accused of trafficking in stolen property. John was the only department member who had met the consignor, but he felt quite strongly that the man was innocent of any nefarious doings. "If that piece is stolen, this guy is not the thief," he told the lawyers firmly. "It's my gut reaction, but there was no artifice in his manner. Besides, *he's* the one who initially sent me on the track of the Joynt table."

Nevertheless, a red flag had been raised, so the following week, when John and I ran into Christie's John Hays at the opening of the Ellis Memorial Antiques Show in Boston, it occurred to us that he might be able to help.

"Congratulations on the table," he said in greeting, unintentionally providing me with the perfect segue.

"John, it seems there's a possibility that the piece was stolen," I said to him carefully. "Without betraying your client, is there any way you could contact him or her and get the real story?"

John agreed to try. A day or so later, when we were back in New York, he called me with good news. "Les, you are free and clear to sell the table," he said. "It wasn't stolen. The former owner knows it's gone."

"But how did it end up in the consignment shop?" I asked, amazed that someone would choose to dispose of such a valuable object in so blasé a manner.

John was cautious in his reply. Understandably, he needed to protect his client's privacy. The little he did say, however, was astonishing. In the past year, he explained, the client had hired an interior decorator to refurbish some rooms, including the one in which the table had been placed. In order to start fresh, the decorator had cleaned out the rooms and shipped the contents to a local consignment shop.

I couldn't help myself—I asked John what kind of person could so casually give away such a costly prize (in addition to whatever else had furnished those rooms). John hinted that the client's lifestyle was lavish and complicated enough that the whole operation might have taken place without his or her knowledge. The implication was that a household manager or private secretary had been the one who gave the decorator the final okay.

So through the oversight of a busy man's (or woman's) busy employee, a table bought for $170,000 at a major New York auction house was sold at a consignment shop for $1,500 and eventually came to sit in the Sotheby's showroom (with an estimate of from $150,000 to $250,000) as one of the stars of the January sale. The table was well received by scholars, collectors, and dealers alike, although a few were curious about a faint yellow stain that was visible along the perimeter of the marble slab. Forgers have been known to mimic the effects of oxidation on marble-top tables by applying a coloring agent to the underside, so these people wanted to be assured that the stain was not created by a scam artist.

"When the old coat of shellac was originally applied to the mahogany frame, the refinisher didn't bother to remove the top because it's so heavy," John and I explained. Then we would point out the line of demarcation (visible when the top was removed) where the stone met the frame and demonstrate how the brushed-on color stopped

there. More proof as to the authenticity of the top lay in the small abrasions and wear patterns visible in the stone. The entire length of the scalloped and molded edge was covered with fine lines and small abrasions that could only have been centuries in the making. Random wear is difficult enough to fake on mahogany, but it's five times harder to produce on tough, durable marble.

Top-level buyers like Peter Brant and Albert Sack, on the other hand, had no concern whatsoever about the top's authenticity. In fact, they ended up engaging in a fierce bidding war for the piece—with Albert the eventual victor. He spent $882,500 (including buyer's premium)—and set the world auction record for both the marble-top form and for a Massachusetts table.

A few months after the sale, I was visiting a private collection out in the Bay Area. During dinner one night with a local appraiser, the conversation turned to the marble-top pier table. "You wouldn't happen to know where that consignment shop is, would you?" I asked.

"I don't know the name, but I think I can find it," the appraiser said. "It's down in Palo Alto."

I was curious to see the place, so the next morning, he and I drove out to the sunny peninsula town that is home to Stanford University. After driving around for a bit, we finally stopped at a small strip mall with a hairdresser's, a watch store, a deli, and the shop we were seeking—Judith A. Frost & Company. True to the description of the table's former owner, the shop really did have some nice antiques amid the bric-a-brac. As I quickly toured the cluttered space, I pictured him wandering toward the good

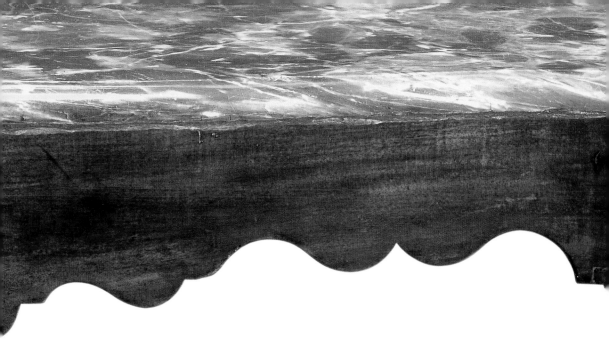

English pieces in the corner, peering at the few strong examples of nineteenth-century Chinese porcelain in the glass case by the window, and chuckling at the large assortment of playful ceramic Fiesta dinnerware from the 1950s that was stacked on a table. As he turned away, still grinning, he would have seen the magnificent pier table standing quietly in an opposite corner, perhaps smarting from its past owner's careless and sudden rejection. I let out a small chuckle, too, at the thought of his good luck, then headed toward the door. Suddenly, I noticed a lonely pamphlet lying on a small table. Its perfectly fitting title? *How to Find Antique Bargains in California.*

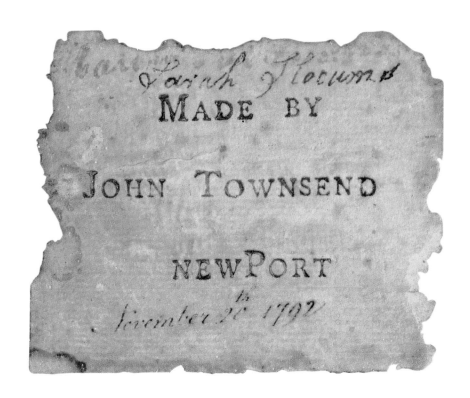

12

The Tacoma Come-On

EVERY WEEK, I SCAN THE AUCTION ADVERTISEMENTS in *Antiques and the Arts Weekly,* one of the mainstay publications of the trade, to see what's coming up for sale. Although I receive dozens of furniture catalogs a month at my shop from auction houses across the country, many of the smaller companies don't have the budget to produce catalogs and instead use illustrated ads to generate interest in their sales. On a bright mid-April afternoon in 1997, one such notice caught my eye. It announced a sale to be held in one week's time at a Tacoma, Washington, auction house called Sanford & Son. Other than the title of an early 1970s sitcom that Leslie and I had watched as kids, the name meant nothing to me; however, the content of the ad was far too compelling to ignore. It began:

To Be Sold: One Lot. The Dr. Thomas Moffatt Newport kneehole, 4 shell, desk w/John Townsend label, (c.1760); the Dr. Thomas Moffatt Newport drop leaf dining table with John Townsend label, (c. 1760); O/C, Portrait of Dr. Moffatt, (c. 1760).

Never in my wildest dreams could I have imagined a more tantalizing collection of objects grouped as a single lot: a four-shell block-front kneehole bureau table and a dining table, both by the Newport craftsman John Townsend, accompanied by an original oil-on-canvas portrait of their first owner. It sounded too good to be true. Throughout this book, Leslie and I have stressed, probably ad nauseum, the importance of the Goddards and Townsends within the realm of eighteenth-century American furniture, but of all the furniture produced by that illustrious group, the work of John Townsend (1732–1809) is probably the most revered. Invariably, his particular brand of perfectionism seems to have extended one step beyond the rigorous standards of his kinsmen (for example, the interiors of his pieces were always finished with the same attention to detail given his exterior work). He had an unerring eye for wood selection and was an exceptionally gifted carver (his deeply hewn versions of the classic large-lobed Newport shell are always breathtakingly sensuous and graceful). When my friend Morrison Heckscher, of New York's Metropolitan Museum of Art, speaks of John Townsend's work, his voice will deepen with emotion. That's the sort of effect Townsend's handicraft has on a man who is intimately familiar with great American furniture.

The ad in the paper also provided a tidy provenance for this trio of pieces, one that claimed the furniture and the painting had remained in the family of the original owner until the present day. It stated:

Dr. Moffatt, a Newport, Rhode Island resident was a "Tory-Loyalist." His house was burned to the ground in 1765. He and his family moved to Halifax, Nova Scotia, via ship, with above heirlooms. Ownership has transferred to first born son for 230 years. [All]. . . are now in Victoria, British Columbia, and will be delivered to Auction House 48 hrs. prior to sale.

Provenance doesn't get much better than that—a pure line of decent in the family of the original owner. It gave the furniture and the painting just the right aura of fresh-on-the-market appeal, which was sure to attract both top-level collectors and dealers like me.

Of the three objects for sale, I was of course most interested in the block-and-shell bureau, or kneehole desk, because it was the rarest item in the bunch. Up until then, I knew of only four documented (meaning signed or labeled) Newport bureau tables, and of that group, only one was labeled by John Townsend. In addition, I couldn't think of a single John Townsend kneehole desk that had come on the market during my professional career. That's not to say great examples of the form haven't turned up. Remember the four-shell desk Leslie found back in 1982 up near Fort Ticonderoga, New York, the one that had descended in the Gibbs family of Newport and was attributed to Edmund Townsend (first cousin to John)? When that piece sold to Harold Sack for $687,500 in early 1983, it set what was then a world record for the form.

Since then, the market has evolved considerably. The current world record for a shell-carved block-front bureau was reached in January 1996, when I paid $3.6 million on behalf of a client for another unlabeled desk by Edmund Townsend, one that was once owned by a prosperous Newport merchant, Capt. Samuel Whitehorne, Jr.

The $3.6 million Samuel Whitehorne desk by Edmund Townsend, in the Birmingham, Michigan, home of its former owners, Adolph and Ginger Meyer.

When the Whitehorne desk first came up for sale at Sotheby's (it was one of the two pieces that Leslie described to Aida Moreno of the *Antiques Roadshow*), part of my argument for convincing my client to fight so vigorously for the piece was that I believed another like it—with a wonderful grungy finish and an ironclad provenance—might never again appear on the market. Now all of a sudden, another example, this one by John Townsend, Edmund's illustrious cousin, had suddenly come to light bearing a maker's label and a great provenance. More astonishing still was the fact that it was being offered with a *labeled* dining table by Townsend, along with a period portrait of the original owner. I was getting ready to eat crow. My mind went into overdrive thinking about the ultimate price this trio of prizes could bring.

I continued to take in the contents of the ad, noticing, for example, that it also included a brief analytical sidebar describing the desk as being identical to one by Edmund Townsend in the M. and M. Karolik Collection at the Museum of Fine Arts, Boston. The text implied that perhaps the two desks were from the same shop. Immediately, I disagreed with this observation, because, to my mind, the block-and-shell bureaus of Edmund and John Townsend are markedly different. I assumed that whoever had placed the ad in the paper had a limited familiarity with eighteenth-century Newport furniture.

Next, I saw that the preview inspection for the pieces had been inconveniently restricted to a single day—the following Friday. Considering the important nature of the pieces and the potential interest they could generate (I was quite certain that across the country, other dealers like me were poring over the ad with equal fascination), I thought the lack of lead time really astonishing. When great objects come to auction, the general rule of thumb is that the longer and more thorough the preauction exposure, the stronger the final sale. Furthermore, a one-day preview was certainly not long enough. I could just imagine the scene at this small Washington State auction house when a slew of jet-lagged East Coast dealers came traipsing in on the appointed day, all demanding individual time with the furniture.

More unusual still was the fact that the ad also included a rather elaborate list of the conditions of sale. It stated that there were to be no phone bids or absentee bids and that buyers should be prepared to issue two checks: one to the auction house and another to the consignor. This, too, I chalked up to what I assumed was the inexperience of a local auction house that had unexpectedly pulled in a lot potentially worth millions. They probably didn't have the staff or even the phone lines necessary to orchestrate such a major operation.

The advertisement also included individual photographs of the furniture and painting, but they were all so dark and of such exceptionally poor quality that it was all but impossible to read any of the objects' details. The kneehole desk, for example, had been shot at an angle, which substantially diminished the impact of its design. Traditionally, a kneehole desk is photographed head-on to highlight the wonderful push and pull of the blocked facade and the bold contours of the carved shells. In the muddy photo in the paper, I could barely distinguish the rise and fall of the lobes rippling across the backs of the shells.

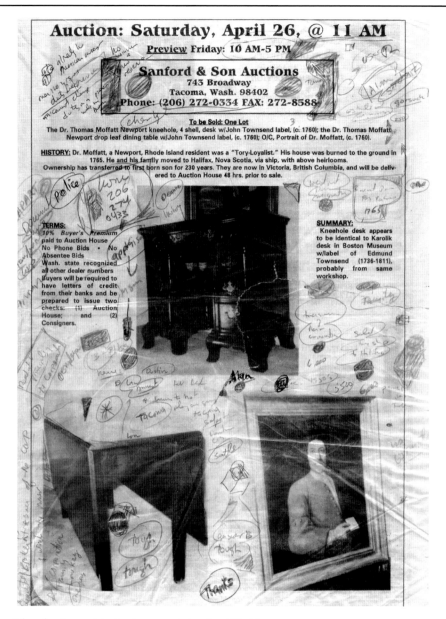

The advertisement in Antiques and the Arts Weekly.
The notes were added during the telephone call.

The photo of the dining table was just as badly staged. It had been shot from the side, with both of its hinged rectangular drop leaves turned down on either end, which left the legs barely discernible against the dark (presumably mahogany) boards. As for the portrait of Dr. Moffatt (which was of the least interest to me), it had been reproduced with the most clarity. Still, in order to learn anything about the age of the painting, I would need, among other things, to study the back of the canvas, including the stretchers (assuming they were original), for any signs of oxidation or period writing.

As soon as I was through scanning the ad, I picked up the phone to call Sanford & Son to obtain some more information. Alan Gorsuch, the owner and principal auctioneer, answered the call himself. After giving him my name and explaining my interest in the ad (Gorsuch immediately realized that I had been the buyer of record for the $3.6 million desk), I asked him if he would please send me some more detailed photos of the furniture. Astonishingly, he turned me down.

I was shocked. It was such a commonplace industry request.

When I asked Gorsuch to explain his refusal, the auctioneer said that the restriction had been placed at the seller's request.

I had never heard of such a peculiar provision. "May I just ask the logic of that?" I said. "Is there something that I am missing?"

"Those were my instructions," he replied somewhat apologetically.

I tapped my desk in annoyance. "But isn't your goal to promote the furniture as much as possible before the sale so that the pieces get seen and ultimately bring more and then you get more and the consignor gets more and everybody is happy?"

"I wish I could tell you otherwise," said Gorsuch. "The seller is an older man and he says he's very familiar with the market. He is certain that the pieces will sell. He wants people to fly out and see the furniture firsthand. He fears that if the pieces are too broadly publicized, there may be collusion."

Collusion? This fellow, whoever he was, sounded truly odd. What did he think would happen? In the old days, dealers were sometimes known to strike preauction deals among themselves, whereby the one person who was willing, theoretically, to bid the highest on a piece would pay off his cohorts so that they wouldn't bid against him. When Leslie and I were teenagers and just beginning to make a name for ourselves in the field of stoneware, we were once approached by a middle-aged collector at a country auction and asked to go in with him and a larger pool of people.

"There's only one collection up for sale here, and we can't all get what we want," the man said, referring to the day's offerings. "Might as well benefit somehow." Naturally, Leslie and I declined the offer, and the man walked away. But a few minutes later, after the auction had begun, the man returned. Having had time to muse over our firm rejection, he was now livid. "You little sons of bitches, I'll break your arms!" he started to scream, seemingly oblivious to the sale going on around him and to our mother, who was sitting in silent outrage beside us.

Needless to say, that man never did follow through on his threat, and today, pooling is illegal. I can't think of a single dealer today who would be willing to risk his or her reputation and enter a pool. From what I could tell, though, Alan Gorsuch didn't think collusion was much of an issue, either. Instead, it sounded as if he didn't want to offend his consignor and risk losing what was clearly a potentially career-defining sale.

But despite this strange obstacle that the seller had effectively thrown in my way, the obvious promise of this furniture group was far too great to overlook. I had no option but to fly out to Tacoma to see the pieces in person prior to the sale. Unfortunately, I already had an unbreakable engagement on the scheduled preview date the following Friday. I had to be at a racetrack in the Poconos because it was the only day left in the year that I could qualify for my racing license and membership in the Vintage Sports Car Club of America. Without that license, I wouldn't be able to race competitively for an entire year. Leslie and I already mapped out a summer of track meets across the country and I was really looking forward to putting our newly purchased 1957 Lotus Eleven to the test. I simply wasn't going to miss the opportunity.

But when I explained my conflict to Alan Gorsuch and asked if I could fly out a few days earlier than the scheduled preview to see the piece—once again, a fairly standard industry request—he said no. After a few futile attempts at persuading him otherwise, I finally said to him in complete exasperation, "Well then, I guess I just won't be bidding on those pieces."

My words were met with a moment of silence and then the auctioneer said slowly, "Look, Leigh, I know that you bought the desk last January for three point six million. . . ." His voice trailed off and then he said, "I think I need to make a phone call."

A few hours later, Gorsuch called to say that he had convinced his client that it would be in his best interest to allow me to view the pieces early. So the following Tuesday, I flew out to Tacoma and checked into the local Sheraton. Right away, I liked the feel of the city, from the constant awe-inspiring backdrop of the snowcapped peak of Mount Rainier to the salty Pacific coast winds that rolled across the city.

Sanford & Son was located about an eight-minute walk from my hotel, along a two-block strip of art galleries and antique and consignment shops locally known as Antiques Row. Prominently displayed in the plate-glass windows fronting the white warehouse-style building was a set of late-nineteenth-century leaded windows in the

*On a real Edmund Townsend desk,
every detail adds up to one perfect whole.*

style of Louis Comfort Tiffany. The windows were vibrantly colored and pretty enough, but for a moment I wondered why anyone would choose to divest himself of an important group of Colonial furniture—potentially worth millions—in such an out-of-the-way setting. Clearly, Sanford & Son was profitable, but it could never compete with the well-oiled machinery of Sotheby's and Christie's.

Seconds after I entered the place, I was greeted by Cheryl Gorsuch, the pretty dark-haired wife of the owner. She had been awaiting my arrival and quickly ushered me toward the back through columns of predominantly late-nineteenth-century furniture and decorative objects, including some heavily carved, large Renaissance Revival sideboards, brass chandeliers, and even an old red-and-white barbershop pole. As we made our way through the merchandise, Cheryl explained that she and her husband had been running the business as a joint auction house and antiques gallery for about twenty-five years. This was the first time in her memory that they had handled such a rare group of Early American furniture. In keeping with the seller's wishes that the pieces remain out of sight until the day before the sale, they were storing them at the back of the gallery in a small office-cum-apartment that they occasionally used as a pied-à-terre.

Alan Gorsuch, a clean-cut, pleasant-faced man dressed in khakis and a well-pressed oxford shirt, was filling out some paperwork on a large table just outside the entrance to the office. After a quick handshake and a few words, he invited me into the room behind him, with Cheryl taking up the rear. At the center of the room, against a decidedly homey setting that included a well-padded couch and a broad-backed easy chair, was the kneehole desk that I had traveled across the country to see.

As I looked at the piece from the doorway, any anticipatory excitement that I had allowed myself to feel up until that time died instantly. Right away, the desk looked problematic. The overall proportions were stocky and heavy, the wood lacked the rich, dense reddish plum color of the expensive, exotic mahogany that I am accustomed to seeing on eighteenth-century Newport furniture, and the surface showed no sign of age-earned darkening or wear. The closer I moved toward the piece, the more certain I became that I was looking at a faked piece. One by one, the various missteps of the forger jumped out at me.

For example, as Leslie previously pointed out in his description of the Gibbs bureau, the vertical blocking on a Newport kneehole bureau begins with the shells, continues through the drawers, and ends with a scrolled curlicue near the bottom of the ogee bracket feet. In order for the blocking to succeed, every element must be in perfect sync with the next. But whoever had designed the piece before me had obviously met with some difficulty resolving the blocking in the feet. Ordinarily, the contour of the projected surface forms a serpentine line that mimics the outer edge of the foot, which means the two lines appear to run parallel. But on the feet of the faked bureau, these two lines diverged, which gave the negative space between them the flared look of bell-bottom pants. It was a significant blunder, throwing off the symmetry of the entire facade.

Note the poor design of the foot on the fake desk. The S curves of the feet are not in sync.

Prior to my arrival, someone had pulled out the top drawer of the bureau and placed it on a nearby table. Next to it lay an open copy of Michael Moses's book, *Master Craftsmen of Newport: The Townsends and Goddards,* which is the field's most thorough compilation to date of their work. I stepped in front of the removed drawer and stared down at the trio of decorative drawer shells spread in an even row across its front. All were stiff and ungainly and completely lacking in any of the renowned sensitivity of the Newport school of cabinetmaking. I was utterly disgusted by the sight and yet I was unable to look away. It was a curiosity born, no doubt, by the same impulse that causes drivers to slow down to view the scene of a highway accident.

Within a few seconds, I had noticed numerous discrepancies in the details of the shells. To begin with, the shells appeared to have more in common with the known work of Edmund Townsend than that of John. They looked like a poor man's rendition of the shells on the Whitehorne desk, which I had purchased for $3.6 million. For example, typical of Edmund's work, each of the shells featured a small raised arch at the center

The real thing.

that swept across the gathering point of the lobes from end to end. By contrast, John Townsend's shells routinely display a central arch that loops inward on itself before curving back and terminating in small volutes at either end. In other words, in Edmund's hands, the energy of the gesture radiates out through the shell's lobes, whereas John's versions provide a more strident, visual separation between the central arch and the lobes above. Now at least I knew why the advertisement in the paper had used the famous labeled Edmund Townsend bureau in the Karolik Collection as a reference. Whoever had made this fraudulent piece had clearly used his work as a model.

Having seen enough of the shells, I moved on to do a quick once-over of the dovetails used to join the drawer sides (which, incidentally, were made of thick, cheap machine-cut pine) to the decorative front. All were crude, uneven, and completely inconsistent with the known perfectionism of John Townsend. Had I really been looking at an example of Townsend's work, the triangle-shaped joints that held the drawer front to the sides would have been perfectly spaced and shaped and identically rendered.

The pretender.

The fake label on the bureau.

The most audacious element of the entire charade, however, had to be the alleged paper label of John Townsend, which was glued to the inside of the open drawer before me. I stared at it, positively dumbfounded. It was a blatant photocopy, freshly cut from a sheet of copy paper and then dipped in a staining agent, such as tea, to simulate age. I stared at this monstrosity with a blend of outrage and mild amusement, reminded of the first time I had ever seen an *authentic* John Townsend label. It was around 1989, not long after I had started my own business, during a house call at the home of a lifelong collector of Americana named Dr. William Serri. Dr. Serri owned a wonderful four-drawer chest of drawers that had descended in the family of the Newport heiress Sarah Slocum, which he had purchased back in the early 1950s. Since then, its picture and history had been published more than once, which meant that I knew I would find the maker's label when I pulled open the upper drawer for the first time. But that foresight did not in any way lessen the sense of awe I felt at the sight of its boldfaced message—MADE BY/JOHN TOWNSEND/NEWPORT—accompanied by the handwritten date of 1792.

The authenticity of the Slocum label was clear on a number of fronts. The paper had the rough, starchy feel of eighteenth-century stock and also displayed some slight foxing (an industry term used to describe the discoloration of paper caused by moisture or mold). The edges of the roughly four-inch-by-two-inch rectangle were mildly tattered, having suffered the natural abrasions of use through the years. And on the drawer bottom, beneath the areas where the paper had crumbled away, there remained the unoxidized shadow of the label, left by centuries of coverage. When Sarah Slocum's chest of drawers sold at Christie's in June 1998, that label, along with the inarguably pristine shape of the piece, helped propel the final price to $4,732,500 (I was actually the underbidder on the chest, meaning that I cast the last bid before the winner). Obviously, the same would never be said for the label on the Tacoma bureau.

Offhand, I was unable to think of a direct source for the faked label displayed in the open drawer. I later learned that had I simply stepped over to Michael Moses's book lying open on the table nearby, I would have discovered its exact origin: an authentic Townsend label displayed on a tidy Federal table made by Townsend in the 1790s that had been reproduced to size in the text. The faked label was a photocopy of the illustration in Moses. The forger was apparently so careless in his copying technique that not only were the same acid stains visible in the paper but so, too, was the background wood grain of the table from which the label had originally been reproduced. The distinctive grain appeared as a darkened printed border on three of the fake label's four sides.

The underside of the fake desk shows no signs of natural oxidation or wear.

Throughout the course of my silent study, Alan and Cheryl Gorsuch had been watching my face with obvious concern, anxiously awaiting my feedback. Now I had a verdict and I wasn't about to mince words. "You've been had," I said. "Someone is using you. There is nothing old about this bureau."

Alan's face went white. Perhaps I had been too harsh. He took a deep breath, glanced over at his wife, and said quite seriously, "Honey, call the caterer; cancel the caviar."

I truly felt sorry for him. It seemed like such a funny response to my words, but then Alan explained that he had planned a sizable postsale party with caviar and champagne and had even lined up some extra security for the event.

The exquisite dovetails found on the drawers of the Whitehorne desk.

The fake desk complete with reproduction brasses.

I waited a moment for the color to return to Alan's face and then asked him where he was storing the alleged John Townsend dining table and the portrait of Dr. Thomas Moffatt.

"Right out here," he said, leading me back to the entrance foyer to the office—an area that I had initially walked through to see the bureau. On my first pass, I hadn't even noticed the nice-enough mid-eighteenth-century portrait of a man holding a letter that was leaning against the wall. Nor had I registered the late George III English mahogany dining table standing next to it—probably because it couldn't have been worth more than a thousand dollars. Often described in period terminology as a

The English drop-leaf table masquerading as a Newport gem.

"falling leaf" table, the straight-legged table featured a stationary rectangular center board flanked by two hinged sides. To verify my on-the-spot-analysis further, I decided to flip the table over to see what the underside looked like. To begin with, the rails appeared to be made of oak (recognizable from its prominent dark medullar rays), a common secondary wood on English furniture, rather than maple or chestnut, which is often found on Newport furniture. Next, the oxidized wood color of the center section didn't even come close to matching the color of the leaves. Clearly, the three boards had not aged at the same rate, which meant they were probably not all original to the base of the table. Furthermore, there were some additional nail holes visible along the edges of the center board, indicating that it had a previous attachment history—quite possibly to another table frame.

Yet another problem with the piece was the issue of the table's single cross-brace, which hung like a narrow bridge between the center of the two longest side rails. For one thing, it had been painted over with a dark rust paint that forever disguised its true origin. But more important, whoever had masterminded this scheme to pass an English table off as a Newport piece obviously knew a little bit—but not enough—about the methods of John Townsend. Typically, Townsend used a series of cross-braces on his tables (usually laid out with three bars placed flush against the top, interspersed by two hanging from the bottom rails) to strengthen the form. Although he occasionally varied this scheme, he never used just a single bar. The proverbial icing on the cake was the sight of another photocopied John Townsend label glued to the underside of the table's central board. The print may have been a bit lighter and perhaps it had soaked in the staining agent a little bit longer, but there was no getting around the fact that the tag was identical to the one on the block-and-shell bureau—right down to the distinct way the copy machine had read the irregularities in the paper.

I briefly explained my observations to Alan and Cheryl and then moved on to the portrait of Dr. Moffatt—or whoever he was. There was nothing about the painting that screamed American to me. It had the stylized, genteel, anonymous look of a classic eighteenth-century English portrait. The clean stretchers and taut canvas told me that the painting had recently been both restretched and relined, which effectively eliminated any evidence of its past. The sitter's attribution appeared to have been from a twentieth-century pencil inscription dashed along one of the new-looking yellow-pine stretchers. I saw no need to waste any more time with the piece. I leaned the portrait back against the wall, turned to Alan and his wife, and asked, "Where did these pieces come from?"

The mysterious "Dr. Moffat."

And that's when Alan launched into a strange story, which, as chance would have it, was far from over. Less than two weeks previously, Alan explained, Cheryl had awakened him from a nap by dropping a sizable handwritten prospectus next to him on the bed. An older white-haired man who had just left the gallery had given her the papers after explaining that he had some eighteenth-century American furniture and a painting that he wanted to sell that were worth in the vicinity of $12 million. The man (whom Alan didn't name, in deference to his request for anonymity) said that he was submitting the furniture on behalf of a family trust called the Carthaginian Financial Corporation, of which he was the treasurer. The trust, which was based in Reno, Nevada, had insurance that would cover the property until it changed hands, and he even said he would pay for an advertisement promoting the sale in *Antiques and the Arts Weekly.* Rounding out the proposal was a detailed marketing plan for the sale, which he stipulated had to occur before the end of the month—the owner was ill and in need of cash.

Having shaken off his sleep in a matter of seconds, Alan listened to his wife with feelings bordering upon cautious enthusiasm and absolute disbelief. "The whole thing sounded fantastical," he said to me. "Twelve million dollars' worth of furniture just landing on our laps? Why us? And yet, I guess I just wanted to believe the deal was true. I mean, aren't we all just optimists at heart?"

Alan then reiterated a point that Cheryl had made to me when we first met—that Early American furniture was not their strength. He said he figured that even if he couldn't verify the authenticity of the pieces beyond a shadow of a doubt—in the photos, they looked fine to him—he felt confident that potential buyers would do their homework. Furthermore, the seller claimed a forty-year background in the field and he used that stated familiarity to impose numerous restrictions on the sale, including the denial of supplementary photographs, the insistence on the one-day preview inspection, and the ban on phone or absentee bidding. In hindsight, of course, it seemed clear that those limitations were set in an attempt to contain word of the fraud from spreading.

In short, by the time Alan was through reviewing the man's proposal, he thought it sounded unusual, although completely nonthreatening to his business. There didn't seem anything in it that could be harmful to Sanford & Son. He had decided to go through with the sale.

"Well, what are you going to do now?" I asked Alan, whose distress at the scheme seemed just too earnest to doubt.

"I don't know," he said slowly. "Cheryl and I need to discuss this. Obviously, we have to get in touch with the consignor. This may all be news to him, as well."

Although that seemed doubtful to me, I could tell that Alan needed a little time to sort things out. He seemed to be nursing some lingering hope that all that I had told him about the furniture wasn't true.

In the end, however, my trip out to Tacoma wasn't a complete waste. Before I left, I asked the Gorsuches for a tour of their place. They took me through canyons of furnishings, all of which seemed to date back to the period of Tacoma's founding in the

1880s. But down in the basement, we came across a wonderful circa 1830 painted Vermont blanket chest with two drawers and a lift top. The piece featured a vividly painted all-over faux wood grain and had come, Alan said, from a family that had moved to the area back in the early twentieth century from New England. I ended up buying the piece for under three thousand dollars and shipping it to New York, where I eventually sold it to a private collector for a price that covered my airfare out west.

It was now nearly three o'clock in the afternoon and I had yet to have lunch. More important, though, I wanted to return to my hotel so that I could call up some of my colleagues on the East Coast to save them the hassle of the trip to Tacoma. Because of the three-hour time difference, I needed to move quickly.

The first call I placed was to Albert Sack.

He greeted my pronouncement that the desk was a fake with a rather extended silence. Finally, he cleared his throat and said, "Leigh, you are either doing me a huge favor or really pulling a good one on me." He said that he had already asked a local Seattle furniture restorer to survey the piece for him and that the report had not been good. "I was still going to fly out," he confessed, "because the potential of the lot was too great to ignore. Thanks for saving me the airfare."

After talking to Albert, I spoke with a small group of dealers, including the Pennsylvania-based Clarence Prickett and sons, the conservator Alan Miller, Wayne Pratt, and, finally, Guy Bush down in Washington, D.C. When Guy heard the news, he said, "Go anywhere you want for dinner. It's on me."

By now, I was ravenous, but I still had one more call to make before I was through. The day before I left for Tacoma, I had received a phone call at my office from a Tacoma-based heart surgeon, who had expressed an interest in the pieces at Sanford & Son. Would I be able to look at them for him? he asked. At the time, I had wavered on his request because the man was a stranger to me and I had no idea if he had the finances to handle such a purchase, if the furniture turned out to be authentic.

Now, at least, I was off the hook, because I only had bad news to report.

"That's a shame," said the surgeon, "Alan and Cheryl are good friends of mine, I'm sure they must be let down." He paused for a moment, then added, "You know, I was actually there at the gallery when the fellow came in—a thin white-haired fellow with a beard. I think his name was Flynn. Cheryl didn't know what to make of him."

Flynn, Flynn, I thought. There was something about the name and the doctor's description of the man that sounded familiar. "Not Don Flynn?" I asked in a flash, remembering a man I had met about ten years earlier on a call to a San Francisco town house while I was still at Christie's.

"Yes," said the doctor, "that was it, Don Flynn."

Well now, things were beginning to crystallize. The Don Flynn I had met (a gaunt white-haired man) had done well in real estate and had evidently poured some of that success into a sizable collection of American furniture. But the collection was poorly conceived and really ran the gamut in terms of condition. Some of the pieces were genuine untouched treasures, but other objects had undergone significant restoration. I was in the house to evaluate the collection, but whenever I pointed out that an object

Don Flynn at the auction.

had a problem, Flynn would cut me off and usher me to another piece. After awhile, I became so frustrated by his utter unwillingness to listen to my analysis that I left. Considering the nature of that past encounter, I wouldn't have been at all surprised if the man in San Francisco and the man who had consigned the furniture in Tacoma might be one and the same.

By Wednesday evening, I was back in New York, but in the days (and indeed weeks) that followed, word of the fraud in Tacoma spread. Journalists such as Laura Beach of *Antiques and the Arts Weekly* and David Hewett of *Maine Antique Digest* began to track the story, and slowly, more details began to emerge about the elusive Mr. Flynn. For example, in 1992, a few years after my visit to his home, Flynn had put some of his collection up for sale at Butterfield & Butterfield, the San Francisco auction house. Included in that sale was an object described as a "Chippendale Mahogany Shell-Carved Block-Front Kneehole Dressing Table in the Newport, Rhode Island Manner." Estimated between ten and fifteen thousand dollars, the piece—which was unlabeled—never attracted a buyer. Had Flynn simply attached a fake label and then thrown the dining table, the portrait, and the Moffatt provenance (which was easily proven a hoax) into the mix in an effort to sell an object he hadn't previously been able to move? There was also an incident back in the mid-1980s, when Flynn had filed a lawsuit against Christie's, claiming that the auction house had improperly sent some of his property to Christie's East, its lower-end division. I was still at Christie's at the time and had actually been deposed for the case, which was quickly thrown out of court.

And what of the fate of the objects in Tacoma? Well not long after I flew home, Alan Gorsuch called his client and told him point-blank that the authenticity of his furniture had been questioned by some top-level East Coast dealers. Don Flynn was apparently unbothered by his words, however, and said that he wanted to go through with the sale. He told the auctioneer that he would accept a minimum of fifty thousand dollars for the entire lot. Flynn also told Gorsuch that he planned to be in the room on the day of the sale but that he wanted his presence to remain under wraps. With that bit of knowledge in his pocket, Gorsuch set a trap. First, he attached disclaimer notes to the pieces, which he decided to offer as three separate lots rather than as one. Then he warned a handful of local television stations and newspapers that a newsworthy event was to take place at Sanford & Son's Saturday sale.

Obviously I did not bother to attend the sale, but according to David Hewett's detailed report of the sale in *Maine Antique Digest,* there were fewer than twenty people in the room that Saturday, including six members of the media and four auction house employees. About ten minutes before the scheduled 11:00 A.M. start, Don Flynn sauntered into the gallery, registered for an auction paddle, and took a seat near the rear. A few minutes later, Alan Gorsuch opened the sale by summarizing the recent sales history of authentic furniture of the Goddard-Townsend school. When he was through, he gestured to the pieces on the podium beside him and then went on to describe them in far less glowing terms. After that, he opened up the bidding on the portrait of "Dr. Moffatt," which ending up selling to—of all people—Don Flynn presumably bidding against the reserve) for one thousand dollars. Next on the block was the drop-leaf dining table, now correctly described as an English piece with a fake label. It sold to a local collector for three hundred dollars.

At this point, Gorsuch halted the sale and officially withdrew the kneehole desk. Then, before rolling television cameras and the smattering of print journalists, he addressed his wily consignor, who was seated in the back of the room.

"Don Flynn," he announced, "as this is the most arrogant counterfeit endeavor in the history of American antiques . . . the entire nation of antiques dealers and collectors would like to see a fitting finale to this piece of furniture." With that, Gorsuch placed a can of gasoline and a box of matches on top of the desk and instructed two of his workers to take the piece outside. Using a hand truck, the two men rolled the desk out of the gallery and onto the sidewalk as the paltry audience—including Don Flynn—filed out onto the curb behind it. There, Gorsuch resumed his speech.

"Don Flynn, I call on you to give everyone involved, directly or indirectly, the closure needed. To avoid prosecution and guarantee that it will never again resurface to deceive furniture innocents, put this article to sleep forever."

Flynn refused the auctioneer's invitation to burn the fake desk, but, oddly enough, he lingered on the street as the crowd dispersed, comfortably lobbing half answers to the numerous questions thrown his way by the reporters who remained. Perhaps the most telling of his responses was his answer to the fact that the desk was a forgery. Hadn't he been concerned about perpetrating a fraud?

Burn this?

Flynn's answer: "No. It's 'Buyer beware' at auctions."

13

. . . Gone!

In case we forgot to tell you, we started our little antique business by searching the countryside for old barns and taking the hardware legaly off of them and selling them to get money. With the money that we got from the hardware, we started to buy other things.

—Leigh and Leslie Keno, journal entry, August 6th 1969

THROUGHOUT OUR LIVES, Leigh and I have taken great pleasure in our shared passion for American furniture and decorative arts. Our love of objects is so much a part of our makeup—our very souls—that I truly cannot remember a time when we were not hunting for and learning about *things*. However deeply I reach back into the past—to our teens, preteens, or early childhood—I come up with memories of interesting and beautiful objects that captured our imagination and sparked our curiosity. Because Leigh and I are brothers, and twins at that, our intellectual connection is bound far more tightly than if we were merely colleagues. Our shared life experience has increased our synchronicity. We have never strayed far from each other—intellectually or geographically—because we have known from an early age the course our lives would take. The trick has been carving out separate yet equal spaces in the world of antiques so that we can grow as individuals but remain bonded as brothers and best friends.

To date, the most important object that I have ever ushered to the auction block remains the gorgeous mahogany secretary-bookcase that I discussed in the first chapter of this book—the one that was found in Paris. I feel it is unlikely that another piece will ever be found that rivals it in execution (though, of course, I'll never rule anything out). For Leigh, the secretary also had milestone potential. I knew he would take great pleasure in helping to place a piece of this caliber with a client. As I said earlier, it was not an object for beginners, which meant there was only a handful of collectors who really deserved the *privilege* of owning it and safeguarding it for future generations. But as the date of the secretary's sale loomed, I remained surprisingly unclear as to Leigh's intentions regarding the piece. It was obvious that he was as captivated by the beauty and grand majesty of the secretary as I—but was he going to take a shot at it? Did he have a client in the wings? What was his goal that day in the crowded salesroom at Sotheby's when the maple bedstead spun out of view on the auction room dais and the towering secretary took center stage? When I looked hard into his eyes just before the bidding opened, I had only my intuition as a guide.

I first saw the secretary in a set of photographs given to me by my colleague Bill Stahl (who in addition to being one of Sotheby's chief auctioneers is also the head of the American Furniture and Decorative Arts Division). A representative from our Paris office had sent him the pictures, along with a request for an estimate. "All the outer hardware is solid silver," Bill said as he laid the pile of snapshots on my desk.

Silver hardware on what looked to be a mid-eighteenth-century Newport secretary—the block-and-shell carved doors of the upper case were a dead giveaway—I had never before seen such extravagance on an American piece. What more did this object have in store? I wanted to see the secretary right away, but I would have to wait a number of years before I was officially invited to do so. (I was later told only half-jokingly by Alexandre Pradère—then the head of Sotheby's French Furniture Department in Paris and now a private art consultant—that the staff at Sotheby's Paris bureau began to dread my near-monthly calls for updates.) The family who owned the secretary was not fully committed to selling the piece until early April 1998. Within days of receiving the go-ahead, I flew to Paris and promptly went to meet the owners and view the secretary in a small apartment on the Right Bank.

Joining me on my visit was Alexandre Pradère, an elegant, erudite man, whose generous smile no doubt served him well at putting potential clients at ease. Was it my eagerness to see the secretary or the many flights of stairs leading up to the apartment that made my heart beat so rapidly? Whatever the cause, I arrived at the threshold literally panting in anticipation. And when the door was opened by one of the two men in attendance that day, I instantly caught sight of the dazzling case piece over his shoulder, standing against the far wall of the living room.

I think the owners enjoyed the look of pure wonderment that instantly crossed my face. After we all filed through the entrance foyer into the living room, I quickly positioned myself directly in front of the secretary and began to drink in the beauty of its details. This was clearly a piece from the Goddard and Townsend school, but the

The Gilder family secretary.

design was anything but traditional. For example, most Early American tall case pieces—Newport or otherwise—feature an S-shaped swan's-neck pediment, such as the one displayed on the Tillinghast high chest of drawers. But this one featured a semicircular, or dome-shaped, pediment, which gave the structure tremendous architectural presence: It looked like the doorway to a northern Italian villa designed by the Renaissance architect Andrea Palladio. Juxtaposed against the angled geometries of the beamed ceiling, the overall sweep was bold and graphic.

I tried to think of a stylistic precedent for a dome-top case piece in the colonies. All I could come up with was a Philadelphia secretary desk and bookcase, once owned by the Gilder family of Burlington County, New Jersey, and Philadelphia, that Leigh had purchased at Christie's back in the early 1990s on behalf of the Dietrich American Foundation. But one Philadelphia secretary hardly constitutes a trend. Furthermore, the interpretation of the dome shape on the Gilder piece was quite different from the version on the secretary before me. The first featured a single recessed panel in the tympanum, whereas the second displayed a smooth-faced pair of side-by-side panels that projected outward toward the viewer.

The pictures that I had kept in my desk drawer in New York had barely revealed the quality of the plum-pudding mahogany used on the Paris secretary. The brilliant mottled pattern of the wood was as vibrant as a leopard's spots. Now warmed by the sunlight streaming in through a set of nearby windows, it had the lush, swirled appearance of freshly poured paint.

I stepped closer to the piece and noticed the reflected movement of my figure in the mirrorlike surface of the long solid-silver escutcheons that surrounded the keyholes of the cabinet doors. I am accustomed to seeing only gold-toned brass hardware on Colonial American furniture, so the contrast offered by the silver-white metal was startling. It offset the coloration of the mahogany in a whole new way, bringing out the purplish undertones in the wood. I bent down to touch one of the pierced Chippendale drawer pulls displayed on the drawers (in outline, it looked like a bat with its wings spread) and gently flipped up the attached bail, or hoop-shaped, handle.

There, on the underside of the pull, I saw the name S. Casey stamped in big block letters. During the course of my examination of the rest of the piece, I would find more than a dozen initialed or scripted markings left by the maker, who was understandably proud of his contribution to the secretary. Casey had even signed the elaborate bird-shaped lopers (meaning the decorative hand pulls that fronted the pocket side runners used to support the hinged slant lid). The pair looked like a whimsical pair of cuckoo birds popping from a clock.

I felt honored to be in the presence of such an unusual and magnificent piece and said as much to the owners, who had retreated to a nearby seating area with Alexandre. I then asked for and received permission to examine the interior of the secretary. I began by opening the block-and-shell carved doors of the upper case. The doors swung smoothly on their small silver hinges, revealing an interior fitted with three graduated rows of pigeonholes, all jam-packed with papers and books. Despite the clutter, the stylish arrangement of the space was undeniable. Each of the dividers that formed the individual compartments was crafted of the same vibrant plum-pudding mahogany used on the exterior of the piece. Furthermore, the scalloped silhouette of each divider seemed to form the profile of a bird, which directly related to the design of those exquisite silver lopers.

Right: One of the secretary's silver bird lopers with green stone eyes.

The secretary's elaborately fitted interior includes bird-shaped compartment dividers that relate to the form of the lopers.

As I scanned the interior of the upper case, my attention was naturally drawn to the decorative compartment—offset by matched Doric columns—that was centered on the second shelf. The trade term for this device is *prospect compartment*, and I have often seen similar ones used on Boston secretary-bookcases from the 1740s and 1750s. Usually, this area masks a hidden compartment or two, so I grasped the sides of one of the columns and pulled to see if it was removable. As I suspected, that column (like its mate on the other side) fronted a small vertical storage compartment. In addition, the three-inch-high serpentine base of the prospect compartment disguised yet a third drawer. Without a handhold to call attention to its facade, however, the drawer was quite literally hidden in plain sight.

Next I turned to the slant-front desk. Before opening the lid, I reached out with both hands to hook my forefingers around the curve of the beak on each of the silver-shaped lopers. The cold metal felt refreshing against my skin. Only the head and shoulders moved when I pulled on the beak to drag the desk's support bars out of their pockets, because the body of each bird was anchored to the desk by a silver screw set in the center of its belly. When the braces were fully extended, I drew down the slant-lid top and began to examine the writing interior. It was organized with two banks of three blocked short drawers (the uppermost ones being fan-carved) centering six pigeonholes capped by delicate arched mahogany valances. A carved fan that matched the two displayed on the side banks of drawers also topped the small prospect door at the center of the desk.

Interestingly, all the hardware on the interior of the desk, and, in fact, on the interior of the entire case piece, was fashioned of brass rather than of the costly silver seen on the exterior. (I guess the client had to draw the line somewhere in terms of extravagance.) As a result, though, the brass brought out the reddish undertones in the wood, just as the silver had drawn out the purple. The cabinetmaker had been so fastidious in carrying out this plan that the three hinges of the slant-top lid (technically interior hardware) were made of silver, rather than brass, because slivers of their rounded backs remained visible along the lid's edge when the writing compartment was closed.

I grasped one of the circular brass knobs and pulled out one of the desk drawers. I was surprised to see that the drawer sides and the back were all crafted of the same vibrant mahogany used on the show surface. Plum-pudding mahogany was among the most costly woods used on eighteenth-century American case pieces (and probably the rarest type of mahogany imported from the West Indies). Out of curiosity, I immediately pulled out a few more drawers in the desk area (all crafted of solid mahogany) and then bent down to the long drawers of the lower case to compare their makeup. The term *secondary wood* simply did not apply to this secretary. It was amazing. Furthermore, the interior woods—which, to my mind, only the mice would see—were finished like a primary surface. Very often, cabinetmakers neglect to sand or plane the back of a drawer or backboard in order to save on time and labor. (At times, I have gone over an otherwise-elaborate case piece, only to find remnants of tree bark on the drawer bottoms or backboard.) Not so here: Even the wedge-shaped dovetails seen on the backs of the drawers were as fitted as the sprockets of a clock by the famous Russian jeweler Peter Carl Fabergé. In a lifetime of viewing masterpieces of Americana, I had never seen such attention to detail.

With the secretary now unfolded before me—the doors drawn open, the desk exposed—I stepped back and assessed the overall design anew. Once again, my eyes traveled to that incredible domed top. Suddenly, it struck me that the semicircular shape served as a leitmotif for the secretary. For example, the pediment was offset with three smooth-sided urn-shaped finials capped by a perfect half sphere before they merged into an unusually elongated spiral twist. (Typically, a Newport finial features more of a fluted, cupcake-shaped body with a short swirl above.) The diminutive wood valances that crowned the four central pigeonholes of the top shelf were also clearly designed in direct visual reference to the domed top—a theme that continued (in variation) in the valanced slots of the prospect compartment and writing-desk interior.

I still wanted to get a closer look at the pediment itself, so I borrowed a tall stepladder from the kitchen and climbed up. It was only from that higher perch that I could see that the backboard of the bonnet had been cut out to echo the front scroll of the tympanum board (often they are not shaped, but simply finished straight across). It was the type of detail that could only be appreciated from atop a ladder, as I was, or on the ground from twenty feet away.

The dome-shaped turnings of the finials echo the form of the bonnet top.

I was now eye-to-eye with the finials, so I wrapped my hand around the urn-shaped body of the right-hand one and gently eased it off the slender fluted plinth, into which it fit like a peg. Despite its small size, it was solid and heavy, which made sense, considering it was made of the same dense mahogany as the rest of the case. The wear patterns on the form (there were a few nicks and scratches) seemed thoroughly in keeping with the distances I knew the secretary had traveled. Still, I turned the finial over to examine the end grain of the peg for signs of checking, the telltale grid pattern that indicates moisture loss and age. (Remember how the marble-smooth pads of the feet on the two chairs I had examined on the Sotheby's loading dock revealed them to be reproductions?) Everything looked as it should.

The more I absorbed of the secretary, the more curious I became about its history. What sort of a person had had the means and inspiration to commission such an object? I turned to the two owners and asked them to fill me in on the history of the secretary within their family.

The Reverend Nathaniel Appleton.

One of the two men acted as spokesperson and carefully began to outline what the family knew. Traditionally, the first owner of the secretary was said to be the Reverend Nathaniel Appleton (1693–1784), the long-serving minister of the First Congregational Church in Cambridge, Massachusetts, from 1717 until his death (he also had significant land holdings in Massachusetts and parts of what would later become Maine and Vermont). I found it surprising that a clergyman would have commissioned what was surely the most expensive piece of furniture made in eighteenth-century America. Curious, too, was why a Cambridge minister would have looked to Newport for such an object when he had the resources of cosmopolitan Boston at his disposal. Perhaps the secretary had been presented to him as a gift.

At this point, the French gentleman produced a small lithograph reproduction of a seventeenth-century portrait, a print that he had taken out in anticipation of my visit. It was a childhood rendering of Henry Gibbs of Boston, the son of a prosperous Boston merchant turned minister, who also became a minister. Gibbs was also the father of seven children, including Margaret, the wife of the Reverend Nathaniel Appleton.

I was amazed to hear of Appleton's connection to the Gibbs family. The portrait was, in fact, already familiar to me because the original oil on canvas is in the collection of the Museum of Fine Arts, Boston. Painted in 1670, the work is considered by many to be an icon of early American portraiture (along with the two accompanying paintings done by the same anonymous artist of Henry's siblings, Robert and Margaret). In each of the paintings, the figures stand against a black-and-white checkerboard floor and are dressed expensively in clothes trimmed with velvet and lace, as befitted the Anglocentric social aspiration of their parents (they could easily be mistaken for the children of an Elizabethan aristocrat). Historian Wayne Craven once suggested that if the religious fervor of the children's father overlapped his success as a trader, then his offspring were probably raised in an atmosphere that reflected the two most powerful influences of their day—mercantilism and the church. Craven's insight gave me some fresh perspective on the secretary. Perhaps Appleton and his wife felt similarly at ease, sliding between the two realms—patrons, one might say, of a new kind of Puritan chic.

The French gentleman explained to me that when Appleton passed away in 1784, the secretary was given to his son, Nathaniel Appleton, Jr. (1731–1789). At that point, Nathaniel the younger was a prosperous businessman; he had started out in general trade but then gradually shifted the focus of his work to the manufacture of candles.

Though the great Boston fire of July 30, 1794, is said to have destroyed Appleton's Walpole, Massachusetts, estate, the secretary survived (along with a John Singleton Copley portrait of his father, which is now in the collection of Harvard University). Soon after the death of Nathaniel Appleton, Jr., in 1789, his second wife, Rachel, may

Mrs. Nathaniel Appleton (1699–1771).

have sent the secretary to their eldest surviving son, John Appleton (1758–1829), then living in France as the American consul to Calais. The frisky John had two children out of wedlock, including his eldest son, John-James Appleton (1792–1864), who, following in his father's diplomatic footsteps, became the American diplomatic envoy to Sweden, as well as the next in line for the secretary. From then on, the secretary descended through three more generations of the Appleton family before passing into the hands of the two men (and their absent sister) before me that day.

It was mind-boggling to think of the distance the secretary had covered since the time it was made in Newport during the 1740s. I thought of carts drawn by horses across cobblestone streets and schooners sailing across wind-tossed seas. And yet there it stood in a modest apartment in the 17th arrondisement: poised, graceful, and surprisingly intact—except, perhaps, for a few inches lost somewhere along the way. Though the Appleton secretary stood nearly nine feet tall, there was something about its overall proportions that appeared a little off. I suspected that, like many tall case pieces (such as the Tillinghast high chest of drawers), its height had been reduced, possibly to accommodate a low-ceilinged room. That height, I assumed, had been taken from the feet.

To prove my theory, I got down on the carpeted floor to peer beneath the secretary with a flashlight. Unfortunately, the tangle of shag wool prevented me from reading any details, although I did notice that the corner blocks (again made of mahogany) behind the bracket feet, which are ordinarily left rough-hewn and imprecise, were sharp and precisely rendered—as if they were meant to be seen. Ordinarily, I would have thought this unusual, if not suspect, but on a case piece crafted entirely of plum-pudding mahogany and decorated with silver mounts, it made perfect sense. Indeed, my entire perception of American furniture—and the level of craftsmanship that it could reach—changed that day in that small, modest Paris apartment. In that sense, the Appleton secretary was more than a masterpiece; it was a revelation.

Though I desperately wanted to spend some more time with the secretary, both Alexandre and the secretary's two owners had other engagements, so the conversation soon turned to the specifics of consignment. From the way in which the owners were talking, I suspected we were not going to get into a competitive situation with another auction house over the piece. To my mind, it wasn't a question of *if* the secretary would go to Sotheby's, but *when.*

I told the owners that I would conservatively estimate the secretary's value at between $500,000 and $800,000, but I hoped it would go higher. Thankfully, the men never questioned my judgment. Very often, I get into a situation in which the consignor will push for an aggressive estimate (New York City consumer laws stipulate that an object's reserve cannot exceed the low estimate—a fact that unnerves some sellers). To explain why a conservative figure is better, I often use the analogy that nobody likes a braggart. Prospective buyers start looking for the problems when the estimate is too steep. A lower estimate provokes the opposite response and encourages people to examine the piece in a positive, hopeful way. As such, estimate levels can really affect the success of a sale.

When I returned to New York, I stopped in to see Kevin Tierney, the head of Sotheby's silver department, to ask him about the name S. Casey. "Samuel Casey," he replied in his sharp British accent. "He was one of the greatest Colonial silversmiths, next to Paul Revere."

I was thrilled by his words. Some additional research for the catalog note revealed that, despite his vast talent, Casey (circa 1724–1779) had led a colorful, if not tarnished, life. After apprenticing to the great Boston silversmith Jacob Hurd (1703–1758), he moved to Exeter, Rhode Island, around 1745 and later to South Kingston, where he went into partnership with his brother (who was fined for passing false money in Philadelphia). Casey later lost his house and shop in a fire that started in his forge. An item that ran in the *Boston News Letter* of October 1, 1764, noted that the "valuable Dwelling-House . . . was entirely consumed [by the fire] with a great Quantity of rich Furniture." (More silver-tipped secretaries perhaps?) In 1770, a bankrupt Casey was arrested for counterfeiting dollars and sentenced to be hanged, but on the night of his scheduled execution, he was rescued from jail by a group of townsfolk "with Faces black'd." In September 1779, Casey's wife petitioned the Rhode Island General Assembly to pardon her husband. She wrote that he had "wandered in exile nine years forlorn and forsaken and destitute of every means of support to make his life even desirable, separated from his wife and offspring." A few days after his wife's plea for mercy, Samuel Casey received a full pardon.

I wanted the Appleton secretary for my all-important January sale (the preview exhibition was scheduled to open Saturday, January 9, but for tax reasons, the piece could not leave France until after the first of the year). Furthermore, the secretary had to be reviewed by a museum committee before it could leave the country—to certify that it wasn't French. The secretary passed inspection, as expected, and on the Thursday before the exhibition opened, it arrived via airfreight in New York.

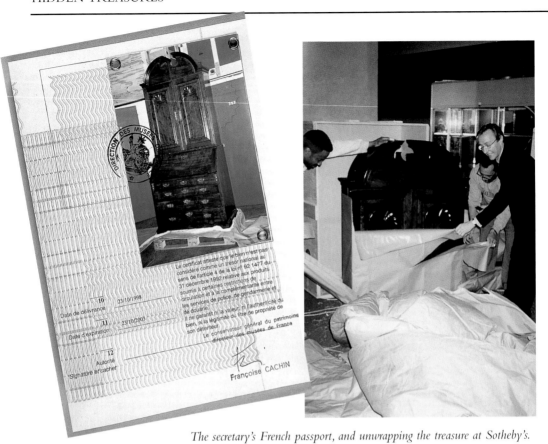

The secretary's French passport, and unwrapping the treasure at Sotheby's.

It took a small team of workmen about half an hour to extract the pieces (the secretary had been separated into two parts for the trip) from their custom-made boxes. I couldn't stop pacing around the workers throughout the entire process (I was almost ready to pick up a hammer myself), because I knew what sort of masterpiece was hidden behind the boards.

The lower section was the first to be freed. At my request, the movers immediately turned the case on its back so that for the first time, I could see the undersides of the bracket feet. I immediately noticed that each foot contained a small square peg hole (formed from the bracket facings themselves and the glue blocks). My early suspicions about the height of the piece were not without merit: The secretary had lost some height through the years—but not because it had been cut. Some additional feet had once been attached beneath those brackets. And from the way the holes were constructed (square rather than round), it seemed clear that whatever had been affixed would not twist. My mind went into overdrive as I thought about the possibilities. What could have been there originally? Ball feet were the traditional form—I had seen the combination of a short bracket paired with a ball foot on a number of English pieces. Claw feet and pad feet were also remote possibilities. In light of the grandeur of the rest of the piece and the square peg holes, could the missing feet have been faced with silver?

The underside of each foot was constructed with two shaped mahogany glue blocks forming a rectangular peg hole—probably to receive a removable ball foot.

My colleague John Nye has a great visual memory for objects and he and I often bounce ideas off of each other. Together, we tried to think of an American case piece on which bracket feet had been used in conjunction with a second foot form—particularly ball feet, which still seemed like the obvious choice, given the understated aesthetic of the secretary (and the ubiquitous dome theme). Between us, we could come up with three Philadelphia slant-front desks, including one that we had sold from a Long Island estate some years earlier. Another object that came to mind was a small valuables cabinet in the collection of the Chipstone Foundation in Milwaukee, a piece signed by John Townsend. The cabinet stands about forty inches tall on delicate ball feet and had been a favorite piece of the collection's founder, Stanley Stone. (He once told me he considered it one of his greatest prizes.)

Of course, when I found out that the secretary was missing its feet, I placed a call to the consignors in France and asked them to check around the house. "Look every-

A London-made pewter-inlaid secretary-bookcase, circa 1710 and attributed to G. Coxed and Thomas Woster, of the type that may have influenced Christopher Townsend. The ball feet are original.

where," I said. "Perhaps you have some other furniture with feet that look out of place—either because of the style or size? They are probably ball-shaped."

Unfortunately, the owners came up empty-handed, but at the end of the day, I received a phone call from John Nye, who at that point was already on his way home to New Jersey. "Why don't we have a set of feet made for exhibition purposes?" he said.

"You read my mind," I said to John with a laugh, for the same thought had begun percolating in my head as soon as I got back the negative report from the consignors. After I hung up with John, I called Colin Stair, who heads up Sotheby's Restoration Department, and asked him if it would be possible to produce four ball feet for the secretary before the exhibition opened on Saturday. Colin said it could be done, and, sure enough, at 9:50 A.M. on Saturday, the Appleton secretary stood for the first time on its new ball feet. Suddenly, it all made sense. The five or six inches added by the feet really unified the design. As the early crowd of collectors and weekend browsers began to stream into the gallery, I stepped back to enjoy their awed reactions to the piece. I felt very much like a proud parent.

Because auction previews are such hands-on events, new information about an object can often come to light, even at the preview stage. The Appleton secretary was particularly ripe for new discoveries, since it had shown up only two days before the preview opening, which left me next to no time to reexamine it (remember that when I saw the piece in Paris, it was packed with books and papers).

For instance, I was convinced that somewhere in that secretary there was a maker's signature or mark. The piece was simply too grand and unusual for there not to have been. In the catalog note, I had attributed the secretary to Job Townsend, Sr. (1699–1765) —based upon the similarity of the secretary to a labeled slant-front desk at the Milwaukee Art Museum and a related dressing table at the Chipstone Foundation—but without a signature or documentation, it could never be proven. Cabinetmakers usually signed their work in graphite or chalk during the mid-eighteenth-century, and experience has taught me that there are a few spots that were typically used for this purpose. These include the backboard, the drawer bottoms or sides, and the top board of the lower case (onto which the bookcase was fitted). To satisfy my own curiosity, I decided to capitalize on the few remaining days that the secretary would be available for public scrutiny.

Further fueling my search was the fact that when furniture consultant Luke Beckerdite viewed the piece during the opening weekend of the preview, he suggested that the secretary was the work of Job's brother, Christopher Townsend (1701–1773), the father of the great John Townsend (who is widely considered the greatest craftsman in the entire Newport clan).

So when there was a lull in the inspection, I brought out a handheld high-intensity light and began to poke around for a signature. On the bottom of the first long drawer, I found what I was looking for—a large letter *T,* written in graphite and with great conviction.

I gasped excitedly and quickly motioned to John Nye and Amy Coes (the researcher who had written most of the catalog entry for the secretary), who were both standing just a few feet away.

"Look at this," I said to them almost breathlessly as I raked the light across the dark mahogany board. "It's a *T*!"

As the three of us leaned into the drawer, another letter revealed itself. "*W!*" we said, nearly in unison. And then as I cast the light at a different angle across the board, two more letters—an *N* and a *D*—seemed to emerge from the swirled grain.

Without the strong raked light, the writing was invisible. I was certain the signature said Townsend, but the question was, Which one? Centuries worth of wear from clothing and papers and whatever else had filled those drawers had worn the letters of the first name away.

Proof that auction houses are really a place where scholarship and commerce can splendidly merge materialized in the figure of Michael Moses, author of the definitive work on the Goddards and Townsends, who just happened to enter the gallery while

A detail of the graphite inscription "Made by Christopher Townsend" on the drawer bottom.

John and I were trying to decipher the signature. When Michael looked at the drawer-bottom, he thought he detected a large letter *C* scrawled about a foot and a half to the left of the *T*. "It could stand for Christopher," he said slowly as he squinted at the faint lettering.

Further supporting that notion was Michael's observation that the size and placement of the signature on the drawer bottom were strikingly reminiscent of the handling of John's signature on a well-known bonnet-top high chest once owned by the early

New York collector Richard DeWolf Brixey. Like his father, John signed the Brixey piece (which is now at Yale) in pencil on the inside of the bottom of a wide drawer. "It's an early piece, dated 1759," said Michael. "John was probably imitating the manner of his father."

I knew of only one other piece bearing the signature of Christopher Townsend. It was a flat-top high chest of drawers with slipper feet, and it offered little direct precedent for the Appleton secretary. In addition, there is very little surviving documentation of Townsend's shop practice. I could recall, however, a wonderful letter of 1738, written by the cabinetmaker to his wealthy client and fellow Quaker Abraham Redwood. In it, Townsend discussed some costly furniture, whose description seemed quite similar to the Appleton example. He wrote, "According to thy Request In thine I indevoured to finish a Desk and Book Case Agreeable to thy directions to send thee by Brother Pope. . . . The Desk and Book case amounts to Sixty Pounds, this currency; includeing the two Ruf cases [or shipping containers]."

He then added for good measure, "I may let thee know that I sold such a Desk and Book Case without any Ruf cases, for £58 in hand this winter. Brother Job, also sold one to our Collector for £59. I mention this, that thou may know that I have not imposed on thee." (Christopher Townsend to Abraham Redwood, February 4, 1738, Library Special Collections, Newport Historical Society.)

Linking the Appleton secretary to Christopher Townsend, I knew, could open up a whole new avenue of research with regard to his work (to say nothing of enhancing the desirability and rarity of the object). If he had made the Appleton secretary, then in it's commanding presence and perfectly finished solid-mahogany interior lay the promise—the very bloodline—of John Townsend's genius. As such, the piece could stand as a prototype to some of the shell-carved secretary-bookcases that his son would execute nearly a quarter century later.

To help clarify matters, I called Leslie Jean-Bart, one of the in-house photographers at Sotheby's, and asked if he could shoot the drawer bottom with infrared film, which might pick up on the signature. It took three days for the film to be developed, but when I opened the manila envelope, I was stunned to see—as clear as day—the inscription: *Made by Christopher Townsend.* I let out such a whoop, they could hear me over in the French Furniture Department. As if in response to my cry, the phone on my desk rang. It was Leigh, calling, in an act of eerie twindom, just in time to share this glorious moment with me.

Later in the week, we detected a second signature by Townsend in another drawer (and sometime after the sale, a third signature would be found). Clearly, Christopher was extremely proud of this piece. I thought he must have viewed the secretary as the culmination of his life's work—which was, in fact, not far from the way I was feeling about selling the piece. I never doubted the Appleton secretary would sell but my deepest wish was that it would sell in the millions. The question in my mind was whether or not it would reach a world record. In order to help that process along, part of my job at the auction house is to build the type of interest in a piece that generates competitive bidding. That means that in addition to drawing in the ultimate buyer, I also need to find an underbidder—a person whose passion for the piece will ostensibly drive the price up.

That led me to think about the roster of potential buyers. The Appleton secretary was a piece for someone who had not just the means but also the *passion* to pursue something that simply had no precedent in American decorative arts. Harold and Albert Sack were, of course, obvious contenders for the secretary because, for one, they represent the out-of-state billionaire, who had bought the Nicholas Brown secretary at Christie's for $12.1 million in 1989. Because that piece had set a world record for American furniture, it generated a lot of unshakable publicity. But the Sacks' client is actually a quiet collector: He avoids the press and is rarely spotted on the Americana circuit. In fact, it is commonly known in the industry that their client has purchased some major pieces of furniture—multimillion-dollar items—sight unseen, so even though he'd yet to surface at Sotheby's during the exhibition preview, I knew better than to eliminate him as a possible buyer. Adding fuel to this thought was the fact that when Harold saw the secretary for the first time at Sotheby's, he exclaimed to Bill Stahl and me, "That's a ten-million-dollar piece." Harold has never been one to throw out such praises, and the comment was later printed in the trade papers.

Also on my mind were Ned and Lillie Johnson, who came to the preview exhibition the day it opened. The Johnsons are veteran collectors, true connoisseurs, and have one of the strongest American collections in the country. They also live in Boston, so I thought the fact that the piece had descended in a local family might strike a personal note with them. Though the Johnsons often place their bids with the Massachusetts- and Ohio-based dealer, Bill Samaha, they visited Sotheby's alone that day.

I was with another client when they arrived, however, so it was some time before I went over to greet them and talk about the sale. I have to admit that I was surprised by the Johnsons' lukewarm response when the conversation turned toward the secretary. My obsession with the piece aside, this was an object that, quite honestly, I felt they should own. I knew it would really complement their already vast and exceptional holdings (their collection is particularly strong in Boston and Newport examples).

I offered to go through the secretary with the Johnsons, and we ended up spending about forty-five minutes together. I wanted them to absorb its beauty on their own terms, without seeming to oversell it. I didn't want them to draw any wrong conclusions—for example, about the use of mahogany throughout the case, which might cause some people to question the authenticity of the piece.

And, in fact, while we were going over the object, another one of the secretary's many wonderful secrets was revealed. As I was discussing the intricate design of the silver lopers, I noticed the right-hand eye on one of the birds appeared to be loose. I fished a paper clip out of the nearby reception desk, wrapped it in a bit of tissue, and gently pushed the green-colored stone back into its place—or so I thought. Instead, the opposite eyeball moved. Contrary to what I had assumed, the eyes were not formed of two individual beads. Rather, they were made of a single cylinder of semiprecious stone—possibly agate—which had been whittled down to about the size of a matchstick and then passed through the head of the bird.

The Appleton secretary as it appeared in the auction catalog, prior to the addition of the missing ball feet.

The Johnsons and I were all astounded by this detail (talk about jewel-like precision!), and I reminded them of a similar pair of bird-shaped lopers on a desk once owned by Thomas Mellon and Betty Evans, which had sold at Sotheby's the previous year, in June 1998. On that desk, which in overall form resembles the lower half of the Appleton secretary, the lopers are made of less expensive brass, rather than of silver, though they also have stone eyes. Because the feet on the Mellon-Evans desk had been replaced, it had been modestly estimated at between $10,000 and $20,000, though it ended up selling for a highly respectable $48,875. In retrospect, I would say that the collector who bought the Mellon-Evans piece owns a real treasure—one possibly made by Christopher Townsend. Indeed, I would later learn that the staircase in Christopher Townsend's home (which still stands in Newport, on the corner of Bridge and Second streets) features a decorative frieze of birds in profile, and these birds greatly resemble the lopers' model. I'd stop short of declaring it a signature device of the craftsman, however, because a quick survey of other Newport furniture turns up two slant-front desks by John Goddard with carved mahogany bird-shaped lopers, as well as a third one, this associated with Job Townsend.

By the time the Johnsons left that day, I felt that they had connected to the piece in a deeper way. In parting, though, they said that they were leaving the country within a day or two and would not be back in time for the sale. That made me nervous. Out of sight, out of mind. I didn't want the couple to lose momentum and I didn't want the catalog photo, in which the case piece was pictured without the ball feet, to be the only image of this masterpiece emblazoned in their minds. As soon as they left the gallery, I called for an in-house photographer to take some pictures of the piece raised on its new ball feet. The next day, I had the photos sent by overnight mail to their London hotel and hoped the effort would make a difference.

I also called their adviser, Bill Samaha, just to make sure he was also thinking about the Appleton secretary. But when I reached him by phone, I was astounded by his nonchalance, which really seemed to match the initial blasé attitude of his clients.

"So what do you think of the secretary?" I asked eagerly.

"What secretary?" he replied.

"Bill, the secretary, the Appleton secretary. Lot 704. Solid mahogany, with silver mounts on the exterior stamped by the maker, Samuel Casey. That secretary."

"Hmm," said Bill. Through the receiver, I could hear him flipping the pages of his catalog. "Solid mahogany. You know, Leslie, you have to be careful with that. Mahogany secondaries show up a lot on those later nineteenth-century pieces."

"Bill," I said, "this is not a nineteenth-century piece. It's the real thing. You have to come in and see it."

When Bill arrived at Sotheby's later in the week, I watched carefully as his initial and obvious skepticism gradually turned to awe. Without any help from me, the secretary was working its magic.

Other people who came to mind included the businessman Ted Alfond, who, along with his wife, Barbara, enjoys a real passion for the history of American craftsmanship (I see them at nearly every major furniture symposium). Also in the running was Tim

Robertson, son of the evangelist Pat Robertson and a fairly new member of this high-level collectors club. (He later told me that as he was examining the piece, he just kept exclaiming to himself, "What a thing! What a thing!") And then, of course, there were the unknowns: the cyberbarons, dot-com princes, and newly minted Wall Street zillionaires. Would the buzz generated by the sale entice an entirely new collector to the scene?

Finally, there was my brother Leigh, whose appreciation for the secretary, I never doubted. Though I was certainly aware that he was keeping his public opinion of the piece in check, I, being a twin, could not mistake the fervor in his eyes when the subject of the secretary came up. When I thought of what I knew of Leigh's client base, at least five possible candidates for the secretary came to mind: Two were from New York, but the rest were from out of state. Many of Leigh's clients enjoy maintaining a close relationship with Sotheby's. They like to examine the furniture during regular exhibition hours (as opposed to scheduling a private viewing) because it gives them a feel for the public perception of the piece that interests them. Others prefer to keep a distance. They feel any obvious signs of interest on their part will spur competitive bidding. (One major client of his has never even been in an auction salesroom.) Since Leigh was obviously keeping his distance from me during the preview week, I assumed that he was working with a client of the latter mind-set. Given the magnitude of the Appleton secretary, I was not surprised. This was the type of object that could inspire great levels of subterfuge.

On the evening of January 15, two days before the sale, there was a party at Israel Sack, Inc.'s sprawling Fifth Avenue gallery in celebration of Americana Week. Leigh and I were both there, in addition to the expected array of top-level collectors, curators, and auction house people. As things were winding down, Leigh and I looked for Albert to say good-bye, but we found his wife, Shirley, instead. We chatted for a few moments and then she graciously offered to take me to Albert. But as we rounded the corner toward the interior office, where he had been holding court, she suddenly halted. I saw past her shoulder that Albert was inside, quietly conversing with the man who bought the $12.1 million secretary.

"Perhaps this isn't the best time," Shirley said to me apologetically.

"That's quite all right," I replied. "Just give him my regards." I think that was the first time I had ever seen the tall, distinguished-looking collector in person, let alone in town during Americana Week.

At a minute before one o'clock on January 17, 1999, I took my place on the dais, which overlooked the standing-room-only crowd in attendance for the sale. There were just over one hundred lots to go before the secretary came to the block, which gave me ample time to survey the scene. At the front of the room, Albert Sack was positioned, as always, within sight of Al Bristol. A few rows behind him and to the left were Ted and Barbara Alfond. Behind them and all the way to the rear was the silver-haired dealer Bill Samaha. I assumed he was there on behalf of the Johnsons, and I made a mental note of his dark purple button-down shirt (it would be easy to spot should he choose to bid). Suddenly, the unmistakable happy chortle of a child floated above the chatter of the auction room. It was my daughter Ashley, not yet two, waving a bag of Cheerios at me as she stood on a chair in the second-to-last row. Steadying her in her eagerness was my wife, Emily, there to lend me support on what she knew was an important day.

By now, Bill Stahl had taken his place behind the auctioneer's lectern, bringing my attention back to the front of the room. Not six feet away from me, Leigh was just settling into a chair on the auctioneer's left, along with our father and Mitchell. It felt good to have so many members of my family close at this career-defining moment.

The afternoon whirled by as a steady stream of highboys and tables, mirrors and chairs had their moment on the dais. Finally, it came down to the maple bedstead preceding the secretary; it sold, seemingly in a flash, for $5,500. Then there was a pause. The lights suddenly dimmed and a slide of the infrared photos of Christopher Townsend's signature was flashed onto a large screen mounted behind the stage.

The audience shifted nervously as Bill Stahl prepared to read what is called a "gold card," meaning an addendum to the text published in the sale's catalog. "Please note an addition to lot 704, the Nathaniel Appleton secretary-bookcase," he began, then proceeded to describe the change in attribution from Job to Christopher Townsend.

When he was through, the overhead lights returned to their normal wattage and the image of Townsend's signature vanished from the stage. I glanced over at the phone bank set up along the right side of the podium. John Nye, Geraldine Nager, and Roberta Louckx (the latter two are both vice presidents in Sotheby's Client Services Division) all stood with phones to their ears, their eyes trained intently on Bill Stahl. Each was connected to a potential bidder, who for reasons of convenience or privacy chose not to be in the room that day. Sometimes, top-level buyers who do not want their collecting habits known to the auction community at large will place their bids through Sotheby's Client Services Division. To maintain their anonymity, they may be known simply by a code name or number, which shields their identity from practically everyone connected with the auction process. In other words, it is possible for a masterpiece of American furniture to sell at Sotheby's for millions of dollars and for neither Bill Stahl nor myself ever to know the name of the buyer.

Sometimes during a pause in the lots, Bill may find reason to turn off his microphone momentarily (perhaps to answer a question from a colleague or to receive some last-minute information). Just after he finished with the gold card and the overhead lights were regaining their brilliance, this happened (though I honestly can't remember why). But right before he turned the microphone on, he said to me in a low, encouraging tone, "Here we go."

As a result, I had a genuine smile on my face as the bidding began. "So, lot number 704," Bill announced to the crowd. "I have $350,000 to start it." He turned to the phones. "$400,000 with Geraldine now. $400,000 . . . I have $400,000 . . . $450,000 . . . $500,000 . . . I have $500,000 on my left now . . . $500,000 . . ."

Slowly, the numbers began to climb.

Bill's practiced eyes roamed the crowd, picking out bidders as the pace and tension grew. Quickly, the numbers were at $600,000 and then $700,000 and then $800,000. Suddenly there was a long pause. "$850,000?" Bill questioned the crowd.

Not a hand moved. Was the secretary of my dreams about to sell within its original estimate? I held my breath and looked into the crowd. Faces, faces filled with questioning. Just then, a paddle flashed from the left-center aisle. It was Ed Lacey, a Richmond, Virginia, collector who looks like Rhett Butler about twenty years after he left Scarlett. This was the first time I had ever seen Ed bid on a piece of case furniture that hadn't been made in Philadelphia or the South. Silently, I applauded the gesture as the pace of the sale resumed.

"I have $850,000 on the center aisle now . . . at $850,000 . . . I have $850,000 gentleman's bid on the left-corner aisle now . . . at $850,000 . . ." Then he said, "Your bid now it's $900,000 . . . I have $900,000 near me . . . $950,000 . . . at $950,000 . . . $1 million."

Now the numbers were rising in increments of $100,000.

"$1 million one." Ed's paddle flashed.

"$1 million two." Geraldine nodded.

"$1 million three." Ed's paddle stayed up.

"$1 million four." Geraldine nodded. "$1 million five . . . $1 million six . . . $1 million seven . . ." Bill's voice remained soft and steady as he pitted the southern collector against Geraldine's client on the phone. "$1 million eight . . . $1 million nine . . . $2 million." Now I detected a flash of movement from the left-rear corner of the room. It was the dealer Bill Samaha, stepping into the game, probably on behalf of Ned and Lillie Johnson.

"$2 million one." Ed Lacey was holding firm.

"$2 million two." Samaha looked determined. "$2 million three . . . $2 million four . . . $2 million five . . ."

At $2.6 million, Ed Lacey was out. At least he could say he had bid on the Appleton secretary. Still, the numbers continued to climb, for now Samaha was facing his own challenge from the phones. Roberta Louckx had just signaled the entrance of another bidder with a flick of her pen.

Front, back, front, back: Bill Stahl was beginning to shift his head from side to side in his characteristic fashion—first toward Roberta on the phone and then toward Bill Samaha in the rear. I was probably moving my head in a similar fashion, though I continued to scan the crowd for other bidders, including my brother. His hands remained still, his paddle down. He was clearly not bidding. The same was true of Albert Sack. Could I have been wrong about his billionaire client? I wondered.

"$3 million three . . . $3 million four . . . $3 million five . . . $3 million six . . ."

Bill Samaha was the only person bidding in the room.

"$4 million one . . . $ 4 million two . . . $4 million three . . . $4 million four . . ."

He held on tenaciously against the anonymous phone bidder.

"$4 million six . . . $4 million seven . . . $4 million eight . . ."

By now, the Appleton secretary had supplanted the Sarah Slocum chest of drawers (which had sold at auction in June 1998 for $4.7 million) as the second-most-expensive piece of American furniture.

Roberta's pen continued to flash, but Bill Samaha answered every gesture. When the numbers passed the $5 million mark, the increments jumped by a quarter-of-a-million a bid.

"$5,250,000 . . . $5,500,000 . . . $5,750,000 . . . $6 million . . . $6,250,000 . . . $6,500,000 . . ."

The audience was now holding its collective breath.

"$7 million . . ." said Bill Stahl.

"$7,250,000 . . ." came the quarter-million counteroffer.

"$7,500,000 . . . I have $7,500,000 . . . at the phones . . . Roberta now at $7,500,000 . . ." Bill Stahl stretched out the bid and looked one last time at Bill Samaha. The dealer shook his head. He had reached his limit. I anxiously scanned the crowd one last time. It is not unheard of for a dark-horse bidder to enter literally in the closing seconds of a sale, when the momentum of the bidding is slowing down. I looked toward Albert and then toward my brother. Both had their eyes trained on Bill Stahl as he announced, "At $7,500,000, then, my bid is on the telephone with Roberta and I'm selling it for $7,500,000. . . . All done. . . . Sold for $7,500,000 with Roberta." And then to the audience at large, he added, "Thank you all."

With the buyer's premium, the final price for the Appleton secretary was $8,252,500. It was only when I felt my body flood with relief that I realized how much tension I had been holding in. I saw my brother's face break into a smile as the packed room burst into applause. I grinned back. We were all clapping for the success of the sale, of course, but also, I believe, in tribute to the secretary itself. When the auction was over, I found Leigh in the exiting crowd and thought I detected a mischievous glimmer in his eyes. I knew better than to ask him, Was it you? And he just smiled, reached out his hand, and said, "Congratulations."

For months after the sale, rumors swirled in the industry as to the winner of the Appleton secretary. The official word from Sotheby's was "Anonymous," and that person really does remain anonymous within the house. In May 1999, a short item in *Maine Antique Digest* announced that Deanne Levison, a respected Atlanta-based dealer who has purchased major items in the past, was the buyer of record for the piece, although on whose behest she was bidding remains secret to the public to this day. One secret that has been exposed: the masterful beauty of an American secretary locked away in a Parisian flat for more than 150 years.

To this day, the Appleton secretary remains the most exceptional piece of American furniture that either Leigh or I have ever encountered. In its gleaming mahogany facade and dashing silver hardware, and in its meticulous construction and curious design details, lie all the majesty and mystery of America's past. Ironically, only modern technology has allowed us to read the faint signatures that its craftsman, Christopher Townsend, left behind as a symbol of his pride across the bottom boards of the drawers. But knowing his name does not satisfy the many questions that the secretary

281

as an object continues to provoke. What were the motivations behind its construction? Why were the design and quality of this piece pushed to such an unheard-of level of excellence? Did the impetus lie with the cabinetmaker, Christopher Townsend, or with his presumed, however strangely matched, client, the Reverend Nathaniel Appleton of Massachusetts? The search for such answers is really a search for the key to America's past. The objects that Leigh and I have pursued with such vigor—from those handwrought rat-tail hinges unearthed in the woods behind our childhood home to those masterpieces that we've been privileged to handle in recent years, such as the Appleton secretary—served as a backdrop to the nation's unfolding domestic life. What's more, they're tangible documents of a truly American character, with their ingenious designs, clever use of local (and imported) materials, and clear evidence of their makers' tireless labors.

Leigh's and my lifelong hunt for American antiques is really an ongoing conversation with these remarkable men, who were not only trying to make their way in a new world but who were intent on leaving their mark for future generations—all the while pursuing a craft they clearly loved.

THE COLLECTORS—The Keno twins, Leslie, left, and Leigh, 14-year-old sons of Mr. and Mrs. Ronald Keno, Mohawk RD 1, are interested in Soft Paste and Redware Pottery and have a collection valued at about $500.

2 Hooked on Pottery

MOHAWK — Two 14-year-old Mohawk boys have discovered that antique collecting can be a fascinating hobby.

To support their discovery, twins Leigh and Leslie Keno now have a Redware and Soft paste pottery collection with an estimated value of $500.

The boys have delved into the origin of these types of pottery that date back more than three centuries.

Redware, made primarily of sand and clay, was commonly used by poorer class people during the 18th century. It included such items as milk pitchers to sgraffito plate banks, Leigh said.

Because it is so fragile, it is scarce.

Soft-paste, popular from about 1750-1850, is distinguished from other types of pottery by its porous and dull appearance, Leslie said.

Types of soft-paste are called Mocha Ware, Leeds Pottery, Liverpool and Splatterware.

The twins, sons of Mr. and Mrs. Donald Keno, Mohawk RD 1, are eighth graders in the Mohawk Central School and both are members of the junior national honor society.

Neither has decided on a career but both say they will be pottery collectors some day who, either for fun or for profit.

Keno Twins Move Up

Leslie Keno and his twin brother Leigh, 26, have both recently been appointed vice presidents of major New York auction houses.

Leslie, who has been an expert in the American furniture department at Sotheby's, has been appointed director of the department, succeeding William Stahl, who has moved up to be director of development and regional operations.

Leigh Keno, who for several years has been the American furniture expert at William Doyle Galleries in New York, has been hired by Christie's where he will be a vice president in the appraisal company.

Both young men are familiar to many M.A.D. readers from their many trips to antiques shows beginning in early childhood with their mother, Norma Keno.

By the age of 13, they had assembled a collection of early stoneware that was exhibited at several museums.

We asked Leslie recently what was the secret of their success. "Don't tell anyone, but we have a triplet stashed away up in Albany who does all the work," he admitted.

Christie's Leigh Keno (left) and his brother Leslie of Sotheby's at the recent Winter Antiques Show.

Glossary

acanthus: Carving modeled after the leaves of the acanthus plant, which is native to the Mediterranean region.

apron: A horizontal cross member or framing element used below a chair seat, table-top, or the understructure of a *case* piece; it is often shaped along the lower edge for decorative effect. Also known as a *skirt*.

back splat: The central upright support of a chair back, often shaped or pierced, which rises from the rear of the seat to the crest rail.

baluster: An upright vertical support found on a table or chair; it has a vase-shaped outline.

birdcage: A trade term used to describe a small open-air boxlike structure with four miniature balusters, or columns, at each corner. It attaches to the center shaft of a pedestal-type table and is configured to allow the top to turn or tilt from a horizontal to a vertical position.

blocking: The decorative division that separates the front of a *case* piece into three vertical sections: two convex outer sections separated by a concave inner one. Occasionally, each section is capped with a carved shell ornament.

bonnet top: A trade term for a broken-arch *pediment* with dust boards at the back.

bracket foot: A support formed by two pieces of wood that join at a corner, with the open side cut to follow a simple pattern (such as an S-shaped outline).

broken-arch pediment: A roughly triangular-shaped *case*-piece top patterned by opposing S-shaped or swan's-neck arches that remain open at the apex. Typically found on American tall *case furniture* of the 1730s through the 1780s.

bureau: A low desk or writing table with drawers.

cabriole leg: An S-shaped furniture leg on which the knee curves out and the ankle curves in, ending in an ornamental foot.

canted: Angled or flattened, as with the slanted corner of a tabletop or *case* piece.

cartouche: A decorative scroll- or shield-shaped ornamental panel.

caryatid: A supporting column in the form of a stylized female figure.

case furniture: Boxlike furniture, often containing drawers, such as a chest.

cheval glass: A full-length mirror fitted on a four-legged frame with crossbars and flanking uprights, which allows it to tilt.

claw-and-ball foot: A foot carved in the form of an animal or bird claw grasping a ball.

compass inlay: A form of *inlay* pattern laid out using a series of arches; it is produced with a compass tool.

compass seat: An eighteenth-century term used to describe a chair seat with a rounded front and incurvate sides, the outline of which resembles a horseshoe.

corner block: A wooden block that is either glued or nailed to the inside corner of a joint to reinforce the juncture of the two intersecting pieces. *See* **glue block.**

cornice: The crowning—typically molded and projecting—member of a *case* piece; similar to the top of an entablature in architecture.

crest rail: The top horizontal rail of a chair, settee, or sofa.

crossbanding: Strips of *veneer* used as a decorative border and often set so that the grain pattern runs perpendicular to the direction of that adjacent to it.

crotch wood: The grain pattern of wood cut from the area of a tree where a branch joins the trunk.

C scroll: A carved scroll-like decorative motif resembling the letter C.

cyma curve: An S-shaped or double curved line, one half of which is concave, the other convex.

demilune: Semicircular, or half-moon, in shape.

desk and bookcase: A tall *case* piece that includes an upper section fitted with shelves and partitions for books and papers and a lower section that includes a writing surface, often with drawers or cabinet doors below. Also known as a *secretary-bookcase.*

dished top: A tabletop, often hewn from a single board, that features a shallow raised rim.

dovetail: A term used to describe a juncture where two pieces of wood are joined together at a right angle with interlocking wedge-shaped joints that in profile resemble a dove's tail.

dowel: A wooden pin, roughly cylindrical in shape, that fits into a hole to join two pieces of wood.

dressing table: A low *case* piece or table with drawers raised on legs; often made en suite with a *high chest*.

drop leaf: A hinged extension that is attached to the stationary top of a table so that it can be folded down when not in use.

easy chair: An upholstered armchair with a winged high back and enclosed padded arms. Also known in the trade as a *wing chair*.

églomisé: A method by which painted or gilded decorative designs are applied to the back of a piece of glass.

escutcheon: A protective metal plate surrounding a keyhole.

fall front: The hinged cover of a desk or secretary that folds out to form a writing surface.

figure: The grain pattern displayed on a cut piece of wood.

finial: A shaped vertical ornament often used to decorate the top of a tall *case* piece.

fluting: Decorative carving in the form of vertical channels. The reverse of *reeding*.

fretwork: A form of openwork or low-relief carving that resembles a geometric grid pattern or latticework.

frieze: A flat or sculpted ornamental band on furniture; it runs horizontally, such as on the *apron* of a table or on the area beneath a *pediment* molding.

gadrooning: Carved ornament in the form of a series of interspersed convex and concave lobes used to accent a horizontal member of a piece of furniture.

gate-leg table: A table form popularized during the first half of the eighteenth century; constructed with legs joined by stretchers that swing out from the frame (like gates) to support the hinged leaves when extended.

gesso: Plaster mixed with a binding material; it is used for relief work or as a ground for painting or *gilding*.

gilding: To coat with a thin layer of gold or a gold-colored paint.

glue block: In furniture, a wood block used to strengthen the juncture of two structural members.

high chest: A tall two-part *case* piece consisting of an upper case with drawers that rests on top of a lower section, also with drawers, that is raised on legs.

highboy: A trade term for *high chest*.

incising: A carving technique in which a fine, sharp instrument is used to produce a shallow thin-lined pattern.

inlay: Ornamentation that involves the insertion of decorative material (such as wood *veneers* or a shell) into the surface of a piece of furniture.

intaglio: Low-relief decorative carving.

kerfing saw: A fine saw used to cut *dovetails*.

kneehole desk: A desk with an open or recessed center flanked by a column of drawers on either side.

lathe: A machine on which a piece of wood can be affixed and spun while being shaped by a cutting tool.

lopers: The decorative handholds that front the sliding support rails of a *fall-front* desk.

lowboy: A trade term for *dressing table*.

molding: A band of wood, either projecting or incised, that has been shaped by a molding plane.

mortise: A recess cut into a piece of wood to receive a *tenon*.

mounts: All the decorative and functional metal hardware, including drawer pulls, *escutcheons*, and hinges, applied to furniture.

ogee curve: An S-shaped or reverse curve; similar to a *cyma curve*.

ormolu: Gilded bronze or brass made in imitation of gold and often used for furniture *mounts*.

pad foot: A simple rounded or oval-shaped carved foot.

patina: Surface texture and color acquired over time from general use and exposure.

pedestal table: A table supported by a central column, commonly leading to a tripod base.

pediment: The ornamental top of a tall *case* piece; commonly triangular or arched in form, it is suggestive of an architectural *pediment*.

Pembroke table: A small rectangular four-legged table with two short hinged leaves supported by swing rails (rather than legs), and often fitted at one end with a drawer.

piecrust table: A common term used to describe a circular *tilt-top* tea table or candle stand with a scalloped, molded edge.

pier table: A side table, often placed in a dining room or parlor between two windows (the architectural term for that wall space is pier).

pigeonhole: A small compartment used in a desk, bookcase, or cabinet for keeping documents and papers.

pilaster: An engaged rectangular column that projects in low relief from a wall or piece of furniture.

pin: A narrow wooden peg used to secure a *mortise*-and-*tenon* joint.

plinth: In decorative arts, a square block that serves as a base for a statue, vase, or finial.

plum-pudding mahogany: A trade term that refers to a rare type of highly figured mahogany, usually reddish purple, with distinctive graining in the form of small oval or circular aberrations.

primary wood: The wood used on the show surface of a piece of furniture.

provenance: A term used to describe the source and ownership history of a piece.

pull: A knob or handle used for opening or closing drawers, cabinet doors, desktops, and other compartments.

rail: A horizontal framing member that extends from one vertical support to another, as in the *crest* of a chair.

rat-tail hinge: A hand-wrought door hinge featuring a heart-shaped terminal with a curled or winding tip that resembles a rat's tail.

reeding: Convex vertical carving. The reverse of *fluting*.

rose-head nail: A hand-forged nail used in America during the seventeenth and eighteenth centuries; it has an irregularly shaped, slightly raised head that in outline resembles an open rose.

sand burning: A method of applying hot sand to an *inlaid* wood design for shading and added dimension.

scroll pediment: A trade term used to describe a *broken-arch pediment*.

secondary wood: The structural wood—thus, unseen—used in furniture construction.

secretary-bookcase: *See desk and bookcase.*

shagreen: The rough, pebbled skin of certain species of sharks or rays that was occasionally put to use in the eighteenth century as an early form of sandpaper.

shoe: A horizontal molded piece of wood attached to a chair's *rail* at the bottom of the back, into which the splat is fitted.

skirt: *See apron.*

slip seat: A removable chair seat, made of cane, rush, or upholstery, that is designed to rest in the four seat *rails* of a chair.

slipper foot: A narrow, elongated foot that is rounded at the rear and tapers evenly to a point at the front.

Spanish foot: A carved scrolled foot with vertical *fluting*; it often curves backward at the base.

spindle: A slender decorative turned piece of wood, similar to a *baluster*, often used on chair backs.

S **scroll:** A decorative motif in the shape of the letter *S*.

stile: One of the two upright vertical side supports in a chair back that support the *crest rail*.

stop fluting: A decorative device that features concave carved channels, or *fluting*, that are filled at the lower end with *reeding*.

stretcher: A horizontal bracing member set between the legs of a chair, table, or the like for added strength and stability.

stringing: A narrow line of decorative *inlay* set into a contrasting *primary wood* on furniture.

tenon: A projecting tonguelike member left by cutting away the wood around it, for insertion into a *mortise* to make a joint.

tilt-top table: A *pedestal table* fitted with a birdcage mechanism or block beneath the top that allows it to tilt when not in use.

toleware: A term of French derivation for paint-decorated tinware.

torchère: A tall stand with a very small top that is intended to hold a candlestick, lamp, or decorative object.

turnings: Furniture elements, such as *balusters* and *spindles*, that have been shaped on a *lathe.*

tympanum: The recessed front-facing board contained within the upper and lower cornices of a *pediment*.

veneer: A thin slice of wood used as a surface covering on a base, or less expensive, wood to give it a finished appearance.

verdigris: A word derived from the French term *vert de Grice,* or "green of Greece," referring to a greenish blue pigment used to simulate an antique bronze green *patina*.

volute: A spiral scroll-shaped form similar to one side of a Greek Ionic capital.

Windsor chair: A chair designed with a multiple-*spindle* back that fits into a wood-plank seat that is supported below by legs that splay outward.

wing chair: *See easy chair.*

Bibliography

Anderson, Mark J., Gregory J. Landrey, and Philip D. Zimmerman, *Cadwalader Study.* Winterthur, Delaware: Henry Francis du Pont Winterthur Museum, 1995.

Barquist, David. *American Tables and Looking Glasses in the Mabel Brady Garvan and Other Collections at Yale University.* New Haven: Yale University Art Gallery, 1992.

Beckerdite, Luke, ed. *American Furniture.* Milwaukee: Chipstone Foundation, 1993–1999.

Bishop, Robert. *Centuries and Styles of the American Chair: 1640–1970.* New York: E.P. Dutton, 1972.

Bivins, John. *The Furniture of Coastal North Carolina.* Winston-Salem, North Carolina: Museum of Early Southern Decorative Arts, 1988.

Bjerkoe, Ethel Hall. *The Cabinetmakers of America.* Garden City, New York: Doubleday, 1957.

Carpenter, Ralph E. *The Arts and Crafts of Newport, Rhode Island: 1640–1820.* Newport: Preservation Society of Newport County, 1954.

Chippendale, Thomas. *The Gentleman & Cabinet-Maker's Director.* 3d. edition. London: 1762. Reprint. New York: Dover, 1966.

Comstock, Helen. *American Furniture: Seventeenth, Eighteenth, and Nineteenth Century Styles.* New York: Viking Press, 1962.

Conger, Clement, and Alexandra Rollins. *Treasures of State: Fine and Decorative Arts in the Diplomatic Reception Rooms of the U.S. Department of State.* New York: Harry N. Abrams, 1991.

Cooper, Wendy A. *In Praise of America: American Decorative Arts, 1650–1830.* New York: Alfred A. Knopf, 1980.

———. *Classical Taste in America.* New York: Abbeville Press, 1993.

Downs, Joseph. *American Furniture: Queen Anne and Chippendale Periods in the Henry Francis du Pont Winterthur Museum.* New York: Macmillan, 1952.

Elder, William Voss, III, and Jayne E. Stokes. *American Furniture, 1680–1880, from the Collection of the Baltimore Museum of Art.* Baltimore: Baltimore Museum of Art, 1987.

Evans, Nancy. *American Windsor Chairs.* New York: Hudson Hills Press in association with the Henry Francis du Pont Winterthur Museum, 1996.

Failey, Dean F. *Long Island Is My Nation: The Decorative Arts & Craftsmen, 1640–1830.* Setauket, New York: Society for the Preservation of Long Island Antiquities, 1976. Reprint. 1998.

Fairbanks, Jonathan L., and Elizabeth B. Bates. *American Furniture: 1620 to the Present.* New York: Richard Marek Publishers, 1981.

Fairbanks, Jonathan L., and Robert F. Trent. *New England Begins: The Seventeenth Century.* 3 vols. Boston: Museum of Fine Arts, 1982.

Fales, Dean A., *American Painted Furniture, 1660–1880.* New York: E. P. Dutton, 1972.

———. *The Furniture of Historic Deerfield.* New York: E. P. Dutton, 1976.

Fitzgerald, Oscar P. *Three Centuries of American Furniture.* Englewood Cliffs, New Jersey: Prentice-Hall, 1982.

Flanigan, J. Michael. *American Furniture from the Kaufman Collection.* Washington, D.C.: National Gallery of Art, 1986.

Forman, Benno M. *American Seating Furniture, 1630–1730.* New York: W. W. Norton, 1988.

Freund, Joan Barzilay. *Masterpieces of Americana: The Collection of Mr. and Mrs. Adolph Henry Meyer.* New York: Sotheby's Books, 1995.

Girl Scouts. *Loan Exhibition of Eighteenth and Early Nineteenth Century Furniture and Glass . . . For the Benefit of the National Council of Girl Scouts, Inc.* (Exhibition catalog.) New York: American Art Galleries, 1929.

Greene, Jeffrey P. *American Furniture of the 18th Century.* Newtown, Connecticut: Taunton Press, 1996.

Greenlaw, Barry A. *New England Furniture at Williamsburg.* Williamsburg, Virginia: Colonial Williamsburg Foundation, 1974.

Gusler, Wallace B. *Furniture of Williamsburg and Eastern Virginia, 1710–1790.* Richmond: Virginia Museum of Fine Arts, 1979.

Heckscher, Morrison. *American Furniture in The Metropolitan Museum of Art, Late Colonial Period: Queen Anne and Chippendale Styles.* New York: Metropolitan Museum of Art, 1985.

Heckscher, Morrison, and Leslie Greene Bowman. *American Rococo, 1750–1775: Elegance in Ornament.* New York: Metropolitan Museum of Art, 1992.

Hepplewhite, George. *The Cabinet-Maker and Upholsterer's Guide.* 3d. edition. London: I. & J. Taylor, 1794. Reprint. New York: Dover, 1969.

Hewitt, Benjamin A., Patricia E. Kane, and Gerald W. R. Ward. *The Work of Many Hands: Card Tables in Federal America, 1790–1820.* New Haven: Yale University Art Gallery, 1982.

Hipkiss, Edwin J. *Eighteenth-Century American Arts: The M. and M. Karolik Collection.* Cambridge, Massachusetts: Harvard University Press, 1941.

Hornor, William MacPherson, Jr. *Blue Book, Philadelphia Furniture: William Penn to George Washington.* Philadelphia, privately printed, 1935. Reprint. Washington, D.C.: Highland House, 1977.

Hummel, Charles F. *A Winterthur Guide to American Chippendale Furniture: Middle Atlantic and Southern Colonies.* New York: Crown, 1976.

Hurst, Ronald L., and Jonathan Prown. *Southern Furniture 1680–1830.* Williamsburg, Virginia: Colonial Williamsburg Foundation in association with Harry N. Abrams, 1997.

Jobe, Brock, ed. *Portsmouth Furniture: Masterworks from the New Hampshire Seacoast.* Boston: Society for the Preservation of New England Antiquities, 1993.

Jobe, Brock, and Myrna Kaye. *New England Furniture: The Colonial Era.* Boston: Houghton Mifflin, 1984.

Jobe, Brock, et al. *American Furniture with Related Decorative Arts, 1660–1830: The Milwaukee Art Museum and the Layton Art Collection.* New York: Hudson Hills Press, 1991.

Kane, Patricia. *300 Years of American Seating Furniture, Chairs and Beds from the Mabel Brady Garvan and Other Collections at Yale University.* Boston: New York Graphic Society, 1976.

Kennedy, Roger G. *Orders from France, The Americans and the French in a Revolutionary World, 1780–1820.* Philadelphia: University of Pennsylvania Press, 1990.

Kenny, Peter M., Frances F. Bretter, and Ulrich Leben. *Honoré Lannuier, Cabinetmaker from Paris.* New York: Metropolitan Museum of Art, 1998.

Ketchum, William C. *American Cabinetmakers.* New York: Crown, 1995.

Kimball, Fiske. *Mr. Samuel McIntire, Carver: The Architect of Salem.* Portland, Maine: Southworth-Anthoensen Press, 1940.

Kindig, Joseph, III. *The Philadelphia Chair: 1685–1785.* Harrisburg, Pennsylvania: Historical Society of York County, 1978.

Kirk, John T. *Connecticut Furniture: Seventeenth and Eighteenth Centuries.* Hartford, Connecticut: Wadsworth Atheneum, 1967.

———. *American Furniture and the British Tradition to 1830.* New York: Alfred A. Knopf, 1982.

Lindsey, Jack L., et al. *Worldly Goods, The Arts of Early Pennsylvania, 1680–1758.* Philadelphia: Philadelphia Museum of Art, 1999.

———, and Darrel Sewell. *The Cadwalader Family: Art and Style in Early Philadelphia.* Bulletin for the Philadelphia Museum of Art #91, nos. 384–385 [Fall 1996]. Philadelphia: Philadelphia Museum of Art, 1996.

Lockwood, Luke Vincent. *Colonial Furniture in America.* 3d. edition. 2 vols. New York: Charles Scribner's Sons, 1926. Reprint. New York: Castle Books, 1951.

McClelland, Nancy. *Duncan Phyfe and the English Regency, 1795–1830.* New York: William R. Scott, 1939.

Monkhouse, Christopher P., and Thomas S. Michie. *American Furniture in Pendleton House.* Providence: Museum of Art, Rhode Island School of Design, 1986.

Montgomery, Charles. *American Furniture: The Federal Period, in the Henry Francis du Pont Winterthur Museum.* New York: Viking Press, 1966.

Montgomery, Charles, and Patricia Kane, eds. *American Art: 1750–1800, Towards Independence.* Boston: New York Graphic Society, 1976.

Morley, John. *The History of Furniture: Twenty-five Centuries of Style and Design in the Western Tradition.* Boston: Bulfinch Press, 1999.

Moses, Michael. *Master Craftsmen of Newport: The Townsends and Goddards.* Tenafly, New Jersey: MMI Americana Press, 1984.

Nutting, Wallace. *Furniture Treasury.* 3 vols. Framingham, Massachusetts: Old America Company, 1928–1933. Reprints. New York: Macmillan, 1954; Dover, 1971.

Ott, Joseph K. *The John Brown House Loan Exhibition of Rhode Island Furniture.* Providence: Rhode Island Historical Society, 1965.

Philadelphia Museum of Art. *Philadelphia: Three Centuries of American Art.* Philadelphia: Philadelphia Museum of Art, 1976.

Puig, Francis J., and Michael Conforti, eds. *The American Craftsman and the European Tradition, 1620–1820.* Minneapolis: Minneapolis Institute of Art, 1989.

Randall, Richard H., Jr. *American Furniture in the Museum of Fine Arts, Boston.* Boston: Museum of Fine Arts, 1965.

Richards, Nancy E., and Nancy Goyne Evans. *New England Furniture at Winterthur: Queen Anne and Chippendale Periods.* Winterthur, Delaware: Henry Francis du Pont Winterthur Museum, 1997.

Rodriguez Roque, Oswaldo. *American Furniture at Chipstone.* Madison: University of Wisconsin Press, 1984.

Sack, Albert. *Fine Points of Furniture: Early American.* New York: Crown, 1950.

———. *The New Fine Points of Furniture.* New York: Crown, 1993.

Sack, Israel, Inc. *American Furniture from Israel Sack Collection.* 10 vols. Washington, D.C.: Highland House, 1981–1992.

Santore, Charles. *The Windsor Style in America.* 2 vols. Philadelphia: Running Press, 1981, 1987.

Schaffner, Cynthia V. A., and Susan Klein. *American Painted Furniture.* New York: Clarkson Potter, 1997.

Sheraton, Thomas. *The Cabinet-Maker and Upholsterer's Drawing-Book.* London: self-published, 1793–1802. Reprint. New York: Dover, 1968.

Stoneman, Vernon C. *John and Thomas Seymour: Cabinetmakers in Boston, 1794–1816.* Boston: Special Publications, 1959.

———. *A Supplement to John and Thomas Seymour: Cabinetmakers in Boston, 1794–1816.* Boston: Special Publications, 1965.

Tracy, Berry B. *Federal Furniture and Decorative Arts at Boscobel.* New York: Harry N. Abrams, 1981.

Venable, Charles L. *American Furniture in the Bybee Collection.* Austin: University of Texas Press in association with the Dallas Museum of Art, 1989.

Wainwright, Nicholas B. *Colonial Grandeur in Philadelphia: The House and Furniture of General John Cadwalader.* Philadelphia: Historical Society of Pennsylvania, 1964.

Ward, Gerald W. R. *American Case Furniture in the Mabel Brady Garvan and Other Collections at Yale University.* New Haven: Yale University Art Gallery, 1988.

Warren, David B., Michael K. Brown, Elizabeth Ann Coleman, and Emily Ballew Neff. *American Decorative Arts and Paintings in the Bayou Bend Collection.* Houston: Museum of Fine Arts, 1998.

Weidman, Gregory R. *Furniture in Maryland, 1740–1940: The Collection of the Maryland Historical Society.* Baltimore: Maryland Historical Society, 1984.

Weil, Martin Eli. "A Cabinetmaker's Price Book." In *American Furniture and Its Makers: Winterthur Portfolio 13,* edited by Ian M. G. Quimby, 175–192. Chicago: University of Chicago Press, 1979.

Whitehill, Walter Muir, ed. *Boston Furniture of the Eighteenth Century.* Boston: Colonial Society of Massachusetts, 1974.

Index

Credits